What a great
Gratwick Guy you
are. Always
remember the fun
times at bowling

Jim Abbott MD

Memoirs of a Volunteer Firefighter

by

Jason A. Borton, M.D.

INFINITY
PUBLISHING

All rights reserved. No part of this book shall be reproduced or transmitted in any form or by any means, electronic, mechanical, magnetic, photographic including photocopying, recording or by any information storage and retrieval system, without prior written permission of the publisher. No patent liability is assumed with respect to the use of the information contained herein. Although every precaution has been taken in the preparation of this book, the publisher and author assume no responsibility for errors or omissions. Neither is any liability assumed for damages resulting from the use of the information contained herein.

Copyright © 2010 by Jason A. Borton
Author photograph: Jenean Mohr

ISBN 0-7414-5989-2

Printed in the United States of America

This is a work of non-fiction. In certain cases, names and other identifying details may have been changed to protect an individual's privacy.

Published May 2010

INFINITY PUBLISHING
1094 New DeHaven Street, Suite 100
West Conshohocken, PA 19428-2713
Toll-free (877) BUY BOOK
Local Phone (610) 941-9999
Fax (610) 941-9959
Info@buybooksontheweb.com
www.buybooksontheweb.com

Dedication

This book is dedicated to several people. I would like to thank my mother and father for their support and belief in me throughout the years. Thanks also go to my Grandma Borton whose many trips to the fire station with me fostered a childhood interest that fired an adult passion. I would also like to thank my wife Sue and my children Alannah, Zander, and Zackary for their patience and support. I am truly grateful to have each of you in my life. Lastly and most importantly, this book is dedicated to the women and men of the past, present, and future who have volunteered and who will someday volunteer to put their own lives at risk to fight fire and make a positive difference in the lives of their neighbors.

Contents

1

Baptism of Fire

A thin veil of acrid smoke enveloped us as we entered the house. Our labored breathing was muffled by our breathing apparatus as we wrestled with a water laden hose, searching for the still elusive fire. As we entered a large room, three doors confronted us. Fred Chilsholm from the career department stopped us, "Wait here." he said, disappearing to the left. Duncan Fanners, who had been a volunteer five years longer than me, looked to the right. He had told me many stories of the interior attacks on fires that he had made in the past. My heart churned as I wondered if he knew that this was my first time inside a real house fire.

I stared at the two doors directly in front of us, wondering if Hell itself was waiting behind one of those portals. A third door stood to the left. For some reason I was drawn to it. I felt it with the back of my partially gloved hand. The skin on my hand retained its protective barrier as the door was cool. I crouched down as I twisted the doorknob, wary but also curious as to what venture I was about to encounter. A bright light radiated towards me from above. Not flame but sunlight illuminating a stairwell. I shouted out to Fred and

Duncan the news of my find. Fred took the lead up the stairs and stopped on the fifth step. A flat hand in our faces warned Duncan and me to step back. Fred's axe met the wall with a thud and a narrow jet of flame burst across the stairwell impinging on the opposite wall. Duncan quickly doused the flame with a cooling spray of water. Fred took a couple of more chunks of drywall out with the axe, but finding no more fire, he ascended the stairwell.

At a landing, the stairs made a one hundred and eighty degree turn up to the second floor of the house. I remained on the landing feeding hose up to Duncan and Fred who had both disappeared into the darkness of the upper floor. I struggled to catch my breath as I was feeding hose, wondering what had ever made me become a volunteer firefighter. Twenty minutes earlier I had been dozing off in front of a Saturday afternoon sports show. Now I was in an unfamiliar building that was on fire, doing a job that usually claimed the lives of just over one hundred firefighters in the United States each year, and I was volunteering to do it. My mind raced as my task of feeding hose had ended. What would I do next? Did I have something to do right now? Were Fred and Duncan alright?

The sound of two ringing bells interrupted my chaotic thoughts. Fred and Duncan appeared at the top of the stairs, their low air pressure alarms still ringing. Fred pulled me over as he walked down the stairs. "Follow the hose up to the nozzle and wait there," he said. I nodded my understanding and crawled on the floor, gripping the hose as if it might be my only chance of getting out of the house alive if something bad happened. I heard new muffled voices of firefighters about twenty feet behind me. They were searching for fire at the front of the house. I reached the nozzle and gazed at the back of the house. Blackened walls released steam upwards and it felt like I had to be in the hottest part of the house. Duncan and Fred had found the fire.

As I stared at the walls, two small orange embers fell to the floor beside me and caught my eye. I looked up and saw that the ceiling was an eerie orange color. I heard the unmistakable sound of crackling wood above me. Then it appeared. A ball of fire that had been hiding in the attic raced to the back of the house. Half frozen from fear, I shouted out at the top of my lungs, "I've got fire back here!"

Someone must have heard the desperation in my voice as a hand touched my shoulder within seconds.

"What's the matter?" the calm voice questioned.

"I've got a lot of fire up above me," I replied.

"Calm down and take a deep breath. It's a simple concept and you can do it. Put the wet stuff on the red stuff, that's all," he said.

"OK, thanks," I said as I regained my lost composure.

I felt the power of the hose press into my body as I opened the nozzle. I directed the water straight up to cool down the ceiling over my head. As that cooled down I shot the water right into the center of the fireball. Within seconds the fire had disappeared and it was replaced by a scorching blanket of steam that enveloped me. I continued to spray water until I was confident that I would not see the menacing face of the fire again. The ringing of my breathing apparatus low pressure alarm startled me and I shut down the hose. I left the nozzle behind me and walked towards the stairs. The group of firefighters that were at the front of the house had just pulled down a part of the ceiling with a pike pole. Looking up into the attic I saw nothing but a sea of orange flame. I stared at it for a second and felt that I had somehow conquered fire that day, even if conquered only meant being able to control it for a short while.

I descended the stairs and the two doors that I chose not to open before now stood wide open. Their previously hidden interior surfaces were heavily charred. The walls of the rooms concealed by the doors were heavily blackened. I wondered how the fire attack would have been different if I had chosen to look behind one of those doors.

I stepped off of the front porch and removed my helmet and mask while I turned off the main regulator of the air tank. The air felt refreshing like a cold Buffalo winter day, even though the calendar declared it was late in the month of June.

Hoards of people had gathered on the street to watch the battle of man and the physical world that was taking place in their neighborhood. Two years earlier I would have been one of those people: watching, standing by, and making no difference at all. Today I was doing something, being somebody in a dedicated group of bodies that had shown up on this Saturday afternoon to bring some relief to a devastated family in the small city of North Tonawanda. I felt great, but a small voice within my head still made me feel uneasy. Why did I hesitate when I was confronted by the fire? Would I freeze up again? The answer to these questions would be uncloaked a few days later while I was at the fire hall.

Steve Jenkins was a member of the fire company who was not well respected by most of the members. He sat at the fire hall for hours on end, drinking beer and lighting up a new cigarette before the previous one had been extinguished. He proclaimed to know something about everything. If he did have one good quality, it was that he was an attentive listener. I had stopped by the hall one afternoon and Steve was at his usual place at the bar. Still being excited about the recent house fire, I started talking to him about my experience. For some reason I told him about my hesitation on the second floor of the building. He sat there for a minute and then smiled as he crushed another cigarette out in an already crowded ashtray.

"Yep, I remember my baptism as if it was only yester-day," he said.

"What does your baptism have to do with fighting fire?" I questioned.

"Everything, because I'm talking about a baptism of fire. You had yours on Hagen Street a couple of days ago. You weren't sure what to do but you kept your calm and stayed in the house. You did what you had to do. Now everything will get easier. You'll be more confident in fires. You won't hesitate so easily. You've been there and done that. Now you're a firefighter." he answered.

I thanked Steve for his insight and left the hall a short time later. This concept of a baptism of fire would not leave my mind. I decided to look up the word "baptism" in *Webster's Dictionary*. One of the entries defined baptism as "A ceremony, trial, or experience by which one is initiated, purified, or given a name."

I stared at the definition in amazement. Steve was right. The house fire had initiated me into the world of firefighting. Fighting fires wasn't about doing controlled simulation burns in a fire training tower. It was about hunting for a fire in an unfamiliar house and containing that fire in whatever way possible at a given time. I had also been purified on Hagen Street. My initial profound fears were washed away with the water that helped me to subdue the fire on that day. But most importantly, my baptism of fire had given me a name. That new name was *firefighter* Jason Borton. This book is the story of my journey as a volunteer firefighter with the Sweeney Hose Company No. 7 of the North Tonawanda Fire Department. Please sit down, relax, and enjoy the journey.

2

Daydreams

If my senior year of high school was anything for me, it was a time of searching and boredom. After thirteen years of school, I had become bored with the material that was being taught to me. It seemed like the school system plagued its students with the same regurgitated information year after year. After graduation I would be traveling to Clarkson University in the small town of Potsdam, New York to study chemistry. My dad approved of the university and their chemistry program seemed competitive to me. I had ranked seventh in my graduating class of three hundred and sixty students. I was on autopilot and coasting through the last months of my high school drudgery.

I took an elective class called advanced composition in the spring of my senior year. It was a class designed to teach the college bound student the complicated process of writing a college level term paper. I sat near the window during this last class of the day and I had a clear view of the traffic on Meadow Drive. The high school, an elementary school, the North Tonawanda Library, and several fast food restaurants occupied the south side of Meadow Drive, while apartment buildings, houses, and office complexes took up its north side. While my English teacher droned on endlessly about the importance of research for a term paper, I gazed out the windows, daydreaming about something, somewhere outside of my seventeen years of North Tonawanda existence.

One day my daydreaming was rudely interrupted by the sound of a distant siren. Suddenly, I saw the North Tonawanda fire chief's car making a mockery of the school zone speed limit on Meadow Drive. The next traffic interrupter was a fire engine. The random staccato blasts of its air horns broke up the wail of its screaming siren. It seemed to move with determination, as if it was daring any car to get in its way. It needed to get somewhere and it needed to get there fast. I looked away from the window and surveyed the classroom. One or two other students were tracking the fire engine. Others were nodding off. Those who were not affected by "senioritis" were actually paying attention to the teacher.

As I looked back over my left shoulder the truck vanished from sight, while the pitch of its siren seemed to change, verifying that the Doppler Effect was still working in North Tonawanda. The sight of the fire engine triggered a reminiscence of a much earlier time in my life. As a child in the mid 1970s, a new adventure could be found around every corner for me. Many of my childhood memories were made from the times that I spent at my Grandma and Grandpa Borton's house.

My grandparents lived in a small section of North Tonawanda known as Martinsville, so named for St. Martin Lutheran Church that was founded in 1843 by German immigrants to the area who sought religious freedom. In the 1950s, my grandfather built a modest white Cape Cod home on Eddy Drive in Martinsville. My grandfather was raised in Adrian, Michigan and he served in the United States Air Force in World War II. After the war he moved to Buffalo, New York to work as an aircraft mechanic for the Curtiss Wright Corporation. It was around Buffalo where he met and married my grandmother, Laura Berner, one of five girls born to a Lutheran minister and his wife. They initially resided in the housing projects of North Tonawanda, later moving to their house on Eddy Drive.

Being asked to sleep over my grandparents' house was always a treat for me and, as I later realized, a welcome break for my parents. Grandma and Grandpa Borton always made me feel welcome at their house. My cousins would often sleep over at my grandparents' house and we would play with the neighborhood kids. Grandma Borton always seemed to be making delicious popcorn. I can't imagine how many games of Candyland and Trouble my grandmother endured playing with me throughout the years. In warmer weather she would take me to a place that would let me glimpse at something I would unwittingly be involved with in my future.

Located two and a half blocks from my grandparents' house was a fire station. The engine that was housed there was Engine 5. The adjoining fire hall was that of the Rescue Fire Company. On each visit to her house, I would beg my grandmother to take me to the fire station. On almost every occasion she would oblige my persistent begging and we would start our short walk to the fire station that seemed to take forever.

As we approached the fire station, I knew the drill. We would cross the street after looking both ways. We would walk up the front ramp and proceed to the man door on the side of the station. I would stand at the door very quietly while I held my grandma's hand. She would knock on the door, patiently awaiting the arrival of an often startled career firefighter. The firefighter would open the door and Grandma would use all of her humble charm. "This is my grandson Jason. He would like to see your fire truck. Could we come in for a short while?" she would ask. I never once recalled the door being shut in our face and Grandma was always sure to thank the firefighter for letting us into his home away from home.

Even as a young child, I distinctly remembered all of my senses becoming sharply focused as I stepped into the truck room. It seemed like hallowed ground to me. A constant crisp overhead buzzing sound let me know that the fluorescent lights were working. When the driver talked, his voice always echoed in the large truck room. The lingering scent of cleaning chemicals hovered in the air and I imagined that the driver spent every waking moment of his shift cleaning something. Engine 5 stood silently and boastfully closest to the side door we had entered. It was the same type of fire truck that kept my attention each week on the TV show *Emergency!* Each firefighter had his own locker with a yellow coat and helmet and a pair of black boots.

Against the outside cinder block wall of the station stood a simple metal desk that had a telephone on it. Some seemingly random numbers always seemed to be scribbled on a notepad on the desk. A second tier to the desk supported two small reels with a thin strip of paper between them. Small triangles in groups were punched out of the paper. A single double wide overhead door shielded the outside world from the inner workings of the fire station on most days. Only small oblong windows were found in the front garage door. Large six foot high windows on the side of the station permitted the entry of some natural light.

Next to Engine 5 was a hook and ladder truck. Although I wasn't an expert on fire trucks, I could tell that this truck came from a different era than the engine. The ladder truck seemed to have a personality all of its own. The front grill consisted of two thickened pieces of chrome that formed a mouth that smiled at me. The eyes of the truck were the headlights that were implanted into the gently swooping front fenders. Right above the grill was a protruding round siren that served as a nose. A white tarp covered the cab of the ladder truck. It was custom designed to protect the firefighters from the North Tonawanda winters. A single red warning light sat atop a short pole above the front windshield. The main ladder came within inches of the back wall of the station. I remembered instinctively ducking underneath the ladder to get to the other side of the truck, even though my head cleared the ladder by at least two feet.

Grandma Borton made it clear that I was not to touch the trucks unless the firefighter specifically told me that I could do so. She also expected me to follow a second rule. I was never to ask the firefighter if I could touch the truck or sit in the cab of one of the trucks. Grandma believed that it was nice enough of the fine firefighter to let us in the door. Many of our excursions probably lasted less than ten minutes with Grandma quietly walking around the trucks while she held my hand.

One day we walked to the station and at the side door we were welcomed by an aging firefighter that I had never seen before. He wore glasses and he had white thinning hair. He used a jack knife to peel away the slender pieces of a pear he was eating. He smiled and asked me my name. I remembered thinking that this guy was awfully nice. Nice to the point that I thought this excursion to the fire hall might hold something special for me. After he talked small talk with Grandma, the firefighter turned to me and asked, "Would you like to sit up in the driver's seat of the fire engine Jason?" I quickly replied, "Yes," as I moved towards the driver's door of Engine 5. The driver put his jack knife down and then I felt his hands engage my armpits from behind. With one quick motion I was then standing in the cab of the engine.

I propped myself into the driver's seat using the large steering wheel in the cab. I looked out over the complicated set of gauges and instruments that were on the floor and dashboard before me. The one thing that didn't seem complicated in the cab was the steering wheel. Even I knew that a counterclockwise turn would turn the fire truck left while a clockwise turn would have the opposite effect. I sat there wondering how the driver did everything while driving to a fire; operating the lights, sounding the siren, blasting the horn. I stared at the overhead door through the large front windshield. Even someone as small as me could see everything in front of the fire truck. I grabbed the wheel and turned it back and forth. I pretended that I was driving to a fire. Grandma and the driver continued to talk despite the urgency of me getting the engine to the house fire in order to save it from complete destruction.

After what seemed to be a lifetime of imaginary driving in the fire truck, the driver broke my intense concentration by calling up to me. "Had enough?" he questioned. I wondered to myself whether someone could ever get enough of driving a fire truck. I knew that this was a hint that the driver wanted me to get down. He reached up into the cab and then gently lowered me to the floor. I think he must have caught the great disappointment in my face, because he immediately asked me if I wanted to go and sit in the hook and ladder truck. My answer was revealed when I beat him to the driver's side door of that truck.

As the pear peeling firefighter opened the door, I glimpsed inside. I was able to climb up into this cab, but the driver followed my movements closely, holding his arms out as a safety net in case I fell backwards. This truck was an entirely different beast from the one I had just been sitting in. A single bench seat spanned the width of the cab. A stick shift and an emergency brake interrupted the jagged diamond plate floor. Even though I was using my best childhood posture to see out through the front window, I couldn't even see the front hood of this truck. An old communications radio was bolted to the dashboard. Two large gauges ornamented the center of the dashboard. Several silver switches formed a line below those gauges.

I grabbed this steering wheel, turning it slightly from left to right and then back again in a repetitive motion. This junior firefighter was now driving the hook and ladder truck to the fire that existed inside his head. I needed to really get going because they needed the tall ladder to shoot water onto the fire. The siren of my mind was clearing traffic as I tore past the miniscule vehicles that pulled to the right. I could see the dark smoke billowing into the blue sky ahead. I was almost at the fire. It was then that Grandma stopped my heroic expedition in its tracks. "Jason, come on down now, we have to go home," she said. My heart sank as I reluctantly stepped down from the cab. It would be nearly thirty years later when I would be able to sit in the cab of a Seagrave fire truck. The firefighter walked behind us as we made our way to the door. Grandma quietly whispered to me and I turned around to face the firefighter.

"Thank you for showing me the fire trucks and for letting me sit in them," I said. "You're welcome Jason, come back anytime," he replied with a big smile on his face. For the duration of the walk back to her house, I repeatedly thanked my grandmother for taking me to the fire station that day.

Another time while visiting my grandmother's house, she took me to a nearby park to play after dinner. The park was just outside of North Tonawanda and it was situated on the Erie Canal. I played for sometime on the slides and the swings. As we prepared to leave, I noticed two yellow fire engines pulling into the parking lot. An Indian head adorned the doors of these fire trucks. These trucks were from the Shawnee Fire Company, a volunteer company from the Town of Wheatfield.

The engine parked near the boat launch and it used thick black hoses to siphon water from the canal. It then sent the water to the ladder truck that had extended its ladder about fifty feet into the air. A firefighter had climbed up the ladder and then he called for water. The nozzle at the tip of the ladder opened with a spurt of air, followed closely by a powerful stream of water. The engine's pump hummed as it fed an endless supply of water to the ladder truck. Grandma and I were on our way out of the park when the volunteers showed up to their drill. I knew that my grandmother understood how interested I would be in seeing fire trucks in action. The spotlights on the fire truck were coming on when we finally left the park an hour later. Once again I kept thanking Grandma when we had left the park. Yes, my grandmother had played a very special part in piquing my interest in firefighting. She even took me to the North Tonawanda Fire Headquarters one day for a change of scenery. Engine 7 was housed there. Little did she or I realize that day that one day, I would respond as a volunteer firefighter to real and not imaginary fires with that fire engine.

"Mr. Borton, could you tell us how we would go about researching information concerning the subject at hand?" an impatient voice questioned. "What?" I instinctively replied. Hushed giggles and loud laughter erupted around me. The teacher repeated her question and I was still unable to answer her question. I had been caught red handed in my reminiscent daydream. The teacher admonished me for not paying attention. Within seconds the bell signaled an end to my torture.

I exited the classroom amid the well meaning jeers of my classmates. I said nothing but I maneuvered down the crowded hallway towards my locker. I couldn't explain it but I felt as though something special had just happened to me. For some reason, I felt that I needed to do something extra with my life. I wanted to be something more than a high school senior. I wanted to really feel alive. I needed some kind of excitement in my life. I realized that sitting in a forty minute English class helped me to discover that I wanted to become a volunteer firefighter. As I fumbled with the lock on my locker, I realized that I didn't know the first thing about becoming a firefighter. One of my teachers was always willing to lend an ear and give well thought out advice. Talking to him was like talking to an old friend. I would talk to him the next day. I was sure that he would help me to think out my decision about becoming a volunteer firefighter. I also knew that his advice would be skewed. He was a well respected North Tonawanda volunteer firefighter.

3

Getting In

I woke up the next day unusually tired. The previous night
had been filled with vivid images of what it might be like
to be a volunteer firefighter. The last check of my alarm
clock before succumbing to sleep revealed that it was 3:30
a.m. Today would be the day that I would take the first step
towards becoming a volunteer firefighter. I would make it a
point to talk to my physics lab teacher, Mr. Frank.

Mr. Frank was a quiet man. He stood maybe 5'4" on a
good day. His usual school attire consisted of cowboy boots,
dress pants, a shirt, a short outdated tie, and a tan corduroy
sport jacket with brown elbow patches. He had been a
member of Sweeney Hose for many years. He worked as a
paramedic for Twin City Ambulance on most weekends.
Although he was short and spoke softly, he commanded the
respect and admiration of his students. Of all the teachers in
the high school, I had never heard a bad remark about Mr.
Frank.

As I was to find out, firefighting was a family affair for
Mr. Frank. His father was probably the most respected
member of Sweeney Hose, having served as the president of

the company. Two of his brothers were members of Sweeney Hose. His brother Greg's love for firefighting had taken him into the career side of the North Tonawanda Fire Department.

My physics lab took place during the fourth period of the day and it was a fun and relaxed time. Mr. Frank traveled from lab table to lab table watching our progress as we launched small metal balls from a ramp towards a target that was set on the floor. Our mission was to use parabolic physics equations to land the ball as close as possible to the center of the target. The winning team would have the most hits on the bull's-eye of the target.

Our class spent forty minutes performing our competition and at the end of the period the bell rang. I strayed behind the other students and caught Mr. Frank's ear, asking him if I could come to his eighth period study hall to talk with him. He obliged, but looked confused by my request as the section of physics we were studying was fairly straightforward. I took the yellow hall pass from his hand, promising to divulge more information to him later on in the day.

The spring day moved along and then it was finally eighth period. I handed my hall pass to my study hall teacher. He looked at it and without even looking at me, muttered for me to go and I did so, walking down the hall and right into Mr. Frank's study hall. He was getting his class under control and he saw me out of the corner of his eye. He motioned for me to come into the room. He offered me a seat next to his desk at the front of the room. He quickly got his class under control and then he came over to sit down at his desk.

"So what brings you here Jason? Do you have some questions about the physics lab?" he asked.

"No," I answered, "I wanted to talk to you about becoming a volunteer firefighter. I've been thinking about it for awhile now and I wanted to get an insider's view as to what it's all about."

He sat speechless as I looked at him. I saw uncertainty, astonishment, and excitement all molded into his unique facial expression. His face then finally showed a smile and he spent the next thirty five minutes explaining all of the opportunities and responsibilities that went along with being a volunteer firefighter. There were drills and training classes and fundraisers that had to be attended. His words scared me. They excited me. Most of all, they intrigued me and I knew that I wanted to learn even more about becoming a volunteer firefighter. Mr. Frank belonged to Sweeney Hose, but he acted in a non-biased way when he let me know about the five other volunteer fire companies in the city that were always looking for new members. The bell put an end to our discussion. Mr. Frank could tell that I was genuinely interested in volunteering. He offered to meet me at his fire hall later that night at 7 p.m. I eagerly agreed to meet him there. I walked towards my advanced composition class with a new bounce in my step. I hoped that the lesson would prove to be more interesting that the previous days'. I couldn't stand to be embarrassed again.

I left for the fire hall that evening at 6:40 p.m., much to the dismay of my parents. Over dinner I had told them of my intention to go to the Sweeney Hose Fire Company that evening to learn more about the fire service. I think they got the impression that I was going to sign up right on the spot. The only reason they let me out the door that evening was that I told them I was meeting with Mr. Frank. They knew that he was a well respected member not only of the school, but also of the community.

I counted the stoplights on the way to the fire hall. There were four. The distance to the hall was 1.7 miles. It took my Volkswagen Rabbit four minutes and fifteen seconds to reach the hall from my house. There was a fire station about four blocks and ninety seconds from my house. That station housed Engine 2 and it also served as the meeting place for the Active Hose Volunteer Fire Company. I could have shown up at Active Hose and asked for information about becoming a member there, but I wanted to see what the Sweeney Hose Company had to offer. If Mr.

Frank had been a member there for so many years, it must have had some redeeming qualities.

I arrived at the fire hall about fifteen minutes earlier than I was supposed to meet with Mr. Frank. Three or four cars sat silently in the parking lot, giving the suggestion that people were inside the hall doing something, possibly even something important, I thought. I did not go up to the door as I didn't want to interrupt whatever was going on in the hall. I would just wait for Mr. Frank to arrive. I glanced at my watch. It was 7 p.m. It was quarter after seven when I spotted a distant figure jogging towards the parking lot. It was who I expected and he was late. I would soon come to find out that Mr. Frank was late for most occasions.

I stepped out of my car as my slightly winded physics teacher greeted me with a handshake. He escorted me through the main entrance to the hall and I immediately noticed the dark wood paneled walls that were adorned with company patches from hundreds of fire companies. A small coatroom was on my right. It housed a beverage machine that not only dispensed soda pop but Genesee Cream Ale too.

The narrow hallway opened into a larger banquet hall with an outdated floor that seemed to be screaming that it needed to be replaced. Four men sat at a table playing Euchre. They did not acknowledge my presence, but cheerfully greeted my sweaty tour guide. I quickly glanced around the social hall. At one end stood a bar with a small television set behind it. The company patch was proudly painted on the wall behind the bar. The hall's interior was painted cinder block. The lower third was dark blue, while a sky blue color rounded out the upper portion of the color scheme. A bingo machine perched atop a platform stood to the right of the bar. Two exit doors interrupted the wall that was opposite from me. A small wall clock was the only thing that graced the distant wall to my right. A stale cigarette smell hovered above that tobacco that was being freshly burned by the players at the card table.

Mr. Frank then introduced me to the Euchre players. Two of them nodded their non-verbal greeting whereas the other two shook my hand and stayed seated at the table. The hand shakers wee obviously brothers as they bore the same last name. The smaller brother carried a small beer gut with slicked back jet black hair. The other brother carried a larger frame that spilled over the sides of his chair. As I wondered how such a small chair could support the weight of this man, his chair vibrated from a very audible and prolonged expulsion of flatulence. The big brother laughed as the other Euchre players reflexively pushed their chairs backwards, as if over the years they had become quite familiar with the effect that the upcoming stench would have on their nostrils.

Mr. Frank quietly laughed at the farting episode and then he cheerfully called the big brother rotten. We left the Euchre game behind to continue my tour of the hall. The kitchen seemed large enough to cater a decent sized party. A small room near the front of the building served as both the bingo office and the janitor's closet. A slightly larger room hosted two tables of bingo players on Sunday nights. During the rest of the week it served as storage room for tables. Once a month, the board of directors of the fire company would hold their board meeting there.

I was then escorted to the rearward exit of the main hall. We stepped out onto a sidewalk and faced a building that was less than twenty feet away from us. The two side entrance doors of this building had thick reinforced glass in them and each door was marked with thick strips of bold fluorescent orange tape. Behind the building two radio antenna towers reached into the air. Each one was surrounded by a fence and a sign bearing the warning of "Danger, High Voltage".

We walked to the side doors of the fire headquarters building. Mr. Frank opened the right side door for me and I stepped up into the building. A buzzer sounded in the distance. We headed right towards the truck room. The door buzzer had assured us a quick greeting by a tall firefighter who noticeably swayed his arms when he walked. The firefighter gingerly took Mr. Frank's hand and greeted him. I was introduced to the firefighter who then proceeded to give me the same warm greeting as he had given Mr. Frank. I learned that his name was Douglas Jarrett. Doug had been a member of the career department for some time, but he was also a member of both the Sweeney Hose Company and the Columbia Hook and Ladder Company. Tim, the name that Mr. Frank insisted I call him outside of the school setting, told the firefighter of my interest in becoming a volunteer firefighter. Doug's eyes lit up. I sensed that he felt like the spotlight was on and he was about to be thrown onto the stage. He knew he had a job to do. He quickly led me to the side of Engine 7.

Doug's tour started out with his description of Engine 7. I learned that it was a 1973 Ward LaFrance pumper. It was made right in Elmira, New York. Doug told me about its booster tank and its booster tank capacity. He then rattled off a fast flurry of additional facts about the engine. The next forty five minutes were used to open every compartment on the pumper. I was also told the name of every piece of equipment in those compartments.

I learned about the red rolled up booster lines that delivered a small amount of water that was adequate for putting out small grass fires. The rig also had tightly woven brooms to mechanically thump out grass fires. AFFF stood for aqueous film forming foam. It came in five gallon containers and was mixed with water to help put out petroleum based fires. There was even an oddly shaped nozzle called a gizmo whose purpose was to deliver a circular shower of water into confined spaces that were inaccessible to the firefighters. I silently felt overwhelmed by the amount of information I was receiving during this whirlwind tour. What would happen if I were asked to retrieve something at a fire? Would I remember what it looked like? If I did know what is was, would I even remember what compartment it was in? Tim calmed my fears as he must have observed the puzzled expression on my face.

"You'll learn all of this again in your essentials of firefighting class," he said. "And you'll also be able to come over here in your free time and go through the truck at your own pace."

"That's good," I said with a half hearted laugh, "I was beginning to think that there would be a test at the end of the night."

Doug took a quick breather after finishing up his tour of the engine. He quickly regained his breath and said, "Jay, let me take you downstairs and I'll show you how this fire department really works."

We followed Doug as we passed in front of Car 10, the assistant chief's command vehicle, and the first siren producer that had distracted my attention in English class just days before. We came to an open door and turned right down a flight of stairs that stopped on a landing. We were confronted with a metallic sign that read, "NO UNAUTHORIZED PERSONS BEYOND THIS POINT". Doug stopped and tapped the sign with his knuckle. "Don't worry Jay. This building was constructed to serve as a fallout shelter in the event of a nuclear attack. Once we get down into the basement you'll have four solid feet of concrete over your head. This is the place to come if the shit ever hits the fan, speaking in a globally shitty kind of way," he said.

We went down another set of stairs and then we immediately turned left down a short hallway. An open door on the left side of the hallway led into a decontamination shower. A small kitchen was further down the hallway. There was an open room at the end of the hall. Desks sat in two silent rows. Numerous doors to offices and locker rooms interrupted the walls of the room. A line of dusty trophies sat forgotten on a large steel girder above our heads. A half podium sat atop a desk to our right. This would be our classroom for our winter drills. Doug escorted us to a room to our right. A closed door greeted us with three stern words, "Fire Dispatcher – Quiet".

Doug tapped twice on the door and then turned the handle. A firefighter in his work uniform had his back turned to us as he watched television. A formidable "L" shaped console sat in front of him and to his left side. A list of many phone numbers was posted to his right and on a sign in front of him. To the left of the door hung a six by six foot map of the city of North Tonawanda.

Doug asked the dispatcher to go upstairs to relieve him from driving the engine so that he could show me the dispatch office. Doug introduced me to the dispatcher who refused my handshake. He literally grunted as he walked past Tim and me. He closed the dispatch door behind him. Doug was silent for a short period of time. He then said, "Jay, that was Andrew Davidson. As you can probably tell, he is a complete prick. Don't think that you had anything to do with his attitude towards you. He hates all volunteer and most of the career firefighters. Hell, he even hates himself." I thought to myself that things couldn't be much worse with any other member of the department if the seemingly biggest jerk would just grunt and walk away from me.

Doug looked comfortably at home when he sat down in the dispatcher's chair. He methodically introduced me to the 9-1-1 system in North Tonawanda. He informed me that all 9-1-1 calls first went to the police department. If the caller to 9-1-1 had a fire to report or needed emergency medical services, the call would be forwarded to the fire dispatcher's office. A small electronic screen would automatically display the caller's address.

Reaching below the desk counter, Doug pulled open a random drawer from a small card filing cabinet. The cabinet contained a card for each street in the city. Doug asked me what street I lived on and I told him that I lived on Chipman Place. He went to the "C" drawer and pulled out the card for Chipman Place. Doug's chest seemed to swell a bit as he spoke. "If there was a fire at your house this card lets me know that Engine 2, Engine 7, Truck 2, Car 10 and Rescue 1 would respond. The fire hydrant nearest to your house is at the corner of Payne Avenue and Stanley Street." I was amazed that all of this information had been compiled for every address in North Tonawanda.

Doug then proceeded to show me how he would set up a box alarm. The "box" in box alarm came from the

Gamewell pull boxes that once adorned nearly every street corner in the city. When a person pulled the lever on a fire alarm box, a four digit number would be transmitted to the fire dispatcher's office. The dispatcher would look at the number that was being sent in. He would then consult a book which showed the location of the box. These numbers would be punched out on a paper tape roll to each individual fire station in the city, so an alert apparatus driver could know the location of the box alarm even before the dispatcher announced its location. Even in the modern day when most reports of fire came in over the telephone, box alarms were still assigned for a fire even though a street alarm box was never activated. This seemed strange to me, but as I would later learn, many traditions were slow to fade away in the fire department.

Doug spent the next thirty minutes explaining the intricacies of dispatching fire trucks. He went into such detail that I honestly believed that I could have successfully dispatched a full complement of fire apparatus to the scene of a fire. Doug's enthusiasm and love for his job was quite apparent. I thanked him for the time he took with making me familiar with the fire equipment and the dispatcher's office.

The buzz of the side door of fire headquarters bid Tim and me farewell just as it had welcomed us two hours earlier. Tim pounded on the steel fire door on the side of the Sweeney Hose hall. The fat brother opened the door. The Euchre game had ended and the players were sitting at the bar and watching TV. Tim asked me if I wanted to talk to any members of another fire hall to see if I would want to join another hall. I quickly told him no. Doug Jarrett had made a great impression on me. I knew Tim and he was one person more than I would know at any other fire hall in the city. I told Tim that I wanted to join Sweeney Hose. The fat brother was quick to produce a membership application. I filled out the application which fit entirely on a four inch by six inch card. To attest that I was a good candidate for membership, two members in good standing with the company would need to sign my application. Tim signed one line and another member sitting around the bar put his signature on the second line. Five dollars guaranteed that my membership application would at least be considered by the company and if I wasn't voted in, I was assured that my five dollars would be promptly returned to me. I would have to go to the North Tonawanda Police Department and request that a police record check in my name be sent to the Sweeney Hose Company.

Tim contacted me about six weeks after my tour of the hall and told me to be at the fire hall on May 7th at 7:30 p.m. My eighteenth birthday would come a day later, but Tim had pulled some strings so that I wouldn't have to wait another month to become a member of the hall. I would become a volunteer firefighter a whole day before New York State would legally allow me to become one.

I arrived at the hall and stood around waiting for the meeting to start. I felt awkward standing among a group of strangers, but the slamming of a gavel at 8 p.m. signaled the start of the meeting. The sergeant at arms escorted another prospective member and me out into the hallway. The fire doors into the main hall were closed and we were instructed to wait in the hallway until we were brought into the meeting. I made small talk with my hallway partner and I found myself nervously pacing up and down the length of the hall. After twenty minutes we were called into the meeting. The members were all standing on their feet. The sergeant at arms led us to the front of the room. We were met by the company deputy. He asked us to raise our right hand and then state our names. We completed that successfully and then he read the following oath:

I, of my own free will and accord, pledge on my honor to faithfully observe the Constitution of the United States of America and the by-laws of the fire company. I further pledge to support and defend the Constitution of the United States of America, to comply with all the rules and regulations for the government thereof, not to divulge or make known any private proceedings of this fire company, to faithfully perform with honesty and integrity the duties assigned to me, to pay all just fines and dues imposed on me by this fire company, to conduct myself at all times as not to bring reproach upon myself or my fire company. This I pledge on my sacred honor as a person and member of the Sweeney Hose Company #7.

After reading the oath, the deputy instructed us to say, "I do". We said "I do" simultaneously and the membership broke a second of silence with applause. The deputy offered his congratulations to us as he shook our hands. The president asked us to find a seat as the rest of the membership sat down. I found a lone seat at the back of the room and sat down.

I sat there at the back of the room listening to the members of the Sweeney Hose Company as they conducted their business. I didn't have a single piece of fire gear or an ounce of training but these men had accepted me as one of their own. At this point I had two men to thank for getting me into this meeting: Tim Frank and Doug Jarrett. Now if only I knew how to fight a fire.

4

Breaking the Tetrahedron

I realized that it would not be enough for me to go down to the fire hall and just keep telling everyone I was a volunteer firefighter. I would actually have to learn how to fight fire. When I joined the fire department every rookie was required to take a course on firefighting – Essentials of Firefighting. The city mandated that this class be taken within two years of joining the fire department. The class had to be completed in its entirety. In thirty nine hours over thirteen weeks we were taught only the basics of firefighting. We learned the names and general uses of pieces of equipment. We learned how to use different spray patterns from a nozzle for different situations. We would learn about the types of ladders and how to safely raise them. We would learn the basic function of the self contained breathing apparatus or SCBA. Hopefully by the end of the course we would have learned how to stay out of the way of trouble. Successful completion of the Essentials of Firefighting course was the only ticket into more advanced firefighting classes.

Tim Frank had prepared me for becoming a member of the Sweeney Hose Company and he took an extra step to make sure that I started off on the right foot. Tim had called up the training officer of the fire department, assistant chief Ken Jarantz. He told Chief Jarantz of my plans to become a member of Sweeney Hose and he convinced him to let me into the Essentials course before I was even sworn in as a member of the fire department. Tim informed me of the date and time of the first night of class. It would be held at Engine 6's quarters, home of the Gratwick Hose Company.

It was a warm and breezy spring evening as I sat along the banks of the Niagara River with the girl I would be taking to my senior prom. She was a soft spoken junior with natural blond hair and blue eyes who had recently broken up with her boyfriend. She was doing a great job of showing very little interest in me. I had brought her to the river to talk about us becoming a couple but small talk and uncomfortable stretches of silence prevailed. After mindlessly picking grass for several minutes I looked at my watch. It was ten minutes to seven. I immediately stood up and explained my need to leave to Diana. I opened her door for her and she got into my passenger seat. Luckily for me her house was a short drive from the river. As I pulled into her driveway, it seemed now that she wanted to talk. My eyes quickly conveyed a silent message that I needed to leave. One of these days I had hoped for a kiss or even a hug. Today, as was the usual, I received a "goodbye" and a promise to talk to me tomorrow.

I sped my car out of her driveway while I looked down at my watch. Five after seven. I was late for my first night of class. The Gratwick Hose Company was less than one minute from Diana's house. I bolted into the parking lot to find about fifteen cars parked there. Walking towards the front of the building, I saw Engine 6 and its rusting body parked on the ramp in front of the station. I walked through the overhead door of the truck bay and into the back of the makeshift classroom. Twenty people were facing forward towards a lanky man with a long sleeved white shirt and a black tie. He wore glasses and his peppered hair was receding. He stopped talking and looked at me. He acknowledged me with a greeting. He questioned, "Who the fuck are you and why are you late?" I stood silent as he motioned for me to come to the front of the classroom. I told him my name. "Oh yeah", he said, as the sarcasm in his voice faded, "Timmy said that you'd be here. Take a pencil, find a seat, and fill this out."

I found an open seat and as I was sitting down a familiar voice whispered from behind me, "Nice job Borton, first class and you're already pissing him off." I looked over my shoulder and saw Vince Adder, a good natured fun loving guy who was a senior in my high school class. I acknowledged him and turned around.

I started to fumble through the sheets of paper that had been handed to me. The State of New York obviously wanted to know everything about me as I was about to become one of its thousands of volunteer firefighters. I started to fill in bubbles on a sheet with my pencil when the training officer started to speak.

"You can and should call me chief. When we're at training, you can call me Ken. You can call me asshole, but the word chief better be in front of it," he said. The class burst out into laughter. Was this the guy that was going to teach us how to get out of a burning building alive?

The chief cradled his coffee mug and walked around the room while we finished our registration forms. In exchange for our completed paperwork, the chief gave us an inch thick stack of papers wrapped in plastic. It had holes for a three ring binder. The front of the book was titled *Firefighting Essentials*. Before we opened the book we were told that we had to complete a pretest. The questions seemed very difficult as I knew very little about firefighting. I guessed the answer to most of the questions and I handed in my test. Most of the other rookie firefighters were still taking their test when I finished. I decided to rip open the plastic surrounding my booklet.

I turned to the first chapter, entitled "Fire Service Organization and Behavior." I leafed through the pages and

27

then a detailed sketch of what appeared to be a large campfire caught my attention. The word "fire" was boldly printed at the top of the page. It seemed that fire, at least according to New York State, was "a self-sustaining rapid oxidation resulting in the release of energy in the form of heat and light." The definition was complicated but at the same time simple. I assumed that as a firefighter it would be my job to interrupt this self sustaining rapid oxidation process so that no energy in the form of heat or light was given off.

The concepts seemed simple so far and I continued to look through the chapter. I came across a picture of a triangle with sides that were labeled: oxygen, heat, fuel. A caption below the triangle read, "Remove one side (one element) of the triangle and the fire is extinguished".

On the bottom of the page there was a picture of a tetrahedron. Not a square or a rectangle, but a tetrahedron. Apparently a triangle was just too simple. Scientists had found that a certain chemical reaction occurred when something burned and lo and behold the fire triangle had turned into a tetrahedron. We would spend the next twelve weeks learning how to remove heat from fires, mainly through the use of water. Even though other sides of the tetrahedron could be removed, I surmised that removing the heat from a fire was the fastest and cheapest way to extinguish it. That principle had existed in America for hundreds of years and it remained the primary method of fire suppression to the modern day.

After everyone had finished the pretest we listened to the monotonous voice of Ken Jarantz for the next two and a half hours. I looked up from my book, trying to give the impression that I was paying close attention to his words but I was not. I kept looking through the book. I read words. I scanned pictures. What things would I be able to do as a volunteer firefighter? Would I be able to set up a forty foot ground ladder and then climb it? Would I be able to hook up a pumper to a hydrant? Could I enter a smoke filled burning building, rescue a child, and then bring her to safety? My thoughts stopped wandering as Assistant Chief Jarantz told us that the remainder of the classes would take place at the fire training tower or at fire headquarters. Our homework assignment would be to find out the names of the assistant chiefs and captains for each of the four platoons. We would also be responsible for getting the names of the drivers for each of our respective company's apparatus. He dismissed us and I walked out to my car.

The next class was held at fire headquarters. I got my second tour of Engine 7's equipment and compartments. Names of pieces of equipment were once again thrown into the air. This time I was jotting down what things came out of which compartments. I could read about its purpose later in the textbook. I knew that if I went to a fire scene I did not want to look like a rookie opening every compartment door if someone asked me to get a tool.

Chief Jarantz also stressed the importance of safety on the fire scene. We wouldn't be useful if we were injured. In North Tonawanda, volunteer firefighters could use blue lights when traveling to a fire scene. These were courtesy lights and they gave us no special privileges on the road. Citizens would often yield the right of way and pull over for a car with a blue light flashing, but they weren't required to do so. We would not even be issued a blue light use card until we had successfully completed the essentials course. We were advised to always walk on fire scenes as falls and minor musculoskeletal injuries accounted for the greatest number of firefighter injuries.

Our third class was an introduction to the use of the self contained breathing apparatus or SCBA. We spent the whole class learning how to perform all the necessary safety checks to make sure that the unit was safe and ready for use. We learned the techniques for putting the tank on and hooking up our masks to life sustaining breathing air. We must have put on and taken off the tank ten times during that class. Chief Jarantz made it abundantly clear that being completely comfortable with the SCBA would be one of the most important steps towards us becoming competent firefighters.

Searching for and rescuing victims while wearing our SCBAs was the topic of our fourth class. There were many things to learn and remember: Why walls were felt with the back of the hand. Why you never switched hands on a wall while doing a search in a building. We "washed" the inside of our masks with alcohol wipes before we handed them over to the next rookie to use. I felt as though I was getting more comfortable with the SCBA as our class was being enveloped in darkness, but I also felt that I needed more training before I would be comfortable going into a real burning building.

In other classes we learned about tying knots. We learned the basic ones and after talking with the career firefighter who was at essentials one night to help Chief Jarantz, we basically forgot about them as he said that we rarely, if ever, needed to tie a knot as a North Tonawanda firefighter.

We learned about fire hoses and North Tonawanda had quite a few of them. The orange supply hose was named "4 inch" because of its diameter. It was made of thickened rubber like material. These hoses carried water from the fire hydrants to the engines which were sometimes quite a distance away. Each North Tonawanda engine carried six one hundred foot lengths of the 4 inch hose.

The two and a half inch hose or the "two and a half" was used for defensive attacks on a fire or when fighting a large volume of fire. It could be maneuvered by two or three firefighters but the girth and weight of the hose severely limited the firefighters' ability to move quickly through a structure. A lone firefighter could control this beast of a line if he looped the nozzle under the other part of the hose and then sat down on the spot where the hose overlapped itself.

The "inch and a half" was the bread and butter hose of the interior attack on a fire. It could be controlled by a single firefighter but two firefighters were needed to snake the line around the obstacles in a house. This hose could deliver up to one hundred and twenty five gallons of water per minute from its nozzle. Taking any hose smaller than an inch and a half into a burning building was considered a dangerous proposition.

Engine 7 had two reels mounted above the pump panel area. One reel was on each side of the truck. Wrapped around each reel was a three quarter inch red hose that was called a booster line. Because of their low water flow, the booster tank, which held the water on board the engine, could usually supply sufficient water to these lines without having to hook up to a fire hydrant. The booster line was used for small grass and rubbish fires. It was also used to wash down small gasoline spills and roadway debris after motor vehicle collisions.

Hoses had male and female parts or couplings. A firefighter was to have the male coupling in hand while dragging a length of hose so that exposed male threads wouldn't be subjected to damage from the ground. For the same protective reasons, the male coupling was always located on the innermost portion of a hose roll. Each coupling had a Higbee notch or indicator that when aligned with the Higbee indicator on the opposite coupling allowed for faster coupling of the two hoses. Discharges for water outflow from the engine had bent necks on them. Intake valves for water flow into the engine were straight and usually lower to the ground.

Shoveled dirt or sand could put out some fires that were small. Water extinguishers could shoot a straight thin stream of water at least forty feet. That was great for hitting an unsuspecting volunteer at your fire hall with, but in terms of fire suppression, a seasoned firefighter would put his thumb over the discharge spout of the extinguisher hose to spread the water.

Hoses could put out straight streams of water or fog patterns. Adjustable nozzles let the firefighter choose any stream in between a straight stream and a fog stream. A well controlled hose could quickly control a fire, but a slithering, unmanned hose with an open nozzle could seriously injure a firefighter. Ideally, a runaway hose was recognized by the pump operator who could shut down the water flow to the renegade hose. A careful firefighter could inch along a hose on his belly with his nose sucking up ground debris in an attempt to shut down an open line.

The number and types of ladders used in the fire department were more numerous than the types of hoses. Ladders looked simple, but each part of the ladder had a specific name. Before becoming a firefighter, my entire ladder vocabulary consisted of one word – "rung". As a firefighter I had to know what tormentor poles were. I stared at a ladder trying to identify the parts I had seen in the textbook. What part was a dog and what was its purpose? What's a halyard? What were toggles, spurs, and tie rods and what did they have to do with the overall function of a ladder?

Ladders could be permanently mounted to a fire truck. The pieces of equipment that they were mounted to were called ladder trucks. In North Tonawanda we referred to our ladder trucks simply as trucks. Pumpers were called engines. There were ladders of many different lengths and many different purposes. To climb into an attic, an attic ladder was used. A roof ladder had special hooks that went over the peak of a roof and allowed firefighters to work somewhat safely on a roof.

Raising a twenty eight foot extension ladder was easy. I had raised one many times with my father. Raising a forty foot extension ladder with tormentor poles was a little more daunting of a task. Six firefighters were needed to hoist a ladder of this size and they needed to be communicating with each other at all times. To place the ladder into the vertical position, the two firefighters at the butt or foot of the ladder planted their foot closest to the ladder on the first rung. These individuals, because of their position were known as the butt men. They bore the brunt of the endless array of butt jokes that were flying their way. Just above the butt men on the joke scale were the tip men who pushed on the tips of the tormentor poles to help to raise the ladder. The center men pushed on the side rail of the ladder to move it into a vertical position while walking towards the butt men. When the ladder was vertical, one of the tip men moved perpendicular to the other tip man and his tormentor pole so that the heavy ladder was stabilized. One of the center men then raised the halyard while the butt men continued to steady the ladder. Once the ladder was raised and up against a structure, the tip men would place their poles parallel to the building.

For me, the biggest challenge and most daunting part of the firefighting essentials course was the chance to climb the ladder of the city's one hundred foot aerial, Truck 1. Before any climbing could occur, the truck needed to be prepared. Four large outriggers had to be extended from the sides of the truck. The outriggers were operated by the apparatus driver who stood on the ground at the back of the truck. A firefighter was assigned to each outrigger and once it was fully extended, a small metal plate was put on the ground beneath the outrigger. Everyone gave the outrigger a wide berth as it was lowered to the metal plate as even the thought of getting a foot smashed was painful. Assistant Chief Jarantz made it very clear that the aerial truck driver was not to be talked to or distracted in any way while he was leveling the truck. He told us that each driver had his own system of setting up the aerial, or big stick as it was affectionately called, and any interruption of his system could cause the driver to miss an important step in his process.

Once the driver was satisfied that the truck was as level as it could be, he stepped away from the controls and directed the firefighters to place a large pin through two holes in the outrigger. This would theoretically prevent the truck from shifting wildly in the event of a hydraulic system failure of the truck. Once the pins were set, the driver ascended a narrow fixed ladder at the back of the truck. He opened a turnstile rope and then closed it behind him as he stepped onto the turntable to the ladder. A rain cover was removed from the control panel and then he was prepared to raise the ladder.

The sun was setting over Grand Island to the west as the aerial ladder began its ascent at one of our last essentials classes. The thunderous sound of the engine lifting the ladder was accompanied by black plumes of spent diesel fuel that bellowed from the exhaust pipes of the truck. The ladder was hoisted to what seemed to be a seventy degree angle to the ground. The driver rotated the turntable one hundred and eighty degrees so that the weight of the truck would offset our weight on the extended ladder. The ladder was then extended to one hundred feet. Chief Jarantz gave us some final words of encouragement and warning before the first person started his climb.

"Now I know that everyone doesn't like heights and you are not required to climb this ladder if you don't want to. If you think you are going to have trouble, then don't climb it," he stated. "Each of you who do climb the ladder will wear a safety belt. Learn how to use it on the ground. If you get nervous and freeze up there, clip it onto a rung and we'll come up and get your sorry ass down from there. When you get to the top, clip your safety belt to a rung and enjoy the view. Take your time and don't tire yourself out," he concluded.

I could feel my heart trying to punch a hole through my sternum. I never harbored any severe aversion to heights, but I never particularly enjoyed them either. The ladder did look quite stable as it was being raised and the still tree leaves didn't show any evidence of strong winds at a higher elevation. At least someone else had volunteered to climb first. He was on his way up the ladder and over the course of the next five minutes he seemed to shrink. He stayed at the top of the ladder for a short time and them he began his slow descent towards solid earth. Nearly out of breath, he climbed down from the turntable and stepped down to the ground. I questioned him how it was and with a smile on his face he said that the trip up was tiring but the view was well worth the trip. I asked him for his ladder belt as a second rookie was now on his way up the ladder. I secured the belt around my waist and gave myself a quick course in maneuvering the clasp while wearing my gloves. I would be the next person to climb the ladder.

When the driver called me to come up to the turntable, I lifted my foot nearly three feet off the ground to reach the stationary ladder that lead to the turntable. I stood silently next to the driver as the firefighter on the ladder was nearly back to the turntable. He reached the bottom and stepped off the ladder. The driver stopped him, putting a hand on his back. He said, "Stand here for a couple of seconds and let yourself get used to the idea that you're not moving backwards and down anymore. When you feel steady, go ahead and get down from the truck."

I looked at the driver for climbing approval and he nodded his head. I stepped onto rungs that were covered with a thick layer of grooved rubber to enhance traction. I slowly but confidently climbed the first twenty five foot section of ladder. There was no sway in the ladder and I felt encased by the thick support beams of this main section. The second section offered little challenge to climbing, but I started to feel somewhat winded as I stepped onto the third section. Peeking down through the rungs I could see the black turnout gear of the surprisingly small firefighters below. They seemed to be moving slightly back and forth with each rung I climbed. I suddenly realized that they were stationary and the ladder was the moving object. I started to feel a breeze that wasn't noticeable at ground level. The thick girders that provided so much reassurance near the bottom of the ladder were now gone and replaced by a thin bar that did little to help my confidence at this altitude. I reminded myself to keep on climbing. I refused to let my mind think about falling. I was now less than ten feet from the top of the ladder. I stopped just below the foot plates near the top of the ladder. These were designed to let a firefighter stand on a flat surface at the top of the ladder. I knew I didn't want to tackle complicated foot tasks ninety five feet above the ground. My feet stayed on a single rung. My hands grasped the upper rung. I decided to forego the ladder belt hook at this point. I glanced out towards the western sky.

Looking over the Niagara River I saw the silhouette of the Holiday Inn on Grand Island. Peering northward, I saw a line of small buildings that were partially hidden by the mist created by Niagara Falls, some fifteen miles away. Looking farther to my right I looked towards North Tonawanda, the city that had been my home for the last eighteen years. Distant traffic signals changed colors for cars that couldn't be heard from where I stood. My town was very quiet at this altitude.

As I slowly descended the ladder, I had time to think about how much I had learned during the past few months in the Essentials class. I felt confident in my abilities, especially after climbing a one hundred foot ladder. I now knew the basics that I needed to know to break the fire tetrahedron. We would learn more skills in the next several weeks, but I was preparing for a big transition in my life. I would be leaving for Clarkson University as a college freshman within a month. I probably wouldn't be able to practice my firefighting skills actively for at least another four years. I wondered if I had joined the fire hall at the wrong time. Would I lose interest in firefighting while I was away at college? I left the training tower that night feeling glad that I had chosen to become a firefighter but sad that I wouldn't be able to actively fight fires. I felt like I would miss out on many things. Only God knew when I would return to North Tonawanda.

5

The NTFD

E very visitor coming to North Tonawanda from the east, south, or west will need to cross a bridge to enter the city. The bridges host green rectangular signs that state, "Welcome to North Tonawanda – Home of the Carrousel". The Herschell Carrousel Factory once crafted carrousels that were shipped all over the United States and the world. History has been preserved in the original factory where a museum now tells the stories of an industry long gone from North Tonawanda. A visitor coming into the city from the town of Wheatfield would not need to cross over a bridge, but a carrousel sign would still greet them upon their entrance into the city. According to the United States census data from 2000, there are 33,262 North Tonawandans living in a city that encompasses ten square miles. The median household income of the citizens was approximately $50,000 in 2000.

The entire western edge of North Tonawanda is bordered by the mighty Niagara River whose waters flow northward to plunge over Niagara Falls. The word "Tonawanda" is actually a Native American word meaning "swift running water". The swift running water is actually that of a creek that sported rapids through the area until the digging of the Erie Canal quelled the rapids forever. The city of Tonawanda lies across the Erie Canal on the city's southern border. The Town of Amherst lies to the east of the city.

North Tonawanda was once proudly known as the "lumber capital of the world". Because of its location along the Niagara River and the westernmost point of the Erie Canal, boats throughout the Great Lakes could offload large quantities of lumber on the city's shores. Because of the lumber industry, the downtown area of North Tonawanda flourished in the latter part of the 1800s and the early part of the 1900s. The hub of the city was located near the junction of the Niagara River and the Erie Canal. Most of the city's early volunteer fire companies were located near the center of the city. Much of what now is housing in North Tonawanda was merely woods or farmer's fields when the city was growing. In time, the geographic locations of some of the fire stations would lead to their ultimate demise and closing.

The North Tonawanda Fire Department currently consists of a career fire department and six volunteer fire companies. The department was initially an all volunteer department until the city realized the benefits of a combined paid and volunteer department to improve response times to incidents. The six surviving volunteer fire companies in North Tonawanda are the Columbia Hook and Ladder Company No. 1, the Active Hose Company No. 2, the Live Hose Company No. 4, the Rescue Fire Company No. 5, the Gratwick Hose Company No. 6, and the Sweeney Hose Company No. 7. When I joined the fire service in 1990, each of these companies had a piece of equipment in service. Today, because of downsizing and powerful political forces, only four of the six companies have an active apparatus responding to emergency calls. The career and volunteer firefighters collectively make up the North Tonawanda Fire Department and they work together in providing the community with fire suppression, rescue, and emergency medical services.

In 1990, there were nine front line vehicles in the fire department. Today there are six. Car 10 serves as the assistant chief's mode of transportation. In 1990 and for several years after, Car 10 was a station wagon. Those station wagons just never seemed manly enough and today Car 10 is a loud diesel burning SUV. Rescue 1 is a light duty rescue vehicle that carries the bulk of the first aid equipment and rescue equipment for the department. It, like Car 10, responds to all emergency medical services calls and all alarms of fire. The career personnel on Rescue 1 consist of a driver, who is a New York State certified critical care technician, and a captain. Currently Engines 4, 6, and 7 cover the entire city of North Tonawanda. Truck 1 is the ladder truck in the city. Truck 2, Engine 2, and Engine 5 have been permanently removed from service.

The career department consists of a fire chief, a fire prevention officer, a training officer, a department secretary, a department mechanic, duty officers and career firefighters. The department is divided into four platoons. Each platoon, when fully staffed, consists of an assistant chief, whose radio call sign is prefixed with the letter "A" followed by the platoon number. The prefix of "B" denotes the captain of the platoon. Each piece of apparatus has one driver on each platoon. Two firefighters on each platoon serve as relief drivers who work at different fire stations and fill in for firefighters who are sick or on vacation. Each platoon works for two days and then they are off for two days. Their shift then moves to nights where they work two night shifts. The day shift starts at 7 a.m. and lasts until 5 p.m. The night platoon comes in at 5 p.m. and leaves at 7 a.m. the next morning.

Volunteer firefighters are issued a monitor or fire scanner when they join the fire department. My first monitor was a scanner that required a crystal of the appropriate frequency to operate. These units had to be plugged into an outlet, which limited the ability to hear an alarm of fire while outside of the house. In later years, the department issued portable handheld scanners that were rechargeable. Dispatching was done by North Tonawanda career firefighters who split their time between dispatching and driving Engine 7 or Truck 2. These dispatchers were eliminated from the fire department when the city made the decision to use dispatching services through the Niagara County Fire dispatch office in Lockport, New York.

Unlike departments that were all volunteer, North Tonawanda volunteers never drove fire apparatus to the scene of an emergency incident. We responded in our own vehicles. This was good in that a great deal of manpower arrived at the scene in a very short period of time. Engine and truck drivers never waited at the station to get a full complement of firefighters to ride the apparatus to a scene. They just took off hoping that there would be enough manpower at the scene. The downside of multiple volunteers responding in personal vehicles was parking problems. North Tonawanda had many narrow streets and if enough volunteers beat an engine or truck to a call, then maneuvering the large piece of apparatus down a narrow street could be a difficult if not impossible task.

New York State allowed volunteer firefighters to use blue lights on their personal vehicles. That being the case, these blue lights didn't afford the volunteer firefighter a single privilege above any other driver on the road. No speeding, going through red lights, or driving the wrong way down a one way street for the volunteers. Courteous drivers would often pull to the right for volunteers whose blue lights were flashing. I would say that this happened about fifty percent of the time when responding to calls in North Tonawanda. Often a blue light would be flashing as a volunteer pulled up to a red light. Concerned and uninformed citizens would stop at their green light and try to wave the volunteer through the intersection. Blue lights attracted a great deal of attention from the public. If we were witnessed performing a traffic infraction with the blue light in operation we were likely to catch hell from the fire chief or even the police. I had used my blue light for several years, but then I packed it away. It was much easier to push the speed limit in the city without having a blue light advertisement for my misdeed.

There were only three tasks that volunteer firefighters could not perform in the fire department. We couldn't drive the apparatus, operate the pumps, or set up the aerial ladder. Besides those things we were trained to do everything on the fire ground that a career firefighter might do. The career firefighters went to a fire academy for several weeks so they were trained to do things that they might never use in their careers while working in North Tonawanda.

Relations between the volunteers and the career department firefighters have improved over time. In 1990 I was told to watch my step around several career firefighters. Today the person who garnered the title of "complete jerk" has recently retired from the department. Rumor had it that he was even a jerk to his fellow career firefighters to the point that he had gotten cold cocked a couple of times. In my years at Sweeney I did hear the story of how a bunch of volunteers from the Rescue Fire Company had duct taped the Engine 5 driver to his chair and then took the engine for a short joy ride, but I was never presented any conclusive evidence to prove this rumor to be true. Aside from the occasional harassment that every volunteer rookie gets from a career firefighter and the occasional and usually well deserved ass chewing by a duty officer, I can think of only one instance when I had a serious face to face confrontation with a career firefighter. And I'm pretty sure that I won.

A bunch of us from the Sweeneys were going to the local all night greasy spoon restaurant Nestors for a late night snack. We were driving separately and about four blocks from the restaurant I heard a one tap come over my portable scanner. I pulled to the side of the road as I always did when I heard a tone in case the call was for Engine 7. By pulling over I wouldn't be driving away from the call.

"Dispatcher to engine four," called the dispatcher.

"Four," replied the groggy Engine 4 driver.

"Tremont near Main Street, report of an MVA with injuries."

"10-4, Tremont near Main".

"I'll be the first one on the scene," I thought to myself, realizing that I was less than two blocks away from the accident. I stopped momentarily at the red light at Oliver and Tremont Streets and made a right onto Tremont. Passing underneath a train viaduct, I quickly stopped and surveyed the scene in front of me. An overturned pick up truck was lying next to a telephone pole that had been freshly sheared in half. Firewood from the back of the pick up truck was strewn all over the street. Low hanging wires prohibited me from driving any closer to the scene. A police car ahead of me turned right off of Columbia Drive, apparently not seeing the accident scene. The caller to 9-1-1 said that the accident was close to Main Street, but in reality the truck overturned closer to Oliver Street. I backed my car up slightly and set my blue light on the roof of my car, hoping that others would see it and realize the true location of the accident.

I exited my car and did a quick overlook of the area believing that there would be at least one mangled body lying in or near the truck. Seeing nothing but a sea of firewood, I opened my trunk and started putting on my turn out gear. I heard nothing except the faint sound of the radio coming from the truck until its intoxicated driver seemed to appear from nowhere and started staggering towards me.

"Stop walking and sit down on the ground," I shouted, half believing that this drunken guy was going to get into a pissing match with me. To my surprise he calmly sat down on the ground. I quickly looked at him and saw no evidence of any major external trauma. "Does anything hurt?" I questioned. "No," he said, "But just look at my truck." "Don't worry about that now; I'm going to check your vital signs," I said.

As I grabbed his wrist in search of his radial pulse, pages of my EMT class book appeared in my head. If I could feel his radial pulse his systolic blood pressure had to be at least 100. I counted his heart rate for ten seconds and then multiplied by six. The rate was 78 beats per minute. He took four breaths in fifteen seconds. If things stayed stable he would finish out his sixteen breaths per minute in the next forty five seconds. The squelch of air brakes announced the arrival of Engine 4 on the scene. Little did I realize that the calmness of this accident scene would soon be banished.

The career firefighter from Engine 4 approached us and he knelt down in front of the patient. I thought that it would be appropriate to give him an update. "One patient, initially ambulatory, radial pulse is 78, respiratory rate is 16. He has no complaints." I said. I expected to hear the Engine 4 driver say something like, "OK" or "Thanks" or "Great, I'll take it from here." What I got was something quite different.

"Who the fuck are you?" he demanded.

"What?" I answered, not believing my ears.

"Who the fuck are you?" he repeated.

"I'm an EMT with the Sweeney Hose Company."

"I didn't ask you what you are, I asked you who you were."

"Well, if you really, really need to know, my name is Jason Borton," I replied with a load of sarcasm in my voice. He stood there huffing and puffing and being pissed off. I finally broke the tension by speaking. "Come on, we're on the same team, now help me take care of our patient," I said.

Reinforcements arrived in the shape of B2, Matt Boyer, and the Rescue 1 driver. My fellow Sweeneys, who were also on their way to Nestors, arrived. The patient was placed in a cervical collar to help to stabilize the cervical spine in the event that he had sustained a neck injury. We secured him to a long hard backboard. He then went into the back of the ambulance. A police car followed the ambulance to the hospital. Blood would be drawn to legally determine if our patient was intoxicated.

Out of the corner of my eye, I could see the Engine 4 driver complaining to a seemingly unimpressed B2. I could have heard him from five hundred feet away. I was fed up with this guy going on a rampage about me providing an emergency medical assessment to a patient because I was first on the scene of the incident. I went over to B2 and the driver and butted in on their conversation.

"Let's just put an end to this. I don't know what the problem is. I did as I was told to do in my EMT class. I didn't harm the patient, and I've never met you before in my life," I said. Captain Boyer stepped in and helped with the formal introductions. He said, "Jason, this is Vince Terabola, the Engine 4 driver." I stared at Vince in cold silence and B2 continued, "Vince this is Jason Borton. I like to call him "doc" because he'll be a doctor in less than a year. When he tells you about a patient, I suggest that you shut up and listen." I grabbed his hand and said, "Vince, it's nice to meet you." I released his hand and walked away before he could say a word.

Although I don't see Vince much anymore, we are now on good speaking terms. Assistant Chief Jarantz invited me to be a guest speaker at the career firefighters' EMT refresher course. I gladly accepted and I did a two hour lecture on trauma. Near the end of the class I asked what organs in the abdominal cavity could be injured during a traumatic event. Each person was naming an organ and by the time it was Vince's turn, organs were running out. Vince said "kidneys" and I let the silence linger in the air for a minute. I replied, "No, sorry Vince, the kidneys are not within the abdominal cavity. The kidneys are retroperitoneal organs." There, in front of all of his co-workers, my "revenge" for his tantrum at the accident scene was executed. He was wrong and I was right.

Today, I know that the volunteers from my company get along much better with the career firefighters than when I first joined the department. Supposedly one reason for the early strife was a thought that the volunteers wanted to take over the career firefighter positions to make an all volunteer fire department. I have doubts as to whether this would ever happen. In the late 1800s and early 1900s, the North Tonawanda Fire Department consisted of all volunteer firefighters. It became a combination department when it was realized that the volunteers, because of their work and family obligations, could not provide consistent twenty four hour a day fire protection coverage for the city.

I took the civil service test to become a career firefighter in North Tonawanda in 1995. I scored a 90 on my test and I was rumored to be second on the list in terms of my score. All the chief had to do was "call for the list" and with some probable minor political "schmoozing", I had a good chance of getting on the career department. It turned out that in the four years that I was near the top of the list for the career fire department, Chief Roger Davis never called for that list.

After that 1995 exam, I never took the civil service test for the fire department again. I had started medical school in 1995 and had chosen medicine as my career path. As I exited the medical school lecture building, the occasional screams of wailing sirens and blasting air horns of the Buffalo Fire Department would remind me of the chance I had to become a career firefighter. I realized though, that I could still be an active volunteer firefighter and practice medicine.

6

N 38

It was the fall of 1990 when I returned home for good from my brief stay at Clarkson University as a chemistry major. I had really thought that I wanted to make chemistry my career choice. Something at Clarkson didn't seem right to me. I seemed to lack the confidence that I had in high school. On my dorm wall at Clarkson was a picture of Engine 7 that a relative had taken during a parade. I wondered what calls it was responding to as I seemed to be wasting my time on an uncertain future five and a half hours away from North Tonawanda.

A day came at Clarkson when everything seemed to overwhelm me. I called home. I knew that I couldn't stay there any longer. With a trembling voice, I told my father that I needed to come home. I spent that night alone in my room packing my clothes as my roommate was out of town for the weekend. I stayed awake for most of the night lying on the floor and wondering what I was going to do next week and for the rest of my life. My parents arrived to pick me up early the next morning. My father greeted me by looking me straight in the eye. He firmly shook my hand.

"I'm proud of you. This wasn't an easy decision for you to make," he said.

I spent the next two weeks in North Tonawanda, pretty much confined to the couch in front of the television. My dad was able to convince me that life indeed was going on and that I needed to get a job if I was going to keep living in his house. I started working at a Dollar Store. I had never worked in retail before and it was very boring for me. It was difficult for me to understand why it was so important to accurately inventory five different styles of underwear.

One day while I was sitting on my front porch, a maroon Dodge pulled into my driveway. Don Rabinski, who I had convinced to join the Sweeney Hose Company, was sitting behind the wheel. I had worked with Don at the Riverside Chemical Company before I had left for Clarkson. Don had heard through the grapevine that I was back in town. He told me that things were still busy at work and he had mentioned my early return to the owner of the company, Rick Peters. Rick had always been a fair boss and after I called him the next morning, he invited me to stop by to talk about what hours I could work. Rick offered me a full time position. My job description would be doing what I had done before. I would prepare orders for shipping. I would re-package chemicals. I would spend my days working while at night I would ponder my future.

With no school responsibilities I had time to go to fire calls. Guys at the hall always seemed to be asking for help on Sunday nights for bingo. When I first joined the hall I never went down on bingo nights, thinking that bingo was for old timers who never went to fire calls anymore. Who would want to go into a smoke filled room that was not on fire and listen to old ladies bitch for three hours? One Sunday night I made the mistake of walking into the bingo hall. The bingo chairman saw me and shot a quizzical look my way, thinking that something must have been seriously wrong with me to have entered the hall on bingo night. Before I could head for the door, an apron full of bingo boards was wrapped around my waist and I was shown to the main floor.

I was now a seller. I walked around the floor selling bingo boards; face down, to players in need of bingo boards. These boards were covered with bingo chips during the games and they were picked up at the end of each bingo night. "Specials", which were a series of five paper bingo sheets that were dabbed with ink markers, were also sold on the floor.

After selling for a couple of weeks, I deduced that there were three types of bingo players. The first type of player was what I called the "blue moons". They came out every once in a blue moon. These people were polite. They would talk with me. They realized that there was much more to life than bingo. The next player was the "occasional". These people might own their own bingo chips and a bingo dabber. These players could occasionally be demanding, but they were not to be feared. The third type of player was by all means the most formidable. This type of player would show up an hour before the hall doors were opened so they could be sure to get in and get "their seat". This player would let the caller and the entire hall know what she thought about the speed of the calling. They are not afraid to pull you over and ask you to sell them a card with a certain numbers on it. These people lived for bingo. They made the bingo workers miserable. They also spent a great deal of their money at our hall. They were to be feared. They were the "regulars".

Sellers had the additional responsibility of reading back numbers to the caller when a bingo was called. A seasoned seller would always move quickly towards a supposed winner and then would raise his hand. The caller would acknowledge the seller over the microphone and the seller would shout out the numbers to the caller. The caller would make sure that the numbers had been called and then confirm, or occasionally deny, a bingo. Letters were never called back and the callers expected the seller to say the numbers in numerical order. This took some practice but over time I learned to call back the numbers quickly.

One night was Harvey Martin's first time calling back numbers. Harvey had grown up around the fire hall as his father had been very active in the Sweeney Hose Company. Unfortunately when it came to calling back bingo numbers, Harvey made a tortoise appear fast. On his first call back of the night after he had read the numbers he said, "Oh yeah, and there's a free space in the middle." I could hear the mumbles coming from the crowd after Harvey had called his first set of numbers back. I looked into the eyes of the regulars and I saw fire. I knew that if Harvey was going to have a chance of making it out of the hall alive that night, he was in need of some quick advice. I grabbed him by the arm and led him to the bingo office.

"What the hell are you doing?" I yelled.

"I'm calling back the numbers," he quietly replied.

"Well you need to do it faster, and any idiot realizes that there's a free space in the middle. If you keep calling numbers back that slow, you're going to need a police escort just to get out of here."

"Sorry."

Harvey returned to the floor with his tail between his legs. He could take some criticism and he always tried his best. By the grace of God and the sheer tolerance of a bunch of regulars, he made it to another bingo night the next week.

The caller of the bingo numbers was truly the unofficial captain of the bingo hall. He alone could set the pace and tone of the game. He verified the accuracy of the numbers called back. Legitimate bingos were determined by him. All bingo power rested in him. He would also be the only one to scream and bitch at if anything in the game went wrong.

Bingo was broken up into two halves that were separated by an intermission. When I was a caller, I always ended up calling the second half. Allen Michalis always called the first half. He did things his way. He would finish the first half and then sell pull off tickets. His health had kept him from being an active firefighter for many years, but he put his heart into all other aspects of the hall.

A new set of bingo balls was loaded onto the bingo machine before the start of the second half. Before the start of each half it was customary for the caller to ask the players if anyone wanted to come up and check the new balls. There was a regular who was a not at all attractive lady who always sat close to the board. She would always check the balls. Being in a particularly tired mood one night, I didn't ask if anyone wanted to check the balls, but I said, "Does anyone want to check my balls?" Without missing a beat she stood up, glanced at the bingo machine, walked to the side of the machine and looking at my crotch said, "Your balls are very nice!" Red-faced she retreated to her seat. Everyone within ear shot of her comment was laughing. After a minute I was able to compose myself and I got on with the business of calling the second half.

The caller was subject to the constant criticism of the crowd. If he went too fast in calling the numbers shouts of "Come on slow down!" would arise from the floor. If calling too slow he would hear, "Hurry it up, we don't have all night!" Over time in my days of calling I tired of the constant nagging. I chose to make fun of the old ladies in my own special way. Polish ladies with thick accents compromised a fair portion of our bingo population. When I had been angered or I was feeling especially punchy and a certain ball, N33, arose from the machine I would have my fun. "N firty free," I would call out as the joke passed right over the patrons' heads and fell onto the smiles of my fellow disgruntled bingo workers.

The most infamous ball in my career of bingo calling was N38. Not that I have anything against that ball, but it happened to come up when I made the biggest bingo blunder as a caller. The incident had occurred when I had routinely called another number. Hearing nothing I looked to the next ball that had been expelled by the machine. It was N38. I called the number N and in the background I heard a quiet voice call, "Bingo!" My mouth kept moving and I called out "Thirty eight". I then said the four terrible words, "We have a bingo." The hall erupted into shouting. I had called out the number "38" when someone had called a bingo, albeit extremely late, from the previous number I had called. What did I do? I chose to incite a near riot by granting the bingo to one winner instead of the multitude of winners who were plentiful after N38 was called. There were things said that night that couldn't be repeated. A guy who looked like he spent every minute outside of the bingo hall lifting weights approached the caller's table and shook fists in my direction. I made the mistake of ticking off one hundred and seventy five people instead of one dimwit who didn't even realize when he had a bingo.

Bingo players, especially the regulars, were a special breed. As a group they tended to be highly superstitious, some to the point where they seemed like professional athletes repeating ritualistic patterns during the course of a sporting event. Many players placed miniature troll dolls with wavy hair on the bingo tables. I observed the players touching the trolls' hair. Trolls were also casually waved in the air before the beginning of each game. Nearly all players believed in the seemingly magical power of prize money. Among regulars, prize money would be grasped in the winner's hand and then swept in the arc of a semicircle for all the surrounding players to touch and hopefully garner some of the luck. Certain regulars just had to have their regular seat. My jaw dropped in amazement the night that we had to physically separate two regulars who were fighting over a seat.

One word that could be used to characterize Sweeney Hose bingo players was "dedicated". One night a women passed out just before the first game of the night was about to start. The career firefighters and the paramedics from Twin City Ambulance came to check her out but she refused to be transported to the hospital. How could she do that and miss her weekly game? On one Sunday night, a regular started bleeding from his nose like a stuck pig midway through the first half of the session. A little nostril pinching wasn't going to stop this epistaxis. He refused to go to get checked out while there were bingo games to be played. A large mountain of bright red and white tissue paper grew next to him during the first half of bingo. At halftime we convinced him that he needed to at least get checked out by the career firefighters next door. We found out that his blood pressure was 210/90 mm Hg and that that he took warfarin, a blood thinning medication that was initially used as a rat poison. He too refused to go to the hospital. Sometime during the second half his nosebleed stopped and he won a game, something that would have never happened if he was at the emergency department.

Our hall had given up running bingo many years ago as other clubs and organizations were offering bigger monetary prizes while we kept our prize money the same. Our number of players declined and we were consistently losing money on a weekly basis. Two other fire halls in North Tonawanda still have a bingo night. After we closed our bingo, I became a blue moon bingo player at either the Rescue Fire Company or the Gratwick Hose Company bingo nights. I initially thought it was because I wanted to win some of the prize money. I soon found out why I really went to bingo. I secretly missed the regulars.

7

Train We Must

When I returned home from Clarkson University, I realized that I would need to start attending city firefighting drills in order to further my comfort level with firefighting. Drills were held on Monday nights for the Sweeney Hose Company. Good weather drills were held on Tonawanda Island at the Niagara County fire training tower. Just like my first Essentials of Firefighting class, I was late for this drill. I carried my gear with me as I timidly walked towards a group of firefighters who were receiving instructions from the city training officer Ken Jarantz, who had basically taught me everything I knew about firefighting up to this point. Ken Rojek, the captain from my company, looked over his shoulder and saw me walking towards the group.. A wave of his arm silently beckoned me to slip into the crowd of volunteers who were receiving instructions. Ken Jarantz didn't see me until my outline grabbed the outermost reaches of his peripheral vision. He turned his entire body to face me. He stopped speaking. I turned towards him and the silence. I knew that I was about to receive a verbal lashing. "I thought you were supposed to be at a pretty boy college hours away from here. What brings you back?" he asked. I knew that I had to be tough and that humor could help me. "Their courses didn't agree with me sir. That's why I'm here to learn about firefighting from you sir," I replied. The short, militaristic tone of my voice gave the other firefighters a chuckle and momentarily stopped Chief Jarantz from badgering me. He countered, "Well thanks for coming to my drill, but from now on, be here on time." I nodded my head in an affirmative manner and listened as he finished off his instructions. There were other Sweeneys around me and I could feel their stares asking probing questions: What was I doing back in North Tonawanda? Did I fail out of college? Was the coursework too much? Did I have problems with the other students there? In reality their questions came out with genuine concern and they almost always ended with a "Well, glad to have you back." What anyone thought didn't matter to me. I had come to the realization that living life was not about black or white, right or wrong. Life was about a myriad of colors and how to deal with them. The fact was that I was back in town and I needed to get more training in the world of firefighting.

The Niagara County fire training tower was conveniently located on Tonawanda Island, a short piece of land that was physically separated from North Tonawanda by a swift moving portion of the Niagara River that had come to be known as the "Little River". The training grounds were fenced in by a barbed wire fence. The eastern edge of the grounds was bordered by the Little River. A long leftward winding driveway led us past old scrap vehicles that were used for extrication practice on the west side of the facility. A circular pit laden with murky rain water was near the left side of the driveway. A four story concrete block tower stood on the right where the driveway ended. Mint green exterior stairs clung to the side of the building. Between the fire tower and a concrete smoke house was a central black topped area. Faded dark green baseball bleachers provided a sitting and rest area for the firefighters. The smoke house had a pitched and a flat part to its roof. There were two sets of concrete stairs on its exterior. One short set led to the main floor of the structure. The other set went down to the exterior door of the basement. A lone yellow fire hydrant was situated halfway between the river and the smoke house. The rest of the training grounds consisted of tall, seldom cut grass. The southern border of the training area was heavily wooded but there were train tracks within fifty feet of the fence. We occasionally noticed a lone box car or tanker car sitting on the tracks. Quaking aspens leaned over the fence and made their presence known to our ears when the winds blew during our drills.

Our drills usually involved some aspect of search and rescue or fire suppression activity. These two activities were the main tasks to be undertaken upon our arrival to a fire scene, so it only made sense that we should become somewhat proficient in performing them. I sometimes wished that our training officer spent more of his down time thinking about creative and fun things to do at the drills. Every once in a while however he did manage to come up with an interesting exercise.

Ken Jarantz once took the reins and decided to show us why we needed to work quickly to rescue people from the inside of a burning building. He told us of the consequences of being without oxygen for even a short period of time. He decided to let us feel the mental and physical fear that a person trapped in a house fire would experience. About ten of us gathered in the main room of the smoke house. Every wall was blackened with a thick layer of soot. A faint odor of burnt wood and kerosene hung in the room. Ken had removed all of the furniture from the room. He asked us to sit on the floor. In the corner was a cut down 55 gallon drum that was filled with hay.

"I'm going to light this hay on fire with you in the room. You won't be exposed to the toxic by-products of plastic combustion like hydrogen cyanide, but you'll feel the heat of the fire. The smoke will get to you. Your eyes will sting. It will become hard to breathe. You'll be able to sit up for a while, but soon the smoke will drive you to the floor. Putting your nose close to the floor will greatly improve your comfort of breathing. When I give you the signal, move out of the room and get outside," Chief Jarantz explained.

Ken put a match to the hay and it started to release a small amount of smoke. A single orange flame appeared and it quickly evolved into a large flame that reached to the ceiling. A blanket of smoke was forming on the ceiling. A slight heat could be felt above our heads. Within two minutes, that blanket of smoke had pushed us to lie flat on the floor. The heat became more intense. Ken told us to remove one of our gloves and raise a hand towards the ceiling. I did this and quickly brought my hand down to the floor level as the heat was painful on my exposed hand. I reached into my bunker pants and pulled out a piece of an old cut up t-shirt. In the smoke divers course we were taught to carry a small rag in our pocket in the event that we ever had to remove our SCBA mask. The rag would not protect us from the ultimate toxic effects of the smoke, but the hope was that the rag would buy us a little time in a dire situation. I thought that now would be a great time to test the capabilities of the rag. My eyes started to sting and water as the smoke hovered just above the floor. An acrid smell filled my nose and made its way to my throat as I began to cough. I heard others coughing in the room and I decided that it was time for me to hold my breath. Thoughts of fleeing raced between my ears but my mind told me to be still. At that moment, Ken yelled out his pardon and commanded us to exit the building.

I got to my knees and started crawling towards the open door on my right and then suddenly I was back down on the floor again. I looked up and saw the pair of boots that had just trampled me to the floor. The other firefighters had all exited but I was still on the floor feeling overcome by the smoke. I belly crawled to the door and sprung myself out onto the stairwell. I started a continuous fit of coughing. Even though I felt terrible, I never imagined that the twenty one percent oxygen and seventy nine percent mixture of nitrogen called air could feel so good. I lied on the ground for the next couple of minutes just breathing in the good air and coughing up all the rotten stuff from my lungs. After that I got up and went to find Ron Billings, the short brother Sweeney who had allowed me to spend an extra fifteen seconds in the smoke house. I hurled multiple defamations at him and told him what I thought of his actions while I coughed in his face. I continued to cough in spurts over the next half hour. My body gave serious consideration to puking, but it recovered remarkably. Since that exercise I always remembered the taste of acrid smoke when packing up to go into a fire. I knew what anyone unlucky enough to be inside the building would be going through while I was on the outside of the building, getting ready to go in.

Drills gave us the opportunity to become familiar with pieces of equipment that we would rarely, if ever, use on the fire ground. Sweeney Hose was considered an engine company, which meant that technically our first job was to find the seat of the fire and attack it. In a big city fire department, the truck company would have the job of searching for occupants and ventilating a structure. Because of the relatively small size of the department in North Tonawanda, we were trained in all aspects of firefighting. It was at the training tower that we engine company boys learned about the world of the truckie.

In the past victims trapped in the upper stories of a building during a fire were sometimes expected to act by themselves to afford a rescue. As evidence of this, many fire departments used life nets for both their own firefighters and for the general public. A life net was a circular piece of canvas that was encircled by a metal frame. Springs attached the metal frame to the canvas. They provided some give to the net when the weight of a jumper's body impacted the canvas. Firefighters on the ground would lift up the net with outstretched arms and hope that the jumper could hit the center of the net.

At one drill, Ken Jarantz decided to bring out the 1955 Seagrave ladder truck to our drill. This truck was in reserve status, meaning that it would only be used to respond to fires if a front line ladder truck was out of service. This was the same ladder truck that I pretended to drive when my grandmother took me to Engine 5's station when I was a young boy. Before long, the truck would be auctioned off at a Saturday morning public auction. Near the back of the truck was a compartment labeled with the words "LIFE NET". Assistant Chief Jarantz told us how we were to hold the life net. When we jumped into the net, out butts were to hit the canvas where there was a red bull's eye. We would be jumping from only one story up, so our risk of serious injury would be minimal if we slipped up. As Ken gave his instructions, some of the older firefighters at the drill recalled how a previous chief had jumped off the top of the training tower into the life net and walked off of it without a scratch. Ken was only going to let us jump from about ten feet, not forty like the former chief had accomplished.

Two or three firefighters had successfully completed their ten foot jumps into the net. Ken asked for the next volunteer and I made my way up the exterior steps of the building. I had unwittingly stepped in some mud at the beginning of my ascent. I was only wearing my three quarter bunker boots and my helmet as Ken didn't want us to get bogged down in our full turnout gear. I arrived on the first landing of the stairs and carefully climbed over the hand railing. I looked at the net below me that was being hoisted up by my brother firefighters. The jump didn't seem like it was very high at all. I knew that this was going to be my first and last time to ever experience the thrill of using this now antiquated piece of firefighting equipment. It required a little skill on my part and a great deal of faith on my part in my firefighting companions. I stepped off the landing and climbed onto the hand railing, increasing my altitude by about three and a half feet. Now I felt like I was about to take a little more of a daring leap. I looked down and called out to make sure the group below was ready.

I could see the group below collectively brace their bodies as I leapt out into the air and pointed my rear end towards the bull's eye. For a second I was free falling and then I hit the life net. The landing was quite comfortable and two firefighters standing next to each other lowered their side of the net to the ground. I stepped off the net and I looked back at the centered red target. I noticed a smudge of brown just to the right of center, the end result of my walk through the mud. Ken saw the mud too and asked the others to be careful where they stepped as he said that I had just tarnished fire department equipment. The jumps lasted another ten minutes and then the slightly less than clean life net was placed back into its storage compartment, likely never seeing the light of day again until the future private owner of the Seagrave possibly became curious one morning while examining his purchase. I wondered if the life net had ever saved the life of a firefighter in the line of duty.

Volunteer firefighters were expected to be able to carry out orders that were given to them by either a line officer from one of the volunteer companies or from an officer of the career department. When an officer gave an order, it was expected that the order would be completed in its entirety. There was no room for the "I'll do it if I feel like it" attitude in the fire service. An uncompleted task had the potential of putting firefighters' lives in jeopardy. Ken decided to hold a drill that would test our ability to follow directions.

Four firefighters had gone through the exercise before my turn came around. They had each been given a three inch by five inch card by Ken. They were instructed to follow the directions on the card. I had observed each of the four firefighters walk across the open field towards the engine that was at the drill. Each firefighter took an axe off the engine and carried it in his right hand back to the starting line. They set the axe down on the ground and then crossed the finish line. They then turned around and took three steps backwards.

My turn was next and Chief Jarantz handed the instruction card to me. It said: "Start behind the starting line and walk quickly to the engine. Remove an axe from the engine and place it in your right hand. Walk back to the starting line and set the axe on the ground using only your right hand. Take three steps backwards. Stop."

Ken Jarantz never did anything without a reason. I had watched every firefighter that had gone before me do exactly what every other firefighter had done. I started my brisk walk at Ken's command and walked next to another firefighter. He was talking and I didn't respond back to him, not because of conceit, but because the instructions had not mentioned talking. Arriving at the engine, I grabbed an axe from its holder on the exterior side of one of the jump seats. I grabbed it with my right hand and started my walk back to the truck. The other volunteer was now far ahead of me. That was alright with me. I slowed my stride and tried to decipher what Ken was trying to get at with this drill. The firefighter who was now thirty feet in front of me placed the axe down on the ground. He then crossed the starting line and took three steps backwards. My eyes suddenly widened as I realized the method of Ken's madness. I approached the starting line. I bent down and placed the axe on the ground. I then looked straight ahead and took three steps backwards, never crossing the starting line. I looked at the other firefighter who was not by my side, but six paces away, facing me. Ken looked at both of us for a couple of seconds. One of us was wrong. Looking at Ken I caught an almost imperceptible grin that came to his face. Some of those who followed in the exercise followed my example. Others still crossed the line. Ken never told us which way was correct after the exercise. He said, "Some people followed the directions and others didn't."

The fire service always seemed to have its latest fads. In the early 1990s, an emphasis was placed on fire departments preparing for rescuing people that were trapped in confined spaces. We had attended one classroom drill on confined space rescues. The drill consisted of watching one of Ken's long boring videotapes in the basement of fire headquarters. These training videos occupied time during the long cold winter months in North Tonawanda. Ken had to fill a drill night with almost three hours of instruction. He could only talk for so long until heads in the back of the room were jerked back into wakefulness by the necks that supported them. In my fifteen years of firefighting, I only recalled seeing one amusing video. A firefighter was working on the roof of a two story house. He attempted to get onto an extension ladder when he slipped off the roof, falling to the ground below. Our class sat in silence as we waited to see what his fate would be. Didn't he get up and quickly look around himself before he started climbing the ladder to go back up to the roof? Our class erupted into laughter, although most of us would have done the same if we were not physically injured. We then saw the firefighter's officer in charge climb the ladder to retrieve him for a rest and to get checked out.

When the weather was warm we had the opportunity to test out North Tonawanda's new confined space rescue equipment. We would be using the tripod, a triangular support that would be placed over a manhole or other confined space. The rescuer would be secured into a harness. The harness would be attached to the tripod and we would be lowered into the confined space. For our drill, the confined space was the ventilation shaft of our smoke house.

Ken asked for volunteers to go down into the shaft. No one came forward, so I stepped into the harness. Straps seemed to be everywhere, including two along my upper inner thighs. I strapped my helmet to my head. I was ready to be lowered into the ventilation shaft and my team began the lowering process. I looked straight ahead as the fading light of the spring night turned into the darkness of the ventilation shaft. The descent was uneventful and then it happened - the shift. My weight had shifted and now my left testicle was caught between my body and the support strap. I instinctively pulled up on the support rope to help relieve the discomfort. Beads of sweat dripped down my face. I felt light headed. I yelled to my team up on the roof telling them of my predicament. Only laughter came back down the shaft. Fortunately the firefighter below me saw the desperation on my face and pushed up on my left leg, easing the compression from the strap. When my feet touched the floor, the nightmare was over. I performed the confined space descent and unfortunately for me, my left family jewel had managed to find its own confined space. Thankfully this was a drill and I only had to descend about fifteen feet.

For me the most exciting thing to do at the training tower was to go up in the bucket of Truck 2. At full extension it put us eighty five feet above the ground. I felt relatively safe inside the encapsulating sides of the bucket. If there happened to be a mechanical failure of the ladder while the bucket was in the air, a long descent down the rungs of the extended arm would have to be made. Unlike Truck 1, there were no side rails on the back bone of Truck 2's emergency ladder.

Truck 2 was a beast. An early 1970s Sutphen, it was very slow to accelerate on the road. On a quiet night, I could hear it grumbling through its gears on its way to a call, even if the truck was over a mile away. It was the loudest piece of apparatus in the North Tonawanda Fire Department fleet. Ken Jarantz didn't trust us volunteers with the operation of the bucket, as we weren't allowed to go up in the bucket at a drill without him joining us for the ride. Only Ken operated the controls in the bucket. These restrictions were lifted when Greg Frank became the training officer.

Truck 2 arrived at the training grounds one Monday night and Greg had us practice ground ladder raises for awhile. We easily raised two section extension ladders and somewhat struggled with the larger Bangor ladders. Greg had us put the ground ladders back onto the truck. He then briefly instructed us in the use of the controls of the bucket and then sent groups of three up into the bucket.

I was eager to be the first to take charge of the bucket's controls. Greg told us to use the throttle handle to move the bucket when we would be doing prolonged moving. I throttled the engine and a big plume of diesel smoke ascended from the truck's exhaust below us. I raised the arm of the bucket to an approximate angle of sixty degrees. I stopped and then activated the throttle again as I extended the bucket to its full length. We were up in the bucket and we were free from the restrictive arm of Ken Jarantz. A loud chirping noise from the bucket let me know that I had extended the bucket to its full length. I stopped for a minute to let my passengers look out at the beauty of the Niagara River. I then decided that it was time to do some rotation to change our view. We went clockwise for a bit and then I decided to stop. I took my hand off the rotation control and the throttle at the same time. We stopped briefly before the bucket was forcefully flung in the opposite direction. We skirted back and forth for what seemed like an eternity. I grabbed the sides of the bucket and bent my knees for fear of being thrown over the side. My passengers did the same. Where was Ken now? This kind of thing didn't happen when he took us up in the bucket. Our heads peeked out from over the top of the bucket once the swaying had stopped. Greg's voice came over the loudspeaker that was inside the bucket. He said, "You have to let off the throttle before you stop moving Borton, you idiot. Let someone else take a turn." I moved to the right of the bucket, allowing Duncan to take over the controls. The rest of the ride, while it provided a unique view of North Tonawanda, was largely uneventful.

Drill nights were always a fun time. We practiced the art of being firefighters. We mingled and joked with members from other volunteer companies. We learned tips from more senior members who had "been there and done that." The relatively controlled environment of the training ground prepared us for the unpredictable and often chaotic scene of a structure fire, motor vehicle collision, or rescue situation.

8

Just for Fun

The Sweeneys always loved a good fire. They also loved to play sports. Early in the existence of the Sweeney Hose Company, the Sweeneys had earned a nickname. The "Fighting Sweeneys" were named so not because of their hard work or their never say die attitude. The name was branded on them because of their tendency to fight amongst themselves. Over time the name had come to symbolize the Sweeneys' dedication in firefighting and sports. While I was an active firefighter, the Sweeneys focused on three sporting arenas: bowling, softball, and water ball.

The first sport I participated in as a Sweeney was bowling. Larry Johnson and Kurt Paulis had taken me under their collective wing as a bingo co-chairperson. I always believed that they had done this so that they could attend Buffalo Bills football games during the bingo season. They would go to the football games and then come to bingo in a minimally sober state to help out with the financial paperwork of bingo. When a spot opened up on the Twin City Firemens' bowling league on Thursday nights, they asked me if I had ever bowled. I proudly told them that I had bowled before, not telling them that all of my previous bowling accomplishments had occurred in a bantam league when I was in elementary school. I had not bowled in a league for over ten years. I think they smelled a high handicap score in me that could help their team. I was possibly the ticket to help them win the league trophy.

The Twin Cities Firemen bowling league was rumored to be the longest continuously running fireman's bowling league in the nation. The league ran every Thursday night from September through April. It was held at Town Lanes, an eight lane bowling alley at the corner of Miller and Oliver Streets in North Tonawanda. The proprietor of Town Lanes was a man named Patrick Thompson. Pat was the owner of the alleys when I was a bantam bowler. He welcomed us to his bowling alley every Saturday morning. He was a true gentleman, showing respect for every person that entered his establishment. As a bantam bowler, I didn't have my own bowling ball. Week after week I used different alley balls until I finally found one that worked for me. As a fourth grader, I approached Mr. Thompson and asked him if I could purchase the ball. I told him that I was bowling well with it. He picked up the ball, briefly looked it over, and handed it back to me. He said, "You can have it for free." I thanked him and never forgot his act of kindness.

The firemen's league consisted of eight teams. The Sweeneys had three teams, the Gratwicks had two, and the Rescues had one team. The Delaware Hose Company from the city of Tonawanda also had one team. The eighth team consisted of a bunch of guys who frequented the bowling alley but were not firefighters. Bowling started at 6:30 p.m. and practice started around 6:15 p.m. Our Sweeney team usually started drinking just before six. Town Lanes was an older bowling alley, so we each took turns keeping score.

On our team was Ken Paulis, who was about ten years older than me. Ken's father, Roy, was a long time member of the hall and had served at various times as both its custodian and its president. Ken worked delivering furniture. Ken had been very active in the hall, even as a child before he was a member. Ken would eventually become less and less active in the hall as the years passed.

Larry Johnson served as the president of our bowling league. Larry was an on and off and on again active member of Sweeney Hose. Although his days of active firefighting had passed, he stepped up to lead the company in many fundraising events. He worked for General Motors as a supervisor and he often joked about how GM paid him a generous salary for doing nothing, although in reality he worked very hard at his job. Larry and Ken were great friends and they drank and partied together often.

Jack Dingens was the third member of our bowling team. He carried a 180 average and often bowled games over 200. He worked overnights as a Niagara County Sheriff. His face always seemed to show a bored expression and he was very soft spoken. He offered bowling advice to me as often as he could. He would help out with fundraisers every once in a while but his career kept him very busy.

The fourth member of our team was Eddy Korzan. Eddy had served time in the Air Force as a firefighter. He worked as an area manager for a chain of convenience stores in the Buffalo area. Eddy liked to talk and talk and talk. Listening to him was always amusing. He could make a story about cutting grass or making a dinner of rice interesting. Eddy could drink just as well as the rest of us. Eddy was going through a nasty divorce but he had a girlfriend who was well liked by all of us.

My memories of bowling did not come from bowling great games or picking up difficult splits. The group of characters I bowled with provided plenty of memories. One Thursday night I casually strolled into the bowling alley. The first snowfall of the year had landed in North Tonawanda that day, blanketing the ground three inches deep. I passed the bar waving to the attractive barmaid behind the bar. I had my classic red hard shelled bowling bag in hand. I was hanging up my coat when Larry came out of nowhere and shouted in my ear.

"What the hell is the matter with you?" he stammered as he smacked the back of my head. I reflexively protected my head and wondered if Larry had gotten to the alley early that day and started drinking at 1 p.m. "Me, what's the matter with you, coming over here and slapping my head?" I said. He then threw questions at me, "Do you want to ruin my whole night of bowling? Look to your right you numbskull. See the pile of shoes and boots? Throw your snow covered shoes in the pile and stop getting the carpet wet." Larry had made me feel as though I had committed the ultimate sin of bowling by walking on the carpet with my wet shoes. I would come to appreciate Larry's advice in the future after I had stepped in water left behind by a novice bowler who had worn his wet shoes into Town Lanes one evening.

Drinking was a big part of bowling for our team. Anyone who didn't garner a strike in the frame when the rest of the team got a strike made an expensive trip to the bar to buy a round of drinks for the whole team. Each of us had our drinks. For Larry, it was a green bottle of Molson Golden and for Ken it was Captain Morgan and Coke. Eddy drank any kind of beer. Jack's vice was Jack Daniels and Coke. I was the underage drinker and tended to drink Labatt Blue. There was one drink that every member of our team drank. That drink was Goldschlager, a cinnamon schnapps that actually had small flakes of gold in the bottle. Goldschlager was poured when the team needed a boost or to celebrate a victory. We assumed that it was good for us and we joked that we increased our net worth by drinking the small flecks of gold.

The Gratwicks had some serious bowlers on their teams. Their senior member team was the most serious. It was OK to have fun with them when they were winning, but a joke couldn't go very far if they were losing. This Gratwick team was so dedicated to bowling that they wouldn't touch alcohol while engaged in the sport. One Thursday near the end of the season we ended up bowling against this team. They were in first place in the league standings and we were in a close second. They had won the first game of the night and we won the second game with the help of our handicap. We were drinking more than usual that night. We seemed to be louder than usual that night too as the Gratwicks shot death ray eyes at our drinking festivities when they returned from taking their turn at bowling. They were under pressure too, as the steam never seemed to stop hovering over their bottomless cups of coffee. At the end of the third game the score was close, but a run of strikes by Jack sealed the victory for us. We were in first place. The Gratwicks checked and rechecked the score sheets from the third game but there was no change. Our captain signed the score sheet, making our match official. We walked out to the bar to celebrate. The senior Gratwicks held their heads down as they left the alley that night, not even stopping by the bar to celebrate our victory with us.

It was close to 10:30 p.m. when we decided to continue our celebration festivities elsewhere. We piled into the front seat of Jack's pick-up truck and drove down Oliver Street to the Stardust Lounge. Ever since I was a child I had heard rumors that Oliver Street was at one time listed in the Guinness Book of World Records. It wasn't reportedly in there for being the longest street in the world, or the widest, or the street with the most curves. Its reported claim to fame was that it had more bars along it than any other street in the world. We arrived at the Stardust Lounge and were greeted by a veil of smoke. People in their forties, fifties, and even their sixties listened to oldies music in the background. We drank for at least two hours recapping how we had won the decisive game that evening.

At one o'clock we left the bar, got back into Jack's truck, and headed towards Town Lanes. I got out of Jack's truck in the parking lot and got into my car. I knew that I could drive, but I was concerned. I only had two blocks to get home to my parents' house. I started the car and turned down an alley that came out onto Oliver Street. I slammed on my brakes at the street entrance. A North Tonawanda cop was coming from my left moving at about twenty miles per hour. I put my turn signal on and waited for him to pass. He slowed down even more. He passed in front of my car glaring at me. I had thoughts of what it would be like to spend the night in jail. A wave of his hand let me breathe again. It must have been one of the three officers that I knew in the city. He sped up and disappeared into the lights of Oliver Street. I turned onto Oliver Street and arrived at my house ninety seconds later feeling very thankful.

Getting out of my car I realized that I had a microbiology test the next morning. I set my alarm to get up at 6 a.m. to study. Sleep came effortlessly, but I woke up with a raging hangover. I studied and then drove the thirteen mile trek to Niagara County Community College for my microbiology test. About ten minutes into the test I handed in my test and ran to the bathroom where I vomited in the toilet. While I was on my knees, the southern orifice was calling and I sat on the seat for the next five minutes. I then felt much better and went into the hall and got a drink of water. I returned to the class and finished my test. The next Thursday I thanked my teammates for being a bad influence on me. I went easy on the drinking that week. I was lucky to have scored a ninety eight on my microbiology test after the binge drinking of the previous week.

Our team ended up winning the league championship that year. The highlight of the season for me and for my entire bowling career was bowling a three game 600 series. They even had a patch for the feat of scoring exactly six hundred for three games. Our league had made a collective decision not to award trophies to the league champions. Instead, we took the money that would have gone towards the trophies and pocketed it. That was the last year I bowled with the Sweeneys. I entered medical school the next fall and my schedule didn't allow for late night drinking on Thursdays anymore. The Twin City Firemen's League permanently disbanded a few years after my last season at Town Lanes. Pat Thompson passed away and several new owners had tried to make the small establishment into a profitable bowling business, but they ultimately failed. A couple of the Sweeney teams joined a men's league on Wednesday nights at a much larger bowling alley. They have done fairly well.

While the Sweeneys always seemed to do well on the bowling alley, the same could not be said of their fate on the softball field. I obviously could not speak of softball teams that were before my time. The softball trophies that filled boxes in our hall storage room revealed a long gone era of softball greatness. In the early nineties a Sweeney softball team was put together by Ron Billings, a short red headed member who was in his early thirties. He was trying to break into the business world and he attended college in an attempt to earn an associates degree. He was always well dressed and he seemed to hate anything dirty. We were always sure to rub a little soot on his turnout coat at every fire scene. Girls loved Ron and we made it a point to embarrass him every chance we had. Rob held some early practices to get us into "softball mode". We actually looked pretty good in practice. Unfortunately, we were never able to bring our hard work to a victory in my first season except for one game during a tournament. We warmed up hard. We stretched hard. We were ready and had ten guys ready to play. The other team didn't. No one from their team showed up for the tournament game. Our only victory that year was by forfeit.

I played a couple of positions during my first year of softball. I usually started playing a game in left field. I was often called in to play shortstop when Ron figured that the older member who was playing the position couldn't bend down quickly enough to field balls that were hit to him.

There were two games during my first year of softball that stand out in my mind. The first game was played on a dark and ominous looking Friday evening. It was being played at Gilmore Field, a one minute walk from Gilmore School where I had attended elementary school. The air was thick with humidity, but no rain had fallen to stop our game. The first two innings of the game went by quickly without any runs being scored. Then it was the top of the third inning. The Sweeneys were in the field. I was playing left field. Our opponents were tearing up our infield with line drive ground balls that ended up being tossed in again and again by the outfielders. The score was soon 7 to 0 and we still hadn't made a single out against our competitors. From the outfield I could see the grins on the faces of the batters as they made their way around the bases at their leisure. Then Ron called me in to play shortstop, hoping that I might stop some grounders from leaving the infield. A ground ball was hit towards me and I stopped it. I threw it to first base for the first out of the inning. The next ball was dinked into short center field. The bases were now loaded. The next batter hit a slow moving grounder right to me. I picked it up and threw it as hard as I could to home plate where Jack Dingens father, Jack Sr., was awaiting my throw. The throw, although slightly low, would be easily handled. The ball hit Jack Sr.'s glove and went through to the backstop allowing another run to score. Under my breath I swore up and down. I knew now that we were probably going to lose the game so I decided to have fun and make the most of it.

I found that standing in the field for this prolonged period of time made me thirsty. During the inning I had caught a glimpse of Stan Lawrence caring a case of Budweiser to our bench. Stan was not normally a generous guy and this offering seemed odd to me. He had four kids at home and it seemed like he was always struggling to make ends meet. I absolutely hated Budweiser beer, but the thought of guzzling a cold beer on this hot day renewed my will to make two more outs. I shouted to my teammates to look alive. Fifteen minutes and five runs later we finally left the field. The score was thirteen to zero but I didn't care at that point. I was only looking for one thing – a cold and crisp refreshing beer. I ran towards the bench knowing that I had at least two minutes before we were back on defense again. I reached into the case of beer as Stan looked on. I thanked him for the beer as other thirsty Sweeneys had gathered behind me. I opened my can and took a long gulp. I quickly spit the beer onto the ground. Apparently Stan hadn't been introduced to the concept of refrigeration. The brew tasted like it had been sitting in the sun all day long. I questioned, "Who's the nimrod that brought the warm Budweiser?" as I stared at Stan. I then continued, "Oh, hi Stan!" Stan wasn't amused with my sarcasm as he quickly gathered his warm case of beer and put it back in his van. We lost the game on account of the mercy rule when the score became 15 to 0. Several members of the team and I left the field and headed to the fire hall to drown our defeat in several cold beers.

The only truly close game that we played in my first season of softball was against the Active Hose Company. Their pitcher was Sam Peterson, who was also an assistant chief for the career fire department. He was tough to hit against, even though this was slow pitch softball. After a couple of bats against him, I discovered his secret. The first pitch he threw to the batter would be perfect and right over the plate. He would throw less than perfect garbage pitches the rest of the time. Later in the game I managed to get a couple of hits off of him. The game was close until the bottom of the last inning when the Actives pulled away and beat us by a couple of runs. All of the members of our team came up with some extraordinary plays, but we still came up short. My best friend Dan was at the game and he gave me crap about not being able to come through in the stretch. My girlfriend at the time was also there. She was slightly more sympathetic, but she gave me flack about ever joining Sweeney Hose. She told me that I should have joined Gratwick Hose because her uncle was a member there. We played a couple of more seasons of softball and then the fire hall took a long break from softball.

In 2003, there were several new young members in the hall who had never had the chance to experience humiliation on the softball field. At a regular meeting of the company, I asked for permission to start up a softball team again. Sponsoring the team cost about three hundred dollars. The floor gave me permission to sign up for softball and eighteen members willingly stepped forward to try their hand at the game. Luke Jones, a young member with less than five years in the hall stepped up and took over management of the team.

Luke was a portly guy who had been very active in the hall. He had even managed to get himself elected to the board of directors. He jokingly picked on people, but he also put up with tons of verbal abuse.

Luke's dad had been a little league baseball coach and helped out at some of our practices. We seemed to improve each week during our practices in April. Then game time started. I had registered the Sweeneys for the advanced league on Tuesday nights. The first game was a blowout against us and after that game I had serious doubts about us being able to compete in the league.

I noticed some major differences between the team I played for in the 1990s and the new team. The first team consisted mostly of older members who had been in the hall for some time. The players were out on the field to have a good time. Winning was not that important to them. The new team had mostly younger members on it. It seemed that nearly every player focused on getting enough playing time. People would literally yell at their teammates when they messed up a play on the field. Talk circled that Luke was doing a poor job of managing the team. I felt that we were too focused on winning and not focused enough on having a good time. A couple of players didn't come back for the second season. I played for the first season and then passed on playing the second season as my kids were giving me more than enough entertainment. By the end of the second season, Luke decided that there was little interest in playing a third season and the Sweeneys hung up their cleats on a third season. I thought that it was quite ironic that people from all different walks of life could come together on any given hour of the day and save someone's life or property from a devastating house fire, yet this same group of people couldn't get together and win a softball game if their lives depended on it. That was the nature of the Sweeney Hose softball team.

The third "sport" that I was involved with as a Sweeney member was a competition called water ball. The Gratwick Hose Company would host a water ball tournament each summer in the early 1990s. The actual event called water ball was the last competition of the day. The tournament had two other events; the efficiency run and the hydrant hook-up.

The efficiency run was an event that tested the abilities of five firefighters from a single company to get dressed into their turnout gear and then run a short distance to the finish line. All of the team members stood behind a starting line. When a starting whistle blew, the participants ran forward to where their gear was lying on the ground. The gear was behind another line. By the time we arrived at our gear, everyone would have kicked off their shoes. We would put our three quarter length boots on and pull them up to our thighs. We would then don our turnout coats, making sure that all of our buckles were clasped. Helmets were then put on and we buckled our chin straps. Gloves went on last. It was important to make sure that the boots were pulled all the way up, all the coat buckles were clasped, the chin strap was buckled and both gloves were on. To cross the next line without being properly dressed resulted in the elimination of the entire team from the event. To help prevent any untimely elimination, teams often kept the first dressed firefighter back behind the line to make sure that his teammates were fully dressed before sprinting about thirty yards to the finish line. The three teams with the fastest times received a trophy for their efforts.

The hydrant hook-up also involved all five members of the firefighting team. The physical implements of the event were a fire hydrant, two lengths of fire hose, a nozzle, a target, and some fast moving water. The hydrant man had the job of connecting the female end of one length of hose to the hydrant. He then had to open the hydrant. At the start of the competition, two firefighters took their place where the two hoses would meet and then they tried to couple them together while running forward. Great care was needed so that the length of hose was not ripped from the grip of the hydrant man. The two firefighters at the nozzle end of the hose had two jobs. They had to attach the nozzle to the end of the hose and then direct the stream of water to hit a target thirty feet away. When the target was hit a mechanical signal was tripped and the clock stopped. It was always fun to watch other teams perform the hydrant hook-up because any one or more of the five team members could end up getting a shower once water was flowing and a connection had not been made. The hydrant man's job was simple. He hooked up to the gate of the hydrant and turned it on. There was no time to look and see if his teammates had made their connections. Trophies didn't go to teams with a timid hydrant man or soaked members.

The third and final event of the firematic game days was water ball. Large back stops that looked like oversized basketball backboards were one hundred and fifty feet apart. They were supported from behind by guide wires that were driven into the ground. A thin wire ran from backboard to backboard. Attached to the wire was a mesh net that contained the water ball, in our case, this was an old beaten up basketball. Again, each team consisted of five members. Each team received their water through a hose line that was connected to the same gated wye so theoretically there was no difference in the water pressure being delivered through each hose. The suspended ball started out in the center of the wire, placed there by a referee who carried a long wooden stick. Each team was in full turnout gear and stood beneath its own backboard. At the referee's signal, the gated wye was opened and a face off took place. The referee directed one nozzle man at a time to direct his hose stream towards the ground near the center of the wire. Hand signals were used to direct the elevation and lowering of the stream. The other team's nozzle man then directed his team's stream towards the center of the wire. Once the streams were aligned in the middle, the referee blew his whistle and quickly stepped backwards.

The water streams were then directed skywards towards the suspended ball. Our main objective was to hit the ball so that it traveled along the wire and hit the opponents' backboard. The major problem for the nozzle man was that in the spray of the other teams' hose line, he was usually helpless to see where to direct his stream. We used our fifth and last firefighter to be his eyes. He would stand towards the side and shout directional commands to the nozzle man. A shout of "go" meant that the nozzle man had given the ball a good push and the team should move forward to move the ball further. The frantic cry of "back" let the team know that the competition had made a decisive hit and it was time to scramble backwards to defend our own backboard and the team pride. An unopposed hit of the water ball could easily send it thirty feet in a second. Two teams that had adept nozzle men could battle in a single game for five minutes or more. The toughest part of playing water ball was playing defense. It was hard to believe that your team could ever win a game when you were almost directly underneath your backboard with a hose stream flowing directly upwards in a frantic effort to not hear the referee's whistle. A stream directed straight upward tended to have an effect of sending the ball into an orbit around the wire. This made it difficult for the other team to get a direct hit on the ball. The defensive team, however, would end up feeling as though they were standing underneath Niagara Falls. To advance to the next round of water ball a team had to win three games against a single team.

Much like the time honored tradition of losing at soft-ball, the Sweeneys always came up a little bit short at water ball tournaments. Our first year of competition was a learning year for us. We struggled to make any headway and we were eliminated early from any chance of taking home a trophy. We had improved by our return trip to competition the following year. We weren't competitive enough to hold practice sessions at our hall all year long, but we communi-cated with each other at the competition. We watched the other teams make mistakes, yet victory was just out of reach in the events.

We performed well in the hydrant hook-up competition. Couplings came together without a hitch. The hydrant was hooked up without a problem. The nozzle was attached to the hose and as I dropped to my belly at the end of the hose, water was flowing from the nozzle. I blew it for the team, taking at least four seconds to hit the target. We ended up in fourth place out of eight teams in the hydrant hook-up.

We were the team to beat in the efficiency run. I was the first firefighter on our team to be completely dressed. I stayed back and watched all the other guys get dressed, keeping an eye out to make sure that every buckle was buckled and every strap was strapped. The last member of our team was geared up and I shouted for him to run. The other three members had crossed the finish line and Mike Mallard and I crossed the finish line a second later. I threw my hands into the air knowing that our time was as good as or better than the teams that had gone before us. We were finally going to bring home a polished piece of hardware called a trophy for the fire hall. We were giving high fives to each other when one of the judges came over. He shouted above our celebration, "Your team is disqualified." I stammered, "What, why?" He replied, "This guy's boot fell down just before the finish line." He was pointing to Mike Mallard. I was sure that his boot was up. It was up when we were looking at it. I argued with the judge, but to no avail. His word was final. I couldn't believe it. We lost because a boot supposedly fell down. I called Mike over and took a look at his boots. They had seen better days and could have fallen down, but I didn't think they would have fallen in such a short distance. We returned to the sideline where Duncan Fanner's wife Cindy held a camcorder in her hand. I asked her to rewind it to our run. She did and we saw the proof right before our eyes. The judge wasn't seeing things. Mike's boot had fallen down before the finish line.

With our luck fading as the competition went on it was now time for water ball. We easily won our first heat and we seemed to gain confidence in our ability. When the first rounds were over there were only four teams left. We had a seventy five percent chance of bringing home a trophy. We lost our next heat and then immediately went into another heat to decide which team would take third place. The team we were up against was good. We traded wins and now the score was 2-2. A single game would decide if we could hang our heads high back at the fire hall that day. I was the nozzle man. We directed our streams towards the middle of the field and I heard a whistle blow. I heard the directions from our fifth man. His voice was calm but it suddenly became tense. He yelled, "Back, back!" The sight of the orange ball completely passing over our heads was the reason for his concern. We quickly backed up as our competition charged towards us. The ball had stopped six feet in front of our backboard and it was being lightly patted by the stream from the other teams' nozzle. I aimed our hose straight up towards the wire, hoping to break up the stream from the other teams' hose. I arrived underneath our backboard and took aim at the ball. Our rivals had really moved forward and the combined forces of our streams had sent the ball in circles around the wire. The orbits seemed to last forever. I could hardly catch my breath. I continuously spit water out of my mouth. Then the sound of water hitting the ball stopped. It was replaced by the sound of a dull thud against our backboard and the cheers of the now third place winners. We had lost. In my disgust I threw the nozzle forward towards the ground giving our opponents a victory shower compliments of the Sweeney Hose Company. We hung our heads low, but we knew that we had given it our all that day.

Bowling, softball, and water ball provided me with many thrills and many disappointments over the years at Sweeney Hose. Looking back they made me laugh at myself. I learned how to occasionally win and to usually lose with a bit of grace.

9

Diving into Smoke

Hollywood has always disappointed me in its portrayal of fire. In a movie version of a structure fire, flames burn vividly and brightly and the atmosphere allows an unmasked firefighter to move comfortably through a fully involved house fire. This is great for the movie studios. The audience clearly sees the movie star being a hero. In reality, any real life firefighter could echo my thoughts that this depiction couldn't be any further from the truth.

The self contained breathing apparatus or the SCBA is the lifeline of any firefighter who performs interior firefighting. It can provide up to forty five minutes of life sustaining compressed air. By wearing an SCBA, firefighters can more safely work in toxic atmospheres. Long gone are the days of firefighters running into burning buildings without full respiratory protection. Unfortunately only the very basics of SCBA use were taught to us in our Essentials of Firefighting class. Volunteers who wanted to truly realize the SCBA's capabilities and limitations attended an intensive thirty two hour course called smoke divers.

The North Tonawanda Fire Department did not offer the smoke divers class but the Niagara County Fire Office did. One of the toughest parts of the class was actually getting into it. Duncan Fanners and I spent a total of $75.00 in application processing fees each and after a year and a half of waiting we were finally called to attend the class.

The structure of the class was simple. Sixteen firefighters from across Niagara County came together for two consecutive weekends. We spent eight hours a day learning how to use the SCBA in a variety of situations. We learned how to trust our brother and sister firefighters. In the last eight hours of the class we suppressed live fires and searched for dummy victims in a house that was slated for demolition. If Duncan and I satisfied all the requirements of the class and didn't collapse from complete exhaustion, we would graduate from the class and then bear the title of a Niagara County smoke diver.

Duncan sat in his car and beeped his horn in front of my house. I emerged from the side door with my fire gear in hand. I saw my breath in the cold Saturday morning air. Duncan popped his car trunk and I threw my fire gear on top of his. The SCBAs that we had borrowed from the fire department were in the back seat. We had a spare air bottle for each unit. Unfortunately we were only able to borrow the reserve SCBAs from the department. These units had old straps and carried heavy steel cylinders as opposed to the newer aluminum cylinders that were much lighter. We were soon to feel like the red headed step children of the class as every other firefighter used a light weight cylinder that their department provided for them.

As we arrived at the Niagara County fairgrounds in Lockport, we saw a fire training tower in the distance. I knew that Duncan and I were wondering what we had gotten ourselves into. "Well, here goes nothing," I half heartedly said as we carried our gear into the classroom. Duncan just laughed.

As with almost any other training class we had attended, the class began with filling out paperwork that needed to be completed. I finished my task and I looked around the table at the other fifteen smoke diver students in the room. I wondered if they were as nervous as me about the class. My thoughts were halted as a tall instructor moved steadily to the front of the room.

"Welcome to the smoke divers class," he said in an authoritative voice. "This will likely be the most grueling and demanding firefighting course you will ever take. You will become exceedingly familiar with your SCBA over the next two weekends. You'll be wearing it all of the time. You will learn tricks that will help to save your life in dire situations. Make it through this course and you'll be a better and safer firefighter. Make sure that you don't act on the urge to go out drinking after your classes. Go home and get plenty of rest. You'll be wearing your masks most of the time during this course. If you puke in your mask because you drank too much the night before, you'll still be wearing your mask. It has happened before. Each and every one of these instructors standing around the room is here because he wants to teach you the skills of a smoke diver. Each one of them is volunteering their time to be here and every one is a graduate of the smoke diver course. Have fun and follow their lead. If you make it through the course you will have the opportunity to become an instructor. With that I'll turn it over to Lee James who will teach you about the basics of the SCBA."

I sat in my chair and shivers went up my spine. This was it. I was going to become one of the elite firefighters. I felt like I was in a scene from the movie *Top Gun* where the pilots were told that the top graduates of the class could come back to be instructors. I was in dreamland. This would be easy. Our first instructor was getting ready to talk. I was ready to soak up everything I could. I knew that soon I would have all the knowledge of the man standing in front of us. The room became quiet as he silently stood in front of the class.

"Whatever you think you know about using an SCBA, forget it. I'm here to tell you that you don't know shit about using an SCBA," he proclaimed. My hopes plummeted through the floor. I wanted to be inspired with knowledge. Now this guy was telling me I knew nothing. Only thirty one hours and fifty nine minutes of this beating left I thought. He would soon show us what he meant.

He ordered us to move and said, "Everybody get up and spread out. Get your turnout gear and put it on, except for your helmet and your gloves." I stepped into my bunker boots and then pulled my bunker pants up around my waist, throwing the suspenders over my shoulders. I clipped the waist shut. Putting on my Nomex hood was the next step and I put it on my head. Donning my jacket, I snapped the inner snaps and clipped its outer buckles.

Lee James continued, "OK, now that you are all finally dressed, I'm going to have you don your SCBA using your normal procedure. Take a few seconds and set up your apparatus the way you want to set it up." I bent down putting the cylinder and harness on its back. The regulator was on the other side of the air bottle. I made sure that all of the straps on the harness were fully extended. The straps on the face piece were also fully extended. I then folded the web like straps over the front of the mask. I stood up, ready for the next instructions.

"Now get ready to don your SCBA, using your normal procedure," shouted the instructor. I hunched over my pack, getting ready to sling the thing on and show Mr. James Lee that I did know something. My heart started racing as James spoke, "The final thing with this exercise that I didn't mention before is that you're going to do this whole process with your eyes closed and we're timing you. Raise your hand when you are in your full protective envelope. Ready? Go!"

I felt lost already as I closed my eyes. I had always used my eyes for guidance, especially when I was doing anything mechanical. Everything in this exercise would have to be done by feel. I would have to trust my instincts. Another movie came to mind as I imagined a tall, elderly, cloaked Jedi speaking to me, "Use the force, Luke."

As my hands fumbled to locate the main regulator valve of the SCBA, I knelt down. Grasping the valve I turned it counter clockwise and a loud bell ringing signified that I was doing my job correctly. My left thumb then found a round piece of rubber. This was the cover for the connection that would attach to the low pressure hose of my face piece. Next, my right hand quickly found the valve that opened the regulator. By sight it was yellow, but its rough rounded surface identified it for me by touch. I turned the valve on and a slight pressure beneath my left thumb told me that air was flowing through the regulator. My right hand went back to the main tank valve and closed it. Slowly I lifted the rubber covering for the face piece connection. Air was escaping and near the end of its escape a bell rang. This was good as the actions I had just performed simulated my SCBA running low on air. My SCBA had passed the test and it was ready to use.

Placing my arms through the straps I lifted the SCBA over my head, the harness coming to rest on my shoulders. I found the chest strap and fastened it across my chest. I hunched up the shoulder straps while simultaneously thrusting the air tank higher on my back. The waist strap seat belt buckle was clicked next. Now it was time for my mask.

I lifted the mask from the ground and placed its strap around my neck. I pulled the webbing of straps over my head and tightened them two at a time until the mask adhered to my face. Placing my sweaty palm at the end of the mask's air tube, I sucked in a deep breath. The mask stayed sucked into my face. My mask seal was good and tight. I fumbled for the regulator on the harness and I found it, screwing my low pressure air hose into it while opening my air supply from the air tank at the same time. I breathed deeply and cool fresh air came through the mask and went into my lungs. The deep mechanical sound of the air always made me think of Darth Vader breathing. I pulled my Nomex hood over my head and then put my gloves on. I raised my arm to signal my readiness for inspection and I opened my eyes.

I saw that there were others still fumbling with their masks. I wasn't the last one finished. An instructor came over towards me and looked closely at my gear. He remarked, "Collar not fully up in back and one exposed strap from underneath your hood, otherwise good." I looked over to Duncan as he had already been inspected. I leaned towards him and breathing deeply I said, "Luke, I am your father." He laughed. We were finally on our way to becoming smoke divers.

The rest of the morning was spent showing us how to stay with our partners during a search. This rule had been drilled into our heads through our training in North Tonawanda. This was no big deal for Duncan and me. On our hands and knees we trudged around in circles in a large room while we wore our SCBAs. We kept in contact with our partners by touching their boot and by talking to each other. The afternoon exercises would test our comfort with the SCBA. They would also reveal something to me that I never knew about Duncan.

After a quick lunch we headed towards the fire training tower that we had seen in the distance earlier that morning. We entered the training grounds and noticed a long rectangular wooden box on the ground. Each end of the box was open. Our instructor for the station started to speak.

"Working in confined spaces with your SCBA is probably something you're not used to. It is important for you to become comfortable in confined spaces. You have to use mind over matter and not suck the air out of your bottle if you become trapped in a confined space. This open ended box over my shoulder is two feet wide and two feet high. It is twenty feet long. Now you'll each go through this confined space in two minutes or less. Tomorrow, to make things more interesting, we're going to put a two by four piece of wood through the slot you can see in the middle. You won't be able to get through the tunnel with your harness and cylinder on your back. When you get to the wood tomorrow, you'll need to remove your helmet and take your pack off over the top of your head. You'll keep control of your mask and your helmet while you push them ahead of you to get out of the tunnel. But that's for tomorrow. Now stay with your partner. You will each go through one at a time. Remember, this will be completed in less than two minutes."

As I was standing closest to the end of the tunnel, the instructor volunteered me to be the first test subject. I attached my mask to the regulator and became prone on the ground. I started belly crawling toward the tunnel. When I arrived at the beginning of the tunnel I was stopped. My air bottle was stuck on the edge of the tunnel. I realized that I would have to turn my body at a forty five degree angle so that my tank would fit into one of the upper corners of the box.

I crept into the tunnel and I immediately realized just how cramped it was. My respiratory rate shot up. I had never been a fan of cramped spaces, but I knew that this was a mind game. I kept telling myself that I was still breathing. Every inch forward was an inch closer to being done. I couldn't lose control here or none of the other firefighters in the group would have any confidence in me, especially when we were inside a building. I could now here the instructor's words of encouragement more clearly. It was getting to be less dark. My glove touched gravel. I kept crawling. "Good job," the instructor applauded, "one minute and ten seconds." I stood up and stretched my arms as the instructor told me to help to guide Duncan to the end of the tunnel.

I stepped towards the tunnel exit to try to coach Duncan. I was startled when I heard a clamoring of noise from the other end of the tunnel. It sounded like a thunderstorm was approaching. The tunnel trembled back and forth. A firefighter emerged from the end of the tunnel. He stood up and ripped off his mask. It was Duncan. He had flown through the tunnel in an amazing sixteen seconds, covering more than one foot per second.

It was time for me to bust Duncan's balls so I walked up to him. I said, "You ass. I was supposed to coach you through the tunnel and offer tender words of encouragement.

You never even gave me a chance to get to the end of the tunnel. What was the big hurry?" He replied as he gasped for breath, "You probably might have figured this out. I hate confined spaces. I get really claustrophobic."

A cloud of worry had parked itself over my head. Here was my partner, who was the company captain at the time, telling me that he wasn't comfortable with confined spaces. I had been with him in numerous structure fires before and he never showed any signs that he could get frazzled. Then again, we had never been stuck in any confined spaces either. I was going to be his partner in the burning building. I would have to take the lead if he lost it in the building. I had enough to worry about thinking of my own limitations. This was double trouble as I was about to find out in our next drill.

For our next exercise we would be making our way through a maze in a converted chicken coup. We were told to make our way through the henhouse as quickly as possible. We would not be required to remove our packs in this exercise. Total darkness would be our companion in the maze. We would have to feel with our hands and communicate with our partners. We would have to trust our instincts. I took the lead into the coup. Talking between our noisy breathing I told Duncan what I was finding. "Narrow passage, turning left," I shouted. "Straight ahead let's go," I urged. Duncan quickly followed. I pounded my hand onto the floor ahead of me. We were taught to always make sure that there was something sturdy in front of us when we were searching a building. This exercise was no exception to that rule.

As I moved ahead I felt myself going up. I crawled upwards and then surprisingly I stumbled forward. I yelped out a shout of fear. Duncan shouted from behind, "Are you OK, what's going on?" "Teeter totter," I called back, "I'll set your end down." I reloaded the trick incline for its next now informed victim.

Duncan made it easily over the incline and we continued our journey through the darkened maze. My helmet and hand then hit plywood with a simultaneous thud. I stopped crawling and I told Duncan to do the same. My right hand felt a wall to my right and I moved it forward and found a corner. My right hand continued moving to the left searching for another corner. There was none. I felt for a floor. My gloved flapped quietly in the air as there was no floor to pound. We were on a ledge. I communicated this to Duncan. I said, "There's a drop down to my left. I'm going to reach down with my hands to see if there's a solid floor below. Hold my legs."

Leaning forward into what in a real fire situation could be an abyss twenty to thirty feet deep, my hands found a solid floor approximately three feet below. The only opening on the wall in the mini abyss turned one hundred and eighty degrees from the direction we were headed. I pounded the floor several times. It seemed solid. Now I had to plan how I was going to navigate this obstacle. As I rested for a couple of seconds my brain kicked in and I called back to Duncan. I said, "There's a drop off here. About three feet down. We're going to be going back in the direction we came. I'm going to go down headfirst and swing myself in the other direction." Duncan replied, "OK, let me know when you're through."

Reaching out with my hands I lowered myself to the bottom level. I turned sideways and starting to crawl through the maze, my lower body flopped to the floor. I continued to crawl forward and I was clear of the obstacle. I called back to Duncan to let him know I had made it through. I encouraged him to take his time.

The next thing I heard was the distinct sound of steel on plywood. Then there was silence. Duncan's frantic voice broke the silence. He yelled, "Jay my tank is caught on the floor and I'm stuck upside down. Help me, I'm getting claustrophobic!" In Duncan's voice I heard the genuine sound of fear. He wouldn't be able to get himself out of this situation. As his partner I would have to get him through this dilemma. I first needed to calm him down.

"Duncan, slow your breathing down. I'm coming back to get you. You have plenty of air left," I said. I did my best contortionist impression as I turned my body around in the narrow passageway. I reached for Duncan's shoulders. "I've got you and I'm going to pull you towards me," I said. Using all of my strength, I pulled Duncan's shoulders towards me. His tank scraped across the floor and then his legs made it past the drop. He was free. "Ready to move on?" I questioned. "Yes," his panting voice answered. We plodded through the maze without further incident and escaped into sunlight.

We stood up and removed our masks. The next group entered the henhouse. Duncan pulled me aside and quietly thanked me for helping him out of his situation. Guys around the fire hall never really talked about their fears when it came to firefighting. For the most part you just did your job and kept your fears to yourself. This seemed like a humbling experience for Duncan. He had let his fear out into the open. Now I knew he really hated tight spaces. He knew that he could trust me to help him.

The next two days of training were filled with exercises that were intended for showing us the limitations of our SCBAs. Nothing demonstrated this better than what I called the run and chop exercise. It looked like a simple task. We sprinted fifty yards and then grabbed an axe. We would then run the same fifty yards back to the starting line and then we used the axe to chop on a telephone pole lying on the ground. Of course the SCBA was worn during the exercise. I was right about the run. It was easy. The chopping however was sheer torture. After about ten chops I could feel every muscle in my body begging for mercy. I felt like the air tank was a villain, robbing my airflow just to make me suffer. After what seemed like a lifetime, the two minutes had ended. I fell to my knees and cracked open the bypass valve on my SCBA. A torrent of air filled my facemask as I recovered from the exercise.

Another drill encouraged us to put faith and trust in our partners. The task that we performed was a hot bottle change. This meant that my partner would take my theoretically empty tank out of its harness and then put a full tank in my harness while I kept the harness on my back. The catch in the drill was that the wearer kept his mask on and held his breath during the entire procedure. Luckily Duncan and I were both fairly dexterous with this newly learned skill and neither one of us lost enough oxygen to pass out during our turns.

The other exercises of the class basically showed us how to escape from dangerous situations. We learned how to get out of trouble in any circumstance. These drills helped us prepare for our ultimate test for the course – burn day.

Burn day started back at the training facility. Duncan and I walked into the classroom without our gear. We received a briefing with fourteen brother would be smoke divers that morning. We then headed out towards the burn house in our cars. The house, located less than a mile from the training facility, was hidden from the road as we approached. Turning down a long driveway, Duncan passed a forty foot wide expanse of trees. Then the burn house, a quaint white two story structure, became visible. Particle board covered every window. The house sat atop a small hill. Three engines from some of the instructors' fire companies sat silently on the grass, looking poised for action. Like our first day of class, we gathered as a group and waited for our lead instructor Lee James to speak. Hopefully we knew something more than shit now about using an SCBA because we were about to go into a building that would have real fires and real smoke in it.

Lee came to the front of the group and started his speech. He said, "We'll have eight burns this morning and eight this afternoon. You and your partner will have different tasks to do. Sometimes you'll be doing a primary search for victims. Sometimes you'll be on the attack line. Other times you'll be on the backup line or you'll act as the outside ventilation team. Above all, stick with your partner. If your partner goes to get a drink, you go to get a drink. If your partner goes for a walk, you go for a walk. If he goes to take a leak, you go take a leak with him. When you're outside the burn house today you can disconnect from your regulators, but leave your masks on. The only time your masks should be off today is if you're getting a drink or eating lunch."

Duncan and I were on the attack line for our first burn. I was the nozzle man. Our job was to find where the fire was burning on the first floor while stretching a water laden hose to the fire room. We would watch the fire and when the signal was given by the instructor we were to darken the fire.

We geared up and got ready to go into the house. We kneeled on the ground. The instructor shouted "go" and my blood really began to pump. The search crew for our floor went in before us. Duncan and I then crawled into the building. Once Duncan was inside the entrance door we stopped. We listened. We were letting the fire reveal its location to us. Its crackles and pops told us it was in the next room. We made our way against the right side of the wall and it came into view. It was a tame fire in the corner of the room and it seemed to beg us to come closer to it.

We claimed our ground in the fire room, sitting back about ten feet from the fire. We watched it as it slowly grew, turning from jumping solitary flickers of light into a unified river of orange power that had started to move horizontally across the ceiling. We had learned that a quick and easy way to control the fire was to squirt a quick shot of water at it. The nozzle was to be adjusted to a ten degree cone pattern and the water would be aimed not at the base of the fire but at the ceiling. The shot of water could only last a brief second or the steam that was generated could provide an unbearable situation for any of the firefighters in the room.

Two minutes had passed as we sat in the room and an instructor approached us from the side. He said, "OK, hit it now, but only with a quick spurt." I aimed the nozzle at the ceiling and fully opened the nozzle. I shut it off quickly. The room became shrouded in darkness as the flame retreated to the bucket from where it was born. Duncan and I both let out an audible gasp of pain as a cloud of scorching steam enveloped us. I had left the nozzle open a tad too long as we weren't supposed to generate any steam. Our instructor told us we had done well and we exited the building with our attack line.

The morning continued on with our evolutions and we quickly found our victim, a baby doll, when Duncan led our search. We were performing primary searches. These searches were done quickly. We were not in the building to be able to describe the texture and placement of every single object we encountered. We were there to find any human sign of life. We had to remove the pretend victim quickly from the noxious atmosphere that it somehow supposedly had managed to survive.

After devouring a much anticipated lunch of sandwiches, we were off to spend an afternoon of smoke diving. One of the members of another team had injured his knee between two hose lines during the morning evolutions. He was unable to continue the exercises in the afternoon. He had spent all of his time training to get to burn day and now he would not complete the course. He would not be a smoke diver.

Our second to last evolution of the day would put us on the second floor of the house. I would lead the search for our victim. When we entered the house, Duncan grabbed my left heel and we used a right hand search to find the stairs that led to the second floor. We entered the room with the stairs and encountered a frightening sight. The fire was burning right beneath the stairs, our only means of egress if things turned ugly. Climbing the stairs we felt immense heat beneath our legs. We got to the top of the stairs and continued our right hand search.

"Got a doorway, turning in," I shouted to Duncan as I went into the first room. The room was small and we scoured it in less than a minute. I touched the wall and leaned towards the center of the room as Duncan spread his body out. He kicked his legs, hoping to encounter our victim. I soon came upon the other side of the doorway we had entered. There were no victims to be found in this room.

Going back into the hall, I quickly found the second room and entered it. On the fourth wall I found a doorway that had a back wall two feet inside of it. It was a closet. I carefully felt along the closet floor, remembering that children often ran from a fire to find a hiding place. I swept my hand up and down the wall hoping to find the victim. We then found the hallway door. We soon entered the third bedroom. It seemed to have the same layout as the first bedroom. There were no closets and no victims. We exited the room and I was surprised when we met the instructor at the top of the stairs.

"Did you find a victim?" he shouted. "No," I replied as I panted through my exhaustion. "Well do another search and don't come back here until you have a victim," he warned.

I was furious with the instructor but I kept my mouth shut. I leaned back towards Duncan and said, "I know where the victim is and we're going to skip the first room. Just follow me." We bridged the doorway of the first room and entered the second room. I hurried past the first three walls and then I came to the closet where I stopped. I took my glove off and raised my naked hand above my head. It was warm in the room, but not dangerously hot. I stood up and found what I was looking for in the closet. It was a shelf, perched about six feet above the floor. I ran my hand towards the left and found the second thing I was looking for – the baby doll victim. I informed Duncan of my discovery and we made our way to the top of the stairs with our victim. It felt much warmer descending the stairs than when we had climbed them. We ended up on the stoop of the house. Duncan was on his hands and knees gasping for air. The lead instructor was standing over us.

"What the hell took you guys so long in there?" he said in a demanding tone. That was it for me. I was exhausted. I had been pushed beyond my breaking point. I stood up and ripped off my mask to address his question. Holding the doll up in front of me, I started asking my own questions.

"How the hell does a baby end up lying on a six foot shelf in a closet? Does he just levitate himself up there? Who hid the victim on the closet shelf?" I queried. The lead instructor immediately understood my point. He left us, looking for the instructor who had hidden the victim on the closet shelf. He used some choice words to admonish the actions taken by this first time smoke diver instructor. The first timer lowered his head and apologized to us. The lead instructor also apologized for the verbal lashing he had given us. Duncan and I accepted their apologies as we continued to work to suck every molecule of oxygen from the outdoor air. Luckily our next evolution, which was the last, only required us to be an outdoor team that would help to feed hose to the interior fire attack team. The last evolution went smoothly and when everyone had exited the building, the day had nearly ended.

The second to last order of business for the day was to have our class picture taken in front of the house. The picture couldn't just be of the house behind us. It had to be totally engulfed in flames. Pictures were taken and the smoke from the blaze started to bank down on us. The house would be allowed to burn to the ground. It had served as a home for one or more families and today it had served to train the men who had vowed to protect the families in their communities. It would burn some more and then the ruins would be wetted down by the volunteers who were manning the pumpers. It was now time for the class to meet for one final time.

Duncan and I got into his car and headed towards the host fire hall which was about five miles from the burn house. We smelled like a burning inferno and now Duncan's car did too. I was considerate enough to bring a towel to put over Duncan's passenger seat as I was drenched from head to toe in stinky, yet refreshing, sweat. The course had been an effective weight loss program for Duncan as he related that he had shed sixteen pounds after the first three days. I, however, didn't even lose half a pound throughout the course.

At the host fire hall, the lead instructor reviewed the main points of the course as we sipped on soda pop and ate doughnuts. There was no grand dinner at the end of the course. No medals were placed around our necks. All we received were doughnuts, pop, a smoke diver certificate, and a patch that read, "Niagara County Smoke Diver". Duncan and I realized that our true prize was in the wealth of information and hands on experience that now resided between our ears. We were exhausted, but we had experienced many things over the last two weekends. We knew exactly what we could and could not do with an SCBA. We could push ourselves. We could help to teach others. We might have thought of ourselves as being a little more than just your average North Tonawanda volunteer firefighter. We knew more. We could now dive into smoke.

10

Making Dough

Volunteer fire companies generally receive some type of stipend for their operation that is paid by the tax money of the community they serve. This was true for the Sweeney Hose Company and we received a meager amount of money paid in quarterly installments from the city fathers. The company had always needed to raise extra funds to support hall projects and we used a variety of fundraisers to acquire our spending money. Our field days and bingo were some of our steady money makers. By far, the Sweeneys' largest source of income was running the beer tent at North Tonawanda's and Tonawanda's largest annual attraction – Canal Fest.

A field day by any other name is still a field day. A church might call their field day a lawn fete. A school could call their field day a carnival. The Sweeneys always called their field day a field day. The first Thursday, Friday, and Saturday of June brought in the Sweeney Hose field days. We had something for everyone: Rides and games for kids and adults, a variety of foods, a beer tent, live music, a gambling tent, and a parade on Saturday afternoon. Because we didn't have acres of usable property like the other two large volunteer companies in North Tonawanda, our field days were held off of our company property. We set up our festivities beyond the outfield of Felton Field, a softball diamond located behind the North Tonawanda Police Station. Bad weather seemed to plague our field days and slim profit margins brought an inevitable end to our field days, but memories of this event abound.

For reasons unbeknownst to me, the line officers of the hall had always been placed in charge of running the field days. The captain and his two lieutenants did everything from making sure there were portable toilets at the field to ordering the beer that would ensure that those vile smelling Johnny on the Spots got used to their fullest extent. Felton Field was about a ten minute drive from our hall and we transported everything to our site. We ran our own food tent and grills, deep fryers, a refrigerator, and a meat slicer had to be brought to our location. A full length outdoor bar and hundreds of plastic beer pitchers were other items we needed to run the field day. We packed up thousands of feet of snow fence to create a double fence around our beer tent so that our cool amber beverage couldn't be easily passed to those outside of our adult fun zone. When I was a lieutenant, a concerned resident had issues with our supposedly inebriated customers urinating on her property. With the suggestion of the North Tonawanda common council we fenced off her yard to ward off the undesired micturitions of our patrons into her flowerbeds. We had lots of material to move each year and luckily one of our members, Ken Rojek, worked at a car repair shop that rented out U-Haul trucks. He would acquire a truck for us each year and he drove the multiple trips back and forth between the hall and the field. He only asked us to sweep out the truck when we had finished our hauling.

During my first field day as a 1st lieutenant, I was at the field on one of our set up days. Some members and I were attempting to set up our ticket booths. These booths, which were constructed from cheap particle boards, had been made by members of the hall. During the field day members would work in the booths and sell tickets for beer. This made for quicker service at the bar and the money stayed in the ticket booths which were locked from the inside. We had three ticket booths in multiple pieces and we were trying to put them together. The pieces were labeled with the letters "A", "B", or "C". I had never put the booths together before, and I was frustrated by the fact that we couldn't seem to get them together. As a lieutenant who was in need of some immediate assistance, I got on my portable fire radio and called up Duncan Fanners who was serving as captain of the company at the time. Duncan had jumped in the U-Haul truck with Ken Rojek to oversee some loading of stuff at the hall.

I called over the radio, "7-2 to 7-1."

Duncan replied, "7-1, go ahead 7-2."

"I'm having some having some trouble with setting up the ticket booths. I've got A, B, and C walls. How are they set up?"

After a long pause, Duncan's reply came back, "Use the A wall for your front, the B wall for your sides, and the C wall for your back."

"10-4," I acknowledged.

I gathered the other members and I explained Duncan's instructions to them.

We gathered one A section, two B sections, and a C section. We attempted to attach the A section to the two pieces of B section. It didn't work. Everyone except the one member who was assisting me had stepped back and watched me in my frustration as I tried in vain to put the pieces of the ticket booth together. I stopped after several minutes of cussing and I looked behind me. A crowd of ten members had gathered. They all stood with smiles strewn across their faces. In the crowd were Duncan, Ken Rojek, and Kurt Paulis who had just returned from their trip. Kurt stepped forward and said, "You stupid shit, A goes with A, B goes with B, and C goes with C." The gallery of observers broke into laughter. My face turned a dark red and I knew that a very entertaining fast one had been pulled on me. After the laughter subsided, everyone went to work and the ticket booths were assembled without a hitch.

A prominent member of the hall who had joined some time before me was a man named Allen Michalis. He was one of the most stubborn men I had ever known. He would argue passionately for anything he believed in. He would fight tooth and nail against those things he opposed. He never had a problem letting the younger members of the hall know what they should be doing. He had retired early from his job as a health condition has limited his ability to work. At times he could be seen pulling a small pill bottle out of his pocket. His cupped hand would then quickly slap its way up to his lips, dropping off a nitroglycerin tablet under his tongue. He seemed to do this more when he got worked up. Duncan found out that he had a Nitro brand bowling bowl and that was it. The paramedic devil came out in him. Duncan addressed Allen as "Nitro" all of the time. Behind his tough exterior, Allen was a gentle and hard working man who always had the best interest of the fire hall at heart. He was always active in hall events and the field days were no exception.

One year during field day set up Allen drove his SUV down the slight incline of a hill into the area of the beer tent. Softball games had been in progress on this night of set-up and a couple of members had asked Al if he wanted to move his truck as several home runs had already been hit over the left field fence. Al laughed at them and said that his truck wouldn't get hit. A short two innings later the distant sounds of some shouting voices were heard followed by a quick thud and the sound of cracking glass. Sure enough, a home run ball had found its way onto and into Al's front windshield, creating a spider web pattern. No member came out and said, "I told you so," but a lot of good natured ribbing was passed Al's way that night. Next February Al was awarded a plaque at the company's Annual Installation of Officers Dinner. His award was a mounted piece of

Plexiglas with a softball embedded in the middle of it. Spider web markings were rightfully included.

The gambling tent for our field day was located at the end of the beer tent closest to the police station. One Saturday night Don Galling, Kurt Paulis, and I were working a gaming wheel. Gamblers would bet on which number the wheel would stop on. We were paying out some money, but we were also raking in a ton of cash for the fire hall. It was about ten thirty at night when a rough looking guy carrying a half empty pitcher of beer walked into the tent. We immediately recognized him. He was a carnival worker or carny for short. He probably had traveled across the country with the amusement rides operator. He probably slept in a trailer for most of the year. He was lacking several of his front teeth and his raspy voice declared that he had probably taken up smoking at the age of seven and he was probably now in his early thirties. He set his beer on the ground and pulled out a thick wad of ten and twenty dollar bills from his pocket. Kurt and I looked at each other and grinned. The carny had just gotten paid. We were betting that his payday would lead to a big payday for the fire hall. I thought that the pitcher of the beer on the ground had to be his second or third of the evening as he was talking loudly among the well mannered gamblers who had been at the table before him.

He started placing five dollar bets down. Five dollars was supposed to be the limit a single person could put down for one spin of the wheel. He won on a couple of spins and he lost on some spins. He kept guzzling his beer. Soon he was putting two five dollar bets down on each spin and although Kurt, Don, and I knew this was outside the rules, we let him continue to play. His bets were technically illegal in New York State's eyes, but we considered them as charitable contributions to the fire hall. He took us for some money when he had bet ten dollars, but then lady luck turned her back on him. Desperation deepened on his face. He lost more and more of his paycheck with each spin of the wheel. Several of the other players now stepped back and watched in amazement as the carny continued to slap money down on the table. He was now placing twenty dollar bets. Kurt was really sweating now as we had completed knocked down any boundaries for the rules. Fortunately, we would be able to cover any payout. The carny lost on a twenty dollar bet and shouted out in disgust. He dug into his pockets and a silence fell over our end of the gambling tent. Nothing but his empty hand came out of his pocket this time. He grabbed his pitcher and said good night to all of the patrons as he exited the gambling tent. I glanced at my watch. It was ten to eleven. Twenty minutes of hard gambling and the carny had blown his entire paycheck. We breathed a sigh of relief and invited the spectators from the great gambling show to step forward to make their donations to Sweeney Hose.

The beer tent was a big part of our field day. Warm weather and a lack of falling moisture ensured a good crowd in our tent. I liked to work the main gate on the security team and I would check people's IDs as they entered the gate.

We rarely had any real need for security intervention at the field days. One year however, a relatively new member of the hall let an unruly patron know that we took security issues very seriously at Sweeney Hose. Chuck Peterson had migrated to North Tonawanda from a nearby state. Chuck had been a career firefighter but his department went through downsizing. He found work in the Buffalo area with a trucking company. He was an outspoken individual who became heavily involved in the social side of the fire hall. On one particular field day night, Chuck entered one end of a portable toilet that contained a trough-like urinal. He immediately smelled marijuana and stepped up to the urinal right next to the patron who was smoking Mother Nature. Chuck could have surely summoned help and we could have notified the police quickly about the incident. In true Chuck style, he simply aimed his stream at the offending agent which was being held in the hand of his urinal counterpart. After extinguishing the joint, Chuck was sure to keep up good relations with our customer. "Whoops, sorry about that," was heard coming from the urinal.

When closing time in the beer tent drew near, the bartenders would briefly flick off the lights in the tent, causing a loud roar from the crowd. This signified last call and people hurried to the bar to get one last pitcher of beer. A second flick of the light switch fifteen minutes later was our way of saying, "now get out of here." The beer taps were shut down. About ten to fifteen minutes later, members from the hall would go through the tent and start to herd the drunks and stragglers towards the gates.

On one Saturday night I was working the gate with Mike Mallard, a young member of the hall who often traveled on business. At times he was very active but at other times, his work and family took control of his time. Mike had been drinking beer throughout the night. He had a half full pitcher of beer in his hand when a scrawny, seemingly malnourished patron with a long beard approached the exit gate. Mike was pretty lit on the beer and he saw the guy coming our way. Mike looked at me with glazed eyes and said, "Watch this." He approached the drunk as he was leaving and said, "Dude, what a party." The drunk gave out a shout, "Yeah!" Mike quickly questioned him, "Wanna funnel some beer?" He held up his half full pitcher with his invitation. "Awesome," said the drunk. Mike helped the swaggering drunk tip his head back and then began to pour beer into his mouth. He kept up with the swallowing for about a quarter of the pitcher and then Mike poured the rest of the beer over his face. The held tilt had thrown the drunk's equilibrium even more out of whack and he took short stuttering steps backwards. He tripped on a section of snow fence and tumbled headfirst into a garbage can, knocking it over on its side. I stood there for a minute in disbelief. The drunk was lying motionless on the ground with garbage strewn around his body. An eternity seemed to pass. Mike was on the ground too, laughing hysterically. I started walking towards our customer, wondering if he had been mortally wounded. He finally started to move and got up to his feet. He turned towards Mike and stared at him. A smile adorned his face. He raised a clenched right fist and shouted,

"Party!" He slowly disappeared into the night as I joined Mike in his laughter.

Sweeney Hose walked into running the beer tent at an annual North Tonawanda and Tonawanda event called Canal Fest. Canal Fest got its start in 1983 with the help of a few prominent businessmen and politicians and the North Tonawanda Chamber of Commerce. It was a week long annual festival held during the third week of July. Conservative estimates had put the yearly crowd attendance between 150,000 and 200,000 people. As one of the largest outdoor festivals in New York State, it had something for everyone. Some of the festivities included live music of every type, car shows, rides, games of chance, waterskiing demonstrations, a build your own boat and race it contest, and a craft show. Every year a Miss Canal Fest and Junior Miss Canal Fest were crowned. Tuesday nights drew an enormous crowd for the Canal Fest parade. From beginning to end a spectator would spend three hours of their life watching the parade. The city of Tonawanda joined in on the money making action in 1984 and the events of the week spilled across the Erie Canal into their city. Several non-profit organizations passed on the idea of running the beer tent for the first Canal Fest. A handful of dedicated Sweeneys took on the challenge of running the tent. Over a decade after the first Canal Fest many organizations were still perturbed about the Sweeneys getting to run the beer tent year after year. They had obviously heard how much money could be made for a week of pouring beer.

Each year the set-up for the beer tent would start on the Thursday before the first day of Canal Fest, which was Sunday. We left setting up the big tent to the tent company guys. A large beer truck was slowly driven into position outside of the tent and behind the bar. Members assembled long narrow wooden bar tables that were fabricated decades ago by Sweeney members for use at the field days. Thousands of plastic cups and hundreds of beer pitchers would be brought down from the storage garage at the fire hall to do their yearly service at the tent. Each year in the early 1990s the company would purchase new pitchers. Each pitcher was adorned by the Sweeney Hose Company emblem. Beneath the company emblem there were two word sayings that changed each year. The sayings never made sense to me. Three of the most memorable of the two word phrases were "coming soon", "getting closer", and "almost here". These phrases confused our patrons and we were often asked what they meant. When asked these questions we shot back equally confused glances at our customers. One day I approached Walt Treziak, who ran the beer tent with his brother, the fat man, Warren. A bunch of people were standing around Walt and Warren that afternoon as business was slow.

I addressed Walt in my usual sarcastic way while I held a slogan pitcher in my hand. I said, "Hey Pollack, what's with all these slogans? 'Almost here', 'getting closer', and 'coming soon'? No one, including me and every drunk in the beer tent, understands what these words mean. It sounds like we're moving closer and closer to some great orgasm. What's next year's slogan going to be? 'Thanks, that was awesome'?" The members that had gathered around burst into laughter. Walt just sat there and said, "You wait mister, you'll see what it's all about." In 1994 the one hundredth anniversary of the Sweeney Hose Company was celebrated. A new company emblem adorned the picture that year and I finally figured out that the slogans, however confusing they had seemed, were getting everyone ready for a great milestone in our company's history.

Sweeney members worked various details during their time in the beer tent. Working security was probably one of the most stressful jobs. The biggest job in working security was checking people for proof of their age. Every night we would hear sob stories of how someone's license had gotten lost or how they didn't want to walk all the way back to their car to get their license. These excuses didn't work on us. One year we denied entrance into the tent to a person who looked to be over twenty one years of age. He had no photo identification on him. He returned twenty minutes later with a court appearance ticket with a name and date of birth on it. I surveyed the ticket and saw a birth date on it. I quickly asked him his date of birth. His answer wasn't even close to the date on the ticket. He failed this easy test and I handed the ticket back to him, wishing him a good night as he walked down the street. There were at least four of us on the gate each night. If any one of us had a doubt as to whether someone was over twenty one or not, they didn't get into the tent.

When working security, it was also our job to make sure that beer didn't leave the tent. One night a tall guy was walking quickly out of the tent with his hand cocked in a strange position. His hat was covering his hand. I knew something was up. As he was passing me I hit his covered hand from underneath, drenching him with the beer that been in his concealed cup. I thought for sure that he was coming back to start a fight and the other guys on security got ready for trouble. Instead, the perpetrator just stood there dripping and smiling and said, "Nice catch," before he walked down the street with his intoxicated friends.

The security detail would also make "pitcher runs". This entailed walking through the hot, noisy, shoulder to shoulder confines of the tent in order to collect empty pitchers. This task was necessary on crowded nights as the pitcher population was usually depleted quickly. Extra men on security would often perch themselves on the Delaware Street bridge that was next to the beer tent. This position gave a bird's eye view of most of the happenings in the tent and if trouble started it would be seen first from the bridge.

Bartenders had a fairly simple job. When a customer walked up to the bar, they asked them what they wanted to drink. They collected the customer's tickets and poured them either a glass or pitcher of beer. They had two choices with the beer – regular or light. By the end of the night it didn't matter which tap the bartenders went to as the majority of the clientele were too bombed to know the difference between the beers. The ladies auxiliary, a group of about six or seven wives or ex-wives of members, helped out at the beer tent.

They provided wine coolers to be sold by the glass only. I thought this was a pain as there were at least three different kinds of wine coolers each year. It took time to explain the choices to the customers. It took more time to twist off the top of the bottle and then put ice in a separate cup for the finicky customers. I had always thought that only beer belonged in a beer tent.

Over the past several years, I created a self appointed position for myself at the tent when I worked there. I unofficially thought of myself as the operations manager. The chairmen were fairly old and they did a good job of delegating responsibilities. They did very little physical labor, but they had put their years in at the hall. They had given of themselves tirelessly for many years and they even took their summer vacation from work during Canal Fest week so they could serve as chairmen of the beer tent. As unofficial operations manager, I made sure that everyone else had the things they needed to perform their jobs easily. If clean pitchers were needed, I washed pitchers. If someone needed cups, I brought them cups. I delivered wine coolers and filled chests with ice. I wiped up spills. Working in the background was enjoyable for me. I didn't have to deal with the drunken public. When a shout of "three's down" went out into the thick summer night air, I jumped into action for my chance at obtaining some forty degree relief.

The shout of "three's down" meant that tap number three had run out of beer. The half keg needed to be changed. The bartender put an empty plastic cup on top of the tap to alert others to its "out of service" condition. I went to the back of the beer truck and opened the back door. I then climbed up into the truck and found tap three. I would shut down the compressed air going into the keg. The beer lines to the kegs were numbered not with actual numbers but with pieces of electrical tape wound around the lines. Line number one had one piece of tape around the line whereas line eight had eight separate pieces around the line. Before unhooking the tap, I always made sure to open a new half keg by pulling the plastic off the top. More often than not the removal of the tap from the keg gave me a quick shower of beer on my torso. This always worried me as I knew I would have to drive home early the next morning and I knew I would smell like a brewery if a cop pulled me over. I would hook up the fresh keg back up as I twisted the tap clockwise while pulling the handle down. I would emerge from the cool oasis of the back of the beer truck and yell, "three's up!" I stepped down onto the ground where my glasses immediately fogged up in the summer night air. I would look out at the crowd of people slowly making their way down the brick-lined Sweeney Street that meandered with the curves of the Erie Canal. I hoped for time to fly as the real fun of Canal Fest for the other beer tent workers and I started after the main attractions of the festival closed down for the night.

The Canal Fest chairmen used the same tactics as the field day chairmen to alert the patrons in the tent that their night in the tent was about to end. Lights were flicked on and off and eventually we would go about doing a trivial clean up of the beer tent. Cups were emptied of warm beer and pitchers were collected. Food was tossed into large garbage cans that would be emptied the next morning by city workers. After this fifteen minute episode of cleaning up, it was time to have a beer or wine cooler as we discussed the night with our brother and sister firefighters. This outdoor drinking lasted for only a short time. We then traveled as a group to one of the bars within walking distance of the tent.

In 1991 I was nineteen years old. Although I was still not old enough to legally get into a bar in New York State, there was no problem getting into Pier 84, a basement bar located right across the street from our beer tent. The ease of entry for me into the bar was because one of our members, Henry Kavinski, worked there part time as a bouncer. A bunch of us jammed our way into the bar and for some reason I abandoned beer and started to drink mixed drinks. The bar was having a contest that night for the best fake orgasm as delivered over a microphone. Girls were lining up and the guys listened intently as their minds wandered to fantasy land as girl after girl gave her verbal rendition of what imagined pleasure felt like. I had been drinking heavily and I felt left out. Guys had the right to express themselves too. I staggered up to the microphone and told the host that I wanted to take a shot at the contest. He promptly laughed and then introduced me. I took the mic and started a long roar that got louder and louder. When I had finished every girl in the place was going wild. I took a bow and at the end of the night I was the unofficial second place winner of the contest.

The rest of the evening was largely a vast blur to me. We had stopped at another bar called the Towpath on the Tonawanda side of the Canal. Sweeney Hose members often went there to celebrate member's birthdays. After finishing up at Towpath we crossed over the Erie Canal again to go to eat at Nestors, a greasy spoon on Webster Street that was open twenty four hours a day. We ate some good high cholesterol breakfast food. Henry and I started walking towards our cars. Henry found his car and sped off into the night. I had a short distance to walk to my car and I felt like I was going to puke. I was not feeling good about having to drive home. I arrived at my car and realized that there was no way I was going to be able to drive home. I opened the door of my Volkswagen Rabbit and I crawled into the back seat after I locked the door. It was 4:30 a.m. Sunlight shining through my window awakened me at twenty minutes to eight. I felt like I could drive now and I could. Nothing was spinning now and although I still felt tired, I didn't feel sick. I drove home to my parents' house where I still lived. I parked my car and quietly opened the side door of the house hoping not to awaken my mother. My father had left for work already. As I tiptoed towards the stairs my mother, who had slept on the couch, was there to question me. "Where in the world have you been?" she asked. I knew that I was in for it and there was nothing to do but tell the truth. I answered, "I drank way too much last night and I couldn't drive home so I slept in my car." My mother agreed with my judgment in not driving but she also seriously questioned the influence that my fire hall buddies were having on me. She reminded me several times that I was not old enough to drink. I apologized to her and made a quick call to my boss at the Riverside Chemical Company. I was honest with him too, explaining that I had been out drinking heavily the night before and that I was too tired and hung over to come into work. He tried to convince me to take a shower and come into work later but I refused to do so. I slept most of the morning and a good part of the afternoon away and then I returned to the Canal Fest to work that night. I went out drinking at the bars after the beer tent closed, but I watched how much I drank and was home by 3:30 a.m.

Canal Fest has continued to be the major fundraiser for the Sweeney Hose Company although profits have decreased somewhat in recent years, most likely due to decreased crowd attendance at the festival. The work that went into running the field day, coupled with the meager profits from the event led to the membership voting to terminate field days as a fundraiser after a particularly cold and rainy weekend one June. The two other large fire companies in town, the Rescue Fire Company and the Gratwick Hose Company, have also disbanded their field days.

The Sweeneys have created some new fundraisers. A weekly Friday fish fry is held during Lent. An annual turkey night where frozen turkeys and other prizes are raffled off has been popular with the people of North Tonawanda. Because our funds from the city tax rolls are limited, the Sweeneys will continue to volunteer their time in the years ahead to help their fire hall to function.

11

Learning to Render

When I joined the fire department in 1990, I expected to hear numerous alarms of fire being dispatched over my fire scanner. A box alarm or a working fire or a supposedly large fire was sent out over the airwaves using two tones, both of the same frequency, with the second tone closely following the first one. An emergency medical services or EMS call would be signaled with the same frequency tone, but there would only be a single tone. It was commonplace for volunteers at the hall to routinely ignore a "one tap" as it usually signaled an EMS call. A "two tap" was far more powerful and could mute a TV or halt a conversation in mid sentence. Silence would await the voice of the fire dispatcher. The dispatcher would call the first due engine to the location over the radio. The fire driver would then acknowledge the dispatcher by answering the radio with his engine number. The dispatcher would announce the nature of the fire along with cross streets for the first due engine. The dispatcher broadcasted the box alarm several times over the radio. A typical broadcast would be:

"North Tonawanda fire dispatcher to all stations and monitors; Truck two, Engines two, four, and seven responding to box 112 at 216 Payne Avenue for a reported structure fire."

The message would be repeated several times over the next several minutes in case a firefighter had missed the initial tones or message but happened to be outside to hear a plethora of sirens screaming around the city.

Unfortunately for those members solely interested in firefighting, the number of actual fires in North Tonawanda were few and far between the hoard of EMS calls that were dispatched on a daily basis. As volunteers we were discouraged from answering EMS calls mainly because the number of people needed for any EMS call was limited compared to the number of volunteers who could potentially show up for a call. Secondly, there were very few volunteers who had actually completed training to the emergency medical technician level. Every career firefighter was required to be certified as a basic level New York State emergency medical technician. Volunteers were encouraged to answer a call for medical help if they were within a block of the address where the aid was requested. We were also allowed to respond to motor vehicle collisions, commonly known as car accidents, as manpower was generally needed during the course of extricating patients from a car wreck.

My initial interest in becoming an emergency medical technician or EMT was fostered from listening to the true stories of EMS calls as told by the paramedics from the Sweeney Hose Company. Ken Rojek, Tim Frank, and Duncan Fanners were all paramedics who worked with Twin City Ambulance, the local commercial ambulance service that provided EMS transport services for North Tonawanda and its several surrounding communities. The three of them could sit at the fire hall bar for hours swapping horror stories in quick succession of mangled bodies that were thrown from motorcycles and cars. They would also tell compelling stories of the people that they had managed to save. Intrigued by their tales, I decided that to become a fully effective firefighter, I needed to become an EMT.

I was attending Niagara University in the spring of 1994. I had earned an associates degree in math and science from Niagara County Community College in May of 1993. I had reduced my spring course load at Niagara so that I could take the emergency medical technician course. It was held every Tuesday and Thursday night from 6:30 p.m. to 9:30 p.m. The course director was Matthew Johnson, a critical care technician EMT, who was also a member of the local volunteer fire department, the Upper Mountain Road Fire Department. Several of his fire hall members were advanced EMTs and they served as ancillary instructors during the course.

The rules of the course were very strict. Matt Johnson was a likeable enough guy, but he didn't put up with any crap either. Our attendance at each and every class was mandatory. If a valid and reasonable excuse was not presented for an absence from the class, we would be learning to become an EMT in a different semester.

Our class seemed to start slowly. We received a course outline with reading assignments. The first two classes were spent on basic human anatomy and basic medical terminology. My two semesters of anatomy and physiology in college allowed me to get an early start on my reading assignments. At the beginning of the third week of our classes, we started to learn some interesting and practical things. We learned how to breathe for a non breathing patient using only our two hands, a facemask, and a balloon like pliable piece of plastic called an Ambu bag. Splinting fractures and applying neck support devices called cervical collars came easy to me. As EMT students we learned to apply supplemental oxygen for patients using different types of oxygen masks. We could even calculate the percentage of oxygen that a patient was receiving based upon the number of liters per minute of oxygen that were flowing out of the oxygen tank. There was even a device called a KED that was used to immobilize a patient's head, neck, and spine when they were being carefully extricated from a car after a motor vehicle collision. The instructor that tested on the application of the KED was a stickler for detail. Placement of the KED around a patient took several steps and each of these had to be followed in order. Many of my classmates, as well as me, felt that the KED application was the toughest practical station in the course.

Even with the many practice sessions that we participated in, we were still not ready to go out and provide actual care for people on the street. We had only read a thick textbook and performed our skills on our instructors and each other. We had become used to lying on the floors in our practical labs. We pretended to be patients and we tried to act out the part. Lying on the floor and looking at the ceiling, we could really never fathom what a real life patient was going through. As providers we dreaded the thought of a patient not being able to respond to our questions. I longed for some practical experience. I wanted to be able to take blood pressures on a person with a real problem. I wanted to try chest compressions on a cardiac arrest victim. We did have ten hours of practical observation to spend in a local emergency department. I hoped to be able to use some of my skills in the emergency department, but I felt almost terrified to go there.

Ever since I was a young child, I had always felt somewhat squeamish concerning the sight of blood or other mangled bodily horrors. I believed that this trait was acquired from my father who was also very uncomfortable with the site of blood. I prepared myself for my trip to the emergency department by eating a substantial lunch and dinner on the day of my first rotation. I sipped on a bottle of orange juice as I drove to the hospital, wondering what interesting things awaited me at the emergency department. I hoped that things wouldn't be too interesting.

I arrived at the emergency department and introduced myself to the greeter at the front desk. I was then introduced to the nurse that would be escorting me throughout the department during the early portion of her overnight shift.

Another student from my EMT class had arrived as I was being shown the layout of the department. She was a quiet but pretty girl from the class whom I had never met. I quickly introduced myself as I awkwardly held out my hand to her. She told me her name as our mentoring nurse rambled on about how we couldn't get in her way.

Near the end of the tour the nurse blurted out, "You guys got here about an hour too late. See that cart over there? Trauma code came in from a car wreck. Open fractures and all. We worked him for about ten minutes when he got here but he was long gone before the EMTs even got to him." The gurney was sitting silently inside a small room. A couple of pieces of clothing littered the floor. Some irregular puddles of blood waited to be mopped up. The sheet had been stripped from the bed. This was an eerie sight but at least there wasn't a mangled body for me to see.

Our evening was going fairly smoothly. I took vitals on some medical patients who graciously acknowledged my need to learn how to take accurate vital signs. I made small talk with them and then quickly moved on, pretending that there was somewhere else that I had to be. I could tell by the nurses' comments that the emergency medicine physician that was working was new to the department. Their attitudes towards him revealed that he was not especially well-liked. He did take time to show us some interesting x-ray findings right before he was called to go to one of the floors to help with a patient in cardiac arrest. The blank expression on his face when he returned ten minutes later told us that his efforts on the floor were unsuccessful.

I had noticed a female patient when I had entered the emergency department. She was sitting quietly in a curtained examination bay with her right hand soaking in a bucket of iced tea colored liquid. From what I could tell, she had not been seen by any physician. My fellow EMT student and I were soon escorted to her cart by our supervising nurse. We were to observe the doctor as he sutured her finger lacerations. We learned that she had sustained them after accidentally slamming her fingers in a car door.

We approached the bedside and watched as the doctor removed the patient's hand from the mysterious brown liquid. The doctor spoke gruffly to the woman letting her know that he was going to give her shots of a medication called lidocaine. Then he began to prepare her hand for suturing. I told myself that what I saw was not gory. Everything was under control. The doctor plunged his curved needle into the lacerated finger and started to bring her skin edges back together. Suddenly it started to feel warm in the room. I felt beads of sweat on my forehead. I kept telling myself that everything was fine. I started to feel light on my feet. I became very thirsty. I needed something to drink and I needed it now. "I need to get a drink of water," I called out as I took a weak step forward.

I woke up and found myself on the cold floor. Everything was blurry. I felt my face and my glasses were missing. Two or three people hovered around me in a semicircle. I wondered why I was looking at the ceiling. I figured out that I must have fainted. After lying on the ground for a couple of minutes, I was helped to a wheelchair. I was given a cup of orange juice and I sipped it slowly. I felt like a fool. I thought that I would make a poor EMT. I imagined scenarios in my head. I heard a voice say, "I'm sorry that your daughter died from the relatively small wound ma'am. A little direct pressure could have stopped everything but EMT Borton always faints at the sight of blood." The rest of the evening in the emergency department was uneventful and I returned to Niagara University at 10 p.m. I wondered how I could go back to the department tomorrow after the syncope feat that I had just performed.

I felt better the next morning and I returned to the emergency department for my second helping of observation. I took some blood pressures and watched the doctor take care of medical patients who didn't possess any recent traumatic wounds on their bodies. I passed on watching another laceration repair and my supervising nurse said she felt relieved about that, although she said she would have been more prepared to catch me if I fainted again. A patient on one of the carts noticed a strange wet substance coming through the sheet on his bed. The patient was removed and a substance finding investigation was undertaken. The sheet was removed from the cart and a blood soaked mattress with a hole in it was exposed. It happened to be the same cart that the trauma victim from the night before had briefly occupied. The patient never learned what the substance was and the cart was removed from the emergency department. I finished the shift without fainting, but doubts still lingered in my mind as to whether or not I was really ready to do the EMT thing.

News of my syncopal episode spread like wildfire through my EMT class. The lead instructor came up to me in front of a small group of students.

"Are you alright?" he questioned.

"Yeah, why?" I replied.

"I heard you fainted at the ER."

"Yeah, that was three days ago. If you really cared you would have asked about me sooner," I said with a grin on my face, trying to lighten up the tone of the conversation in front of my classmates. I felt red and once again ashamed.

Our class continued to learn more and more EMT skills and then we were set to take our practical examination. For this we would each rotate separately through skill stations that tested our practical competency. There was an airway management station, an oxygen administration station, and a splinting station. We would also need to correctly apply a cervical collar as well as a KED. There was another station that would be the toughest of all – the physical assessment station.

The physical assessment station was to be feared and for good reason. It encompassed all of the skills that would be needed to perform as an EMT. The student had to literally know their ABCs. The "A" stood for airway, the "B" for breathing, and the "C" for circulation. Two additional letters were also incorporated into our assessment. Logically they were D and E. "D" represented disability and "E" stood for exposure.

The reason for the alphabet mnemonic was to make sure that the EMT was addressing all of the patient's needs in their order of importance. We were told of instances where people had died unnecessarily because a caregiver had paid too much attention to a broken limb while forgetting about a patient's airway. If a person could not maintain a patent airway then they could not breathe. If they could not breathe on their own then they could not deliver life sustaining oxygen to their lungs. A person who could not breathe on their own needed our help to breathe for them. A person who had a weak pulse or a low blood pressure had a problem with their circulation. A traumatic injury could cause massive bleeding whether the bleeding was external and obvious or internal and hidden. A person with a new disability could have suffered damage to their nervous system. An EMT could use certain devices to prevent further disability from occurring. Injuries often remained hidden beneath a person's clothes. The cutting and removal of shirts and pants allowed the EMT to expose injuries that were initially hidden from view.

The patient assessment skills testing station was run by Matt Johnson's wife, a tough cookie who had worked umpteen years as a registered nurse. Nothing could get past her. Everyone seemed to be studying patient assessment before the practical stations. Everyone knew that her station would be tough to get through.

I waited outside the game room at the Upper Mountain Road Volunteer Fire Company. The room usually only hosted a pool table and a dart board but today it would host many EMT students. My classmate who had entered the room before me exited after a twenty minute period that seemed to last forever. Nothing but a blank expression cloaked his face as he left the room. The SA node of my heart kicked into high gear. Was I next in line for a helping of the doom that had obviously just been served?

I greeted the chief instructor's wife as I entered the room. She bore an evil grin on her face looking as though she had just finished a gourmet helping of EMT student soul for dinner. She presented a clinical scenario to me. She let me know that my patient, a volunteer firefighter, was lying on the floor in front of me. She asked me if there were any questions before I began. I told her that I had none and she prompted me to begin my assessment of the patient.

I began my encounter by introducing myself to the patient and I identified myself as an EMT. I asked the patient what his name was. He replied, "Bob." I said, "Bob what happened today and what hurts?" In a strained voice he said, "I was in a car accident and I think I was thrown from the car. My belly hurts, that's it."

I approached Bob and told him that I was going to take a look at him. I put my stethoscope in my ears and listened to his lungs. I then put my hand on his wrist and felt for a radial pulse. He had one and it was beating strong at eighty four beats per minute. I proceeded to put my hands on Bob's belly and he pretended to moan in pain. The instructor then interrupted me.

"Stop! What in the world do you think you're doing?" she shouted.

"My patient skills assessment test," I smugly replied.

"What have we been teaching you for the last three months? How do you start your initial patient assessment?"

"Well, you start with the airway and then move on to breathing and,"

"Exactly. So can you tell me why you did not assess his airway or his breathing or his circulation?" she questioned.

At this point I was confident that I had done everything correctly. I now had to explain my actions to her.

"I came into the room and started talking to Bob. He was able to clearly talk back to me. That meant that his airway was stable. I then continued to talk to him and noted that his respiratory rate was twenty. His respirations were not labored. I listened to his lung sounds and they were equally clear. I asked Bob what hurt and he told me that his abdomen was killing him. I thought that it might be likely that he had sustained severe abdominal trauma. Because I could palpate his radial pulse, I knew that his systolic blood pressure was greater than one hundred. His pulse rate was eighty four. I was about to determine if he had any neck pain or neurological deficits when you stopped me. What was wrong with my primary survey?" I finally questioned.

She sat in her chair for an extended moment pondering what I had just said to her. Finally she said, "I see your point and I think you are going way above what you're expected to know here. What I would like you to do is start over and go through each evaluation step carefully and systematically, showing me how you would fully evaluate the patient in each step of the survey. Talk to me out loud. Verbalize what you are thinking."

I stared at her for about five seconds realizing that I, a lowly EMT student, was not going to win any battle with this instructor who had seen it all. I reluctantly said that I saw her point and that I would follow her advice. I started my new assessment of Bob and performed a dog and pony show for the next fifteen minutes. I completed my assessment with the report that I would give to the hospital staff if I were bringing Bob to the hospital in an ambulance.

I finished my report and caught my breath. The instructor tallied up my score on the sheet in front of her. She looked up from her clipboard and smiled. She was not frowning. There was no look of concern on her face that I could detect. Did I pass her station? Would an obligatory second shot at patient assessment be avoided? After looking down at her clipboard a second time she spoke saying, "You did an excellent job of assessing this patient. You passed my station. Have fun with your other practicals." I thanked her with a big grin on my face. I walked out of the room and smothered my grin as I opened the door. I put a concerned look on my face. I didn't want the next student to think he was walking into an easy test.

The rest of my practical exams on that day went rather smoothly and I passed each station. I would be able to take the written exam. I needed to study for this. Our textbook was over seven hundred pages long and we could be asked practically anything from those seven hundred pages.

Ken Rojek had been my Sweeney Hose captain when I became a member. He had recently been hired by the North Tonawanda Fire Department as a career firefighter. He served as a paramedic class instructor at another college. I decided to visit him one day when he was working at fire headquarters. "Hey Jas, what's up?" Ken questioned as I walked in the side door of fire headquarters. I told him of my upcoming test and asked him if he had any helpful hints. He said, "Follow me," as we walked to his locker. He pulled down a stack of stapled papers and began to sift through them. He gave three piles to me. "These are retired state questions for the basic EMT test. Look through them and get a feel for how the questions are worded. Answer them but don't mark up my papers. Make sure that I get them back when you're done. You won't have any problem with the written test," he concluded.

I studied hard for the test, mulling over my textbook, class notes, and Ken's questions. I arrived at Dunleavey Hall on the night for our final exam. Everything was very formal and serious on this night. Jackets and book bags had to be left outside of the testing room. Instructors who we had joked with all semester asked us for our drivers' licenses for proof of identification as we entered the room. We were required to have at least two number two pencils on our person at all times.

The test booklets were handed out and we were told not to turn them over until the head instructor had finished reading the test directions. Matt finished reading the directions and he asked if there were any questions that needed to be answered before the test started. No one raised a hand. Matt gave the official signal for us to begin and the simultaneous sound of booklets slapping desks echoed in the auditorium. We had three hours to finish the test.

After two hours of taking the one hundred question test, I had finished. I had gone through the test and checked my answers. I was fairly confident in my answers. Two people had already finished the test and handed in their booklets. I was the third and I shook Matt Johnson's hand as I walked out of the room. Now I had to play the waiting game to see if I had answered at least seventy questions on the test correctly. New York State was in no hurry to score our tests. Our instructors had mentioned that it could take anywhere from six to eight weeks to get our results.

About two months later I entered the post office at Niagara University and put my key into my mailbox slot. I opened it. There was an envelope that had a return address of the New York State Department of Education. It was fairly large and I wondered what the department of education wanted with me. Didn't they know I was a biology major? I wasn't planning on becoming a teacher. I opened the envelope and saw a certificate that had my name across it. It said that I was certified as a New York State emergency medical technician – basic. I quickly memorized the number 191148 – my EMT number for life.

I had done it. I was now not only a firefighter but an emergency medical technician. I was confident that I could use my newly acquired skills to save humanity as long as their injuries didn't bother my sensitive nature and cause me to find solace with the ground. I was sure that I would see interesting things as an EMT. What I could not imagine at that time was just how interesting some of the things that I would see could be.

12

Street Rendering

The world of emergency medical services was largely sheltered from the volunteer firefighters of North Tonawanda. The fire chief never wanted volunteers racing across the city to park on narrow city blocks when they had no practical EMS skills. For a long time North Tonawanda had practiced at the level of a basic emergency medical technician. Basic EMTs did basic things. They stopped bleeding and breathed for people that were not breathing. They performed CPR and immobilized and packaged patients for transport to the hospital. Twin City Ambulance, a private ambulance company staffed with paramedics, was always simultaneously dispatched with the North Tonawanda Fire Department for EMS calls.

North Tonawanda Fire would dispatch Car 10, Rescue 1, and the nearest engine to any call for first aid. First aid came and it came fast. Whether someone had suffered a paper cut to their finger or suffered a cardiac arrest, lights and sirens were the only mode of response. The first arriving unit was almost always on location within two minutes. The hidden cost of quick arrival was the risk of motor vehicle collisions between the responding units and the general public. Driving lights and sirens had been proven to always be a dangerous activity. To me the risk seemed senseless, especially when the benefits of a quick response rarely outweighed the risks. A process called emergency medical dispatch had been available since the 1980s. A trained emergency medical dispatcher would dispatch units to use lights and sirens or no lights and sirens based upon the answers to a series of questions posed by the dispatcher to the citizen who dialed 9-1-1. The North Tonawanda Fire Department did not use this system however.

By becoming an EMT I enabled myself to further explore the world of the career firefighters who answered EMS calls on a daily basis. I would often ride on Engine 7 to first aid calls when I was down at the fire hall. I would also go to first aid calls that were within a block or two of my house. I almost always responded to motor vehicle collisions or MVCs as extra manpower was needed to help with the extrication of patients from their cars.

One seemingly mundane EMS call for help turned out to be an interesting one. I was at the fire hall and I had made arrangements with the Engine 7 driver to ride the rig in the event of a call. While I sat at the hall, a one tap went out over the hall monitor. I moved towards my gear as the dispatcher called Engine 7. I jumped into my bunker pants and headed out the side door of the hall as I put my coat on. I stopped before crossing in front of Car 10's overhead door and waited for him to begin his response to the call. As he exited the station I went through his open door and climbed into Engine 7. I put my helmet on and I buckled my seat belt. The driver had climbed into the rig and the roar of the diesel engine starting was accompanied by a thick cloud of black smoke that filled the station. We pulled left onto the street with lights and sirens blaring. As we started down Zimmerman Street I turned to the driver.

"What was the nature of the call?" I questioned.

He answered back, "Sunburn."

"You're kidding right?"

"Nope, sunburn."

"This is BS, people calling 9-1-1 for sunburn."

We arrived at the house and the driver grabbed his first aid jump bag out of the EMS compartment of the engine. We entered the dimly lit house and found our patient sitting in a recliner. He looked like he should have been sitting on a plate as a lobster in a four star restaurant. He was red from head to toe. He had started blistering and he was barely able to respond to our questions. I felt his radial pulse. It was thready and beating at one hundred and forty beats per minute. I felt bad about saying this call was BS. This guy was obviously sick and dehydrated. The paramedic from Twin City Ambulance arrived and questioned the wife about what had happened. She told her that they had been out on their boat all day. Swimming trunks were the only article of clothing that our patient had been wearing. He had consumed at least half a case of beer throughout the day. He started puking when he got home and his wife said he seemed to be confused so she called 9-1-1. The paramedic started two IVs on the patient and opened them up so the hydrating normal saline could course through his veins. The patient screamed whenever he moved or was touched. As he got up from his chair to get on the stretcher, I could see that his entire back had started to blister. We helped the ambulance crew load him into the ambulance. They ended up taking him to the regional burn center at the Erie County Medical Center. This BS call ended up spending two days in the burn intensive care unit.

Lounging at the hall led to another interesting EMS call for me. My gear sat ready by the door if a call for Engine 7 went out. The TV was on as I sat at the bar drinking pop. A call for a police officer came across the police scanner. Apparently a woman had called 9-1-1 and told the police dispatcher that her son was trying to hang himself. The address that came over the scanner was about a five second drive and a ten second sprint from fire headquarters. I ran to the door and put my gear on. I opened the door and saw Car 10 coming out his door and I followed him on foot. The career captain bolted out of his car and raced into the house. I opened the door to the house to see the captain supporting the weight of a man who was suspended from the ceiling with a rope around his neck. The captain ordered me to get something to cut the man down as he didn't think that he could support his weight much longer. I ran back out through the door and headed for Engine 7. Meanwhile, a police officer by the name of Karl Rollata, who had been a volunteer with the Rescue Fire Company, arrived on the scene. He sprinted into the house. I grabbed a pair of bolt cutters off the engine, hoping that they would be able to cut through the rope. I arrived back in the room to see Karl cutting the rope with his pocket knife. I helped the captain lower the patient to the floor. Our suicidal patient had a dusky color to his face and he was barely breathing. The captain suggested that we move the patient outside. There were stacked beer cans throughout the trashed room. We knocked over piles of junk as we struggled to exit our surroundings.

The Engine 7 driver was coming to the front door with his first aid bag. I stabilized the patient's neck while the captain breathed for him using an Ambu bag. This bag allowed oxygen to be pushed through a face mask that was placed over the patient's mouth and nose. After a minute of "bagging", the patient's color improved and he started flailing around. The captain, Mike Davies, who always had a dry sense of humor, started talking to him. "Hey guy, settle down, we're just trying to help you. What were you doing tonight? Just hanging around?" he questioned. With this I let out a burst of laughter and a wry smile came over the captain's face. We had successfully prevented this man from violating New York State law by killing himself. Within minutes he was in the back of a Twin City Ambulance. Ahead was a slow ride to the Niagara Falls Memorial Medical Center. There he would receive a medical screening examination followed by a compulsory two day admission to their psychiatric ward.

EMS calls often came in at inconvenient times. We responded to many box alarms at the old Roblin Steel Plant on Oliver Street. There wasn't really a plant there anymore – just some steel framed buildings that still had roofs over them. Roblin Steel had basically ceased to exist on July 4, 1987 when a general alarm fire consumed most of the buildings on the property and left behind eerie ruins. On a particular summer day we had been called out to a box alarm in the complex. Fire had consumed the bodies of several junked cars that were stored under a roof. Kids with nothing better to do than practice arson gave us something to do on a hot North Tonawanda summer afternoon.

Engines 2 and 6 had easily beaten Engine 7 to the call as their stations were both about ten blocks away from the Roblin Steel plant. While these engines drove deep into the bowels of the complex, Engine 7 stayed at the street and pumped water from the hydrant to the other rigs. I had arrived late to the call and noticed that Ken Rojek was at the pump panel. When I arrived he got the radio order from the assistant chief to shut down his pumping operations. Ken was also told to "pick up and return". This meant that all of Engine 7's gear and equipment was to be returned to the rig. Ken would then return to fire headquarters.

A Sweeney Hose member, Mike Mallard, was on the scene with me. We started to pick up what little Engine 7 had off of it at that time. Only a hydrant wrench and a ten foot section of pre-connected soft suction hose had been used in the firefight. Mike slowly shut the hydrant down. I removed the hose from the hydrant and a small stream of water flowed on Oliver Street as I drained the water from the hose. A one tap came across the radio as I finished folding the soft suction hose back into its place within the front bumper of the rig. The call went out for Rescue 1 to respond to 15th Avenue for an unresponsive female. Unfortunately, Rescue 1 would have to snake its way out of the narrow roads of the Roblin Complex. Being the seasoned paramedic that he was, Ken quickly keyed his radio, "Seven can take the call, responding from Ninth and Oliver." The dispatcher responded, "10-4. Engine seven responding to 15th Avenue." Now Ken could have left us in a cloud of diesel smoke as he tore off towards the EMS call, but he understood what it meant to be a volunteer. He realized that any extra set of hands would be helpful on this call, especially since the other units would be delayed. Mike and I could have walked back to our cars and left the scene but we knew Ken could probably use some help. Ken told Mike and me to hop on the rig, and after a three point turn we were screaming towards 15th Avenue. We arrived at the house within a minute. Ken told me to go check on the patient. He went to grab the EMS bag.

To my surprise, I was met at the front door by a volunteer from the Rescue Fire Company in full turnout gear. He wasn't doing anything for the patient. He stepped aside for me and pointed me to the living room. There, half propped up in a chair, was a short elderly woman with enough make-up on for the entire line up of the Rockettes. Her dress was gaudy. She looked like a clown that was stoned. Her eyes were open but she wasn't moving. I stood in front of her and said, "Ma'am! Ma'am?" She did not respond to me. I counted her breaths and she was only breathing six times a minute. Ken came in the front door with a bag in each hand. He placed them on the floor and I said to him, "Help me get her on the floor, I've got to bag her." Ken lifted her feet as I slid my arms underneath her armpits. We lowered her to the floor. Ken tossed me an Ambu bag and then he hooked it up to an oxygen tank. I placed the mask over the patient's face and after tilting her head back slightly, I squeezed as much air into her lungs as I could. Ken placed his fingers on her wrist. Fifteen seconds later he called out, "Pulse is 82." The patient's dusky face had gotten somewhat pinker in color with my bagging but she still wasn't becoming responsive. Ken got a blood pressure but it was only 98/62 mm Hg.

Shortly after taking the patient's blood pressure, a female paramedic from Twin City Ambulance walked in the door. She started to speak in a semi-authoritative and fully condescending voice. She questioned, "What's going on here guys, why are you bagging her?" Ken responded, "Well she was breathing at a rate of only six breaths a minute and that's why we're bagging her. She's got an altered mental status and she's hypotensive. Her color improved with bagging but her mental status didn't. That's when you walked in the door and now you're up to speed." Ken looked at her and then glanced back at me rolling his eyes. I knew he didn't trust her. I kept bagging the patient.

The medic looked through the patient's pill bottles and called out the name of each medication when she read it. She called out the name on the first medication bottle. It was hydrocodone. I thought to myself that an overdose of that medication could be causing the patient's symptoms. Hydrocodone was a narcotic painkiller medication that could cause respiratory failure if too much was taken. Our patient was exhibiting respiratory failure. Paramedics carried a medication called nalaxone that could completely reverse the sedative effects of hydrocodone. The paramedic spoke, "Yeah, hydrocodone, that's a heart medication." Ken and I stared at each other with bug eyes. Ken corrected the paramedic but she just moved on to the reading of the next pill bottle. Bupropion was the next medication. It was a relatively new antidepressant medication which could make some people more prone to have seizures. Was it possible that our patient had suffered a seizure and then entered a period of unresponsiveness called a postictal state? Sure it was. The paramedic then lifted up the third pill bottle. She was about to read the third name when I interrupted her.

"Excuse me, I don't mean to sound rude but I've been bagging your patient for over five minutes now. You haven't even examined the patient or offered to intubate her. You're not sure exactly what's wrong with her and we're at least seven minutes away for the nearest hospital. Do you mind if we get going?" I said. A flabbergasted look came over her face. She paused a second and then seemed to realize just how valid my suggestion seemed. As we were loading the patient into the ambulance Ken whispered in my ear, "You're going to the hospital with the patient. I don't trust

127

this medic. Keep the patient safe. I'll have someone pick you up at the hospital."

As we rode in the back of the ambulance the patient became slightly more conscious but she still required assistance with her breathing. The paramedic once again called hydrocodone a cardiac medication. I said nothing but kept my eyes focused on the patient's breathing. I glanced out the side window of the ambulance and noticed some historic mansions appearing along Payne Avenue. That was good. It meant that we were close to DeGraff Memorial Hospital.

We stopped and I heard the EMT who was driving the ambulance click off the battery to the vehicle. The rear doors swung open and we carefully but quickly rolled the patient to an open cart in the emergency department. The patient was quickly assessed by the emergency department physician and then she was quickly intubated. I was within earshot of the paramedic as she once again decided to give her mistaken opinion about the "cardiac" medication hydrocodone.

I could not hold back my words any longer. She needed to be corrected. I walked over to her and said, "That's the third time in fifteen minutes that you said hydrocodone was a cardiac medication. I would strongly suggest you get a drug identification book and use it." She reached into her cargo pants pocket and pulled out a drug identification book. She replied, "Don't tell me what to carry because I have the book right here." I remarked, "You need to open the book and study it. You're confident ignorance is going to kill someone."

Fred Chilsholm was driving Rescue 1 and he arrived at the hospital to take me back to my car at the fire scene. He had caught the end of my conversation with the paramedic. He asked me what had happened to ruffle my feathers. I told him that I had a great respect for people like Duncan, Tim, and Ken because they were good paramedics. I told him that I had an encounter with a person that bore the same title of paramedic, yet degraded the meaning of the word by the actions she had just shown.

In North Tonawanda, cars seemed to be attracted to touch each other on almost a daily basis and responses to car accidents were plentiful. One winter evening I stopped by Galassi's pizza and sub shop. Galassi's was originally owned by Larry Galassi. When he died the day to day operations of the shop were handed over to his daughter. Some of my earliest childhood memories were of my father and me walking three blocks to Galassi's to pick up a pizza. As my taste buds matured, I realized that I could get better pizza in town, but their subs were some of the best. Several of our new members in the Sweeney Hose Company were employed at Galassi's. I stopped to grab a sub to eat and to see what everyone was doing later on in the evening. I was introduced to another couple of guys who worked at Galassi's who would soon be joining the hall. They were easy to talk to and seemed pretty relaxed. That was a good sign that they would fit into the hall. One of the hall members stepped outside as I got ready to leave. I got into my car and started it. I looked ahead of me and towards my right and I suddenly saw headlights way above street level. A thick cloud of snow then dimmed the lights.

When I got out of the car I heard nothing but eerie winter silence. Mark Donaldson had heard the crashing of metal and ran towards Payne Avenue. I fumbled with my car keys and opened the trunk. I walked towards the accident while putting on my fire gear. I asked Mark to go inside, remembering that I could be outside forever alone if someone didn't call 9-1-1. I walked into Payne Avenue to see a car with moderate front end damage resting perpendicular to the length of the street. The other car, which had briefly shown me its headlights, was perched on the side of a snow bank. The driver of the car that was still on the street walked towards me as I approached the car on the snow bank. He started talking and a strong odor of alcohol emanated from his mouth. His demeanor told me that he was going to become a nuisance if I didn't take control of the scene quickly. By triage definition he was a walking wounded person and he could wait for full medical assessment until more help arrived. I turned towards him and said, "Go over to the curb, sit down, and don't move." To my surprise he followed my directions. I asked Mark to keep an eye on him to make sure that he didn't flee the scene before the police arrived.

I had at least one more person to assess now. From the street I looked into the car that was on the side of the snow bank. The driver and only occupant of the car was someone that I knew. Hilary Humbard was the mother of one of our former members who had left the hall to join the Active Hose Company. She had a death grip on the steering wheel. She stared straight ahead. She was either scared out of her mind or she could have been critically injured, or both. Her driver's side door was smashed into the passenger compartment of the car. I called to her but she only stared straight ahead.

I knew that I had to get into the car to fully assess her. I tried to open the back seat door on the driver's side but it wouldn't open because of the impact. I trudged up the snow bank from the sidewalk and climbed my way up to the passenger's side of the car. The back passenger's side door opened easily and I slowly entered the car which was sitting at a forty five degree angle. I could hear Hilary breathing very quickly. I called her name several times and then she answered back. In a startled voice she replied, "Yes, who is this? How did you know my name?" I said, "Hilary, its Jason from Sweeney Hose. You were in a car accident. What hurts right now?" She told me that she just hurt all over. I then told her that I was going to put my hands around her head to help to stabilize her neck. As I did that Car 10 pulled up and the 4th platoon assistant chief walked up to the car. His name was Nicholas Mickens and among the volunteers he was the most feared assistant chief. He came across as harsh and rude. He would never hesitate to let you know if you were out of line or if you messed something up. I was lucky that I had all of my turnout gear on as well as my medical gloves. Chief Mickens asked me if everything was alright. I told him that Hilary and I were doing OK for the moment. He told me that the other firefighters were going to be putting wood cribbing under the car to help to support it. I continue to stabilize Hilary's cervical spine while the firefighters stabilized her car. Rescue 1 arrived and the driver placed a cervical collar around her neck while I continued to stabilize it. The jaws of life were then used to pry open Hilary's driver side door. A backboard was placed underneath her rear end and three other firefighters helped me to put her down flat on the board. Hilary was secured to the board with straps and once her head was taped down with foam blocks on either side of it, I was finally able to let go of her head. I stretched my left leg out as much as I could in the back seat to relieve the awful cramp that had developed from my awkward position. I crawled to the front seat and exited out of the driver's door. I continued to stretch after I made my exit.

I looked over towards the curb to see Mark looking on in amazement at what our team of firefighters had accomplished. Now I knew that there was no turning back for him. He got a fire department preview right before his eyes. He became a member of the hall at the next meeting. Hilary was transported to DeGraff Memorial Hospital. She was found to only have minor contusions and she was discharged that same evening. The driver of the other car was transported in handcuffs to the police station where he was charged with driving while intoxicated.

Another car accident that was memorable for me occurred not more than thirty feet from Rescue 1's quarters. A group of us were sitting around at the hall when a call came in for a two car accident at the corner of Walck Road and Payne Avenue. We got into our cars and formed a line that followed Car 10 and Engine 7 to the scene of the accident. After parking in a dentist's office parking lot, I donned my turnout gear and dashed across Payne Avenue and saw a car with major damage to the driver's side door. The trapped driver was an elderly male. Rescue 1 had pulled out onto its ramp and now sat no more than ten feet from the wrecked car. The firefighter from Rescue 1 was inside the car stabilizing the driver's cervical spine. Duncan had picked up the Jaws of Life and was moving towards the driver's door when he was stopped by Stan Pollenberg. The assistant chief of the third platoon, Stan had initially been a volunteer with Sweeney Hose. Stan called out to Duncan and anyone else who was within earshot, "I need a guy in full turnout gear to work the jaws and get this guy out." Duncan was only wearing his bunker pants and his gloves. I was standing next to Duncan and quickly relieved him of the Jaws. I jammed the points of the tool between the door and the body of the car. I turned the handle of the tool, allowing the powerful arms to spread apart from each other. The arms slipped out after widening the space between the frame and the door by about three inches. That was alright. I had created my purchase point, an area where I could place the Jaws again, this time hopefully getting a large enough space where I could pop the door open. The arms of the Jaws came back together and I jammed the pointed tips deeper into the flesh of the mangled car. The arms then began to slowly spread apart. I could feel the steel begin to give way. With a jolt of force the crumpled door separated from the body of the car. We were now able to get more access to the patient. I had done my job and I stepped backwards and placed the tool on the ground.

I went back to the car to see how the patient was doing. The medics were having some trouble getting a blood pressure on the patient. They thought he was having some difficulty breathing. I tore the patient's shirt open and borrowed a stethoscope from one of the firefighters. I asked the patient to breathe deeply. He did. His lungs filled with air equally. I felt no broken ribs or air beneath his skin that would signify a pneumothorax, commonly known as a collapsed lung. His abdomen was not tender to my touch. Despite this, he looked pale. He was quickly extricated from the car and placed in the back of the ambulance. The paramedic asked me if I wanted to take a ride to the trauma center as he had yet to get an IV line started. The basic EMT then shouted out a good blood pressure reading. The paramedic was then successful on his second attempt in getting the IV started. The paramedic and I then both agreed that the patient was more stable than he initially thought. They would take the ride to the trauma center without me.

It was then that I felt that something was wrong with me. Something hurt. That something was my right leg. It felt like it had been hit with a massive sledgehammer. The adrenaline from the accident situation was dissipating in my body and I realized what had happened. When the door had been popped open, there was a backward force on the Jaws that went directly into my right leg. I was seeing stars and sweat poured off of my forehead. I felt thirsty. I wanted to faint. I limped into Rescue 1's quarters and went to the kitchen. I grabbed an empty coffee cup and filled it with water. I drank two full cups and I sat down at the table while I lowered my bunker pants. The area just above my knee had become very swollen and tender. It hurt to walk. At least my knee cap was safe. If the Jaws had struck me just a couple of inches lower, I would have surely been nursing a fractured patella. I mulled around the scene for the next ten minutes hoping that I wouldn't faint.

When I returned to fire headquarters I filled out an injury report, just in case something was seriously wrong with my leg. I had to miss two days of work due to my injury. When I did return to work, I looked up the car accident patient's name on the computer. He had been discharged from the emergency department on the day of the accident and it seemed like he fared better than me. I had rested on the couch for two days vowing that I would forever have respect for the Jaws of Life and Newton's Third Law of physics.

Truly one of the most memorable and personally most tragic EMS calls that I went to occurred during my first year of medical school. It was December of 1995 and I had returned to my house after taking a morning exam in biochemistry. I had an exam the next day but my previous night's studying had worn me out, so I decided to take a nap. Just as I started to fall asleep, I heard a one tap go out over my fire monitor. The dispatcher called for Engine 2. The call was for a possible cardiac arrest. When I heard the address I was sure that I was dreaming. My ears perked up when Engine 2 called on location. Forty five seconds later the driver transmitted a message to the dispatcher, "We have a code." A code meant that someone had suffered a cardiac arrest and the driver was starting CPR on the patient. My heart fluttered as I feared the worst. I threw my clothes on, headed out my side door and sprinted down the street. I knew the address that had been called out over the fire monitor. I had been to that address hundreds of times. It was my best friend Dan's house.

When I approached Dan's house Rescue 1, Car 10 and Twin City Ambulance had arrived on the scene. The call had come in for a female who was not responding. It could have been for Dan's mother, but I had just talked to her two days ago and she had seemed fine. Maybe it was one of the neighborhood ladies that came to visit Dan's mom. People would always stop over Dan's house to visit his mother. She was a good friend to many people, me included. She didn't seem like a friend's mom to me. I could sit down with her and talk about anything at all. I always felt comforted by the fact that she lent a truly attentive ear to what I was saying. I never felt that judgment would be coming from her mouth once the conversation was over either.

I stood outside the house shivering in the cold and not knowing what to do. They surely had enough help inside. I stood in front of the neighbor's house, hoping for news that was good. Dan's front door opened and the Rescue 1 driver appeared. He saw me and told me to grab a spare oxygen tank. I went to the driver's side compartment of Rescue 1 and pulled out a green oxygen cylinder that I hoped would help give life back to whoever was in cardiac arrest in Dan's house. Walking up to the front door, I was met by Dan's father. He looked at me and said, "It's Mrs. Stevens. Dan is upstairs. Could you go talk to him?" I said that I would. I entered the house and passed Dan's mom who was sprawled out on the living room floor. An endotracheal tube was carrying oxygen to her lungs. Paramedics had been performing CPR and pushing medications in an effort to restore her pulse. She did get a faint pulse back. She was going to be transported to DeGraff Memorial Hospital.

I went upstairs to find Dan. He was pacing back and forth in his room. He looked up at me and I saw that he was panic-stricken. He shouted at me, "What are you doing here? Can't you see this isn't a good time?" He nervously kept talking. He wondered how this had happened. He recalled how his mother had sat down in the living room to watch TV before making dinner. She asked him to rub her shoulders as she had felt unusually tired. He did and then went upstairs to his room. About ten minutes later he needed help with something and he called downstairs to her. There was no answer. He walked downstairs to find her slumped over in the chair and not breathing.

Now Dan's world was collapsing around him and I was there with him. I didn't try to make sense of it. I didn't try to calm him down. I just listened. In all of my training in my EMT class, there was never any mention on how to comfort family members of a dying patient. I could have gone downstairs to deliver perfectly timed compressions to his mother's lifeless chest, but I struggled to find words of comfort for my best friend in his time of need. Dan's mother died a few days later in the hospital. It was through her death that I slowly started to learn the art of rendering compassion.

13

Catching the Plug

Every fire scene had jobs that had to be effectively accomplished so that everyone remained safe. Not everyone could operate the pump panel or take a hose line into a building or operate the aerial ladder. People were needed to shuttle equipment from the rigs to the structure and set up that equipment. There were a number of things that a firefighter needed to know how to do on the fire ground. Training provided the opportunity to learn how to do these things in a non-emergency situation.

Most firefighters tended to like doing certain things more than others. Many firefighters liked putting on an SCBA and taking a nozzle into the building. Others felt perfectly at home sitting on a roof and chopping holes in it to ventilate a structure. Some were happy just to be on the scene lending a hand wherever they were needed.

My personal favorite job was to put on the SCBA, make entry into a burning building, and then search for a victim or put out the fire. For my tastes, all of the action was inside of the house where it was hot. In winter going inside was much better than standing out in the cold.

It seemed to me that everyone in my company only liked going into burning buildings on the fire scene. One day I decided to ask Duncan Fanners, who had been my partner in the smoke divers class, what his favorite fire ground job happened to be. I was surprised when he said, "I like catching the plug."

"Plug" is a shortened term for fire plug or water plug. In modern times the term plug translates to "hydrant". Catching roughly means "hooking up a hose to". Fire plugs were initially just that – a plug. In colonial America, water was carried throughout cities in underground water mains constructed of hollowed out logs. When fire broke out, firefighters would locate a water main by putting a hole in it with a pick. This supplied the water for the hand engines to receive. Once the firefighting activities concluded, the hole in the water main was sealed with a piece of wood or a plug. If another fire occurred in the same area and a fire company found the plug, they could easily remove it and get water.

Duncan had been a good friend of mine ever since I joined Sweeney Hose in 1990. I was his 1st lieutenant when he was a captain. I played golf with him, ate at his family picnics, and he was a groomsman in my wedding party. Duncan however was a fairly quiet man. I pestered him again and again as to why hooking up to a hydrant at a fire was his favorite job. The only thing he would say to me was, "When that fire comes and you're hooking up to the hydrant and then you get it done, you'll know why."

Operating a fire hydrant was a fairly simple task and an advanced monkey could probably operate one just as well as a seasoned firefighter. With a hydrant wrench in hand, the firefighter decided whether the large steamer cap would be removed from the hydrant or if one of the side discharge caps would be removed. Once one or all of the caps were removed a device called a gate could be threaded onto the discharge so the flow of water through a hose could be stopped without having to turn off the hydrant. The hydrant operating nut, located on top of the hydrant, was then slowly turned in a counterclockwise direction. Large amounts of crappy brown sediment then usually spilled onto the street for a short time. Once the water ran clear, the hydrant was shut down and the supply line, which was usually four inch diameter hose, was connected to the hydrant. The hydrant was then opened up again, this time sending water to the engine. In some dire emergency situations hydrant flushing could be omitted, but the pump operators usually frowned upon sludge being sent into their pumps.

About a year after talking to Duncan about his favorite fire ground job, an alarm of fire came in for a structure fire on Oliver Street. This street, once rumored to be world renowned for having the most taverns on a single street, now boasted multiple apartment buildings with many tenants on welfare. As I found a parking spot near the front of the building, I saw the apparatus arriving on the scene but I saw no evidence of fire. I figured that I had left the warmth of my house for yet another false alarm. There did seem to be a bustle of activity near the corner of Oliver and Thompson Street that told me that this wasn't likely to be a false alarm.

I walked quickly and carefully over the ice covered sidewalks and turned the corner. Other firefighters were doing their own careful penguin walks towards the back of the building. My right ear informed me that Engine 7 was coming up behind me but slowing down. I looked over my shoulder and Paul Dennison was driving the engine. I was walking with two others now and Paul called out to us, "Meet me at the hydrant. I'm going to lay into four." In firefighting slang, Paul's message was easy for us to understand. He wanted us to meet him at the hydrant he was driving towards. We would pull off about the first thirty feet of four inch hose from the hose bed. We would wrap the hose around the hydrant as Paul drove towards Engine 4, spilling his four inch hose onto the ground as he went. He would hook up the hose to Engine 4 and we would hook our end of the hose to the hydrant.

Once Paul stopped at the hydrant, everything seemed to go into slow motion like a dream. The two firefighters I was with pulled the four inch hose out of the hose bed of the engine. I snagged a hydrant wrench. I went towards the hydrant and then looked back at the other two firefighters. They held the hose in their hands and they were showing off their "deer in headlights" look. The red triangles adorning the front of their helmets told me their story. They were rookies. For all I knew this was there first real fire. I recognized this as my opportunity take the baton and lead the orchestration of this water supply effort by myself. I grabbed the hose and then wrapped it once around the hydrant. I then stepped on the hose while I shouted "Go!" at the top of my lungs. Paul heard my cue and started driving towards Engine 4.

In a thick transient cloud of diesel smoke I removed the steamer cap from the front of the hydrant. I then slammed the hydrant wrench on the top of the hydrant and slowly turned the operating nut in a counterclockwise direction. Thick brown liquid poured out of the hydrant but within ten seconds it turned into a fluid commonly recognized as water.

The wrench moved in a clockwise direction as I turned off the water to hook up the four inch line. I looked up to see smoke billowing out of the house about a hundred feet away. I had a feeling in my gut that I wasn't moving quickly enough. I screwed the coupling of the four inch onto the front of the hydrant. The side of the hydrant wrench helped to secure my connection. I hoped that everything was going smoothly on Paul's end of the hose. I again looked towards the house and caught sight of Paul. He was drawing circles in the air with his arm and he let out a simultaneous call of "Water!" This was my green light to open up the hydrant. A low rumbling noise let me know that water was going into the hose. The hose turned from a flat lifeless piece of orange rubber into a taught cylindrical conduit for supplying water to Engine 4. The rookie firefighters had watched me as I hooked up the hydrant. I remembered that I would have frozen up just like they did when I was a rookie. They were learning. They next time they would be able to hook up the hydrant.

Satisfied that I had done my job at the hydrant, I walked quickly along the length of the supply line towards the fire. A continuous and plentiful supply of water was now entering Engine 4. Water flowed to the numerous hand lines that had been pulled from the engine. I saw no soaked bodies or disgruntled faces. Paul had done a good job of hooking up his end of the line.

I now knew what Duncan had meant when he said that catching the plug was his favorite fire ground activity. I realized that almost everything that happened in a fire attack was totally dependent on the hydrant hook-up. If the hydrant was not tapped, the engines would run out of water from their booster tanks within minutes. A fire could go unchecked and houses and dreams and even lives could be destroyed.

I stood next to Engine 4 for a second or two after I had hooked up to the hydrant. I had to admit that it was an exhilarating experience to supply water to the entire firefighting operation. Although I felt somewhat proud, I also felt something else – cold. I went to the back compartment of Engine 4 and found an SCBA. Within two minutes, I was inside the burning house, out of the cold and in the hot and smoky environment that I truly enjoyed as a firefighter.

14

Above and Beyond

In the far back recesses of every firefighter's mind was the realization that what they did was inherently dangerous. Shortly after joining the fire department in 1990, there was a widely publicized news story in which two firefighters were killed when a roof collapsed on them. This tragedy occurred in another state. My Essentials of Firefighting training gave me the statistics that unfortunately seemed to be repeated on an annual basis. Each year in the United States just over one hundred firefighters die in the line of duty.

Many of these deaths occurred when firefighters suffered a cardiac arrest while working at a fire scene. Quite a few firefighters had left a fire scene not feeling well only to die the next day while at home. Vehicle accidents in responding or returning fire apparatus also killed a significant number of firefighters each year. It had been my hope that I would never have to attend the funeral of a firefighter who had fallen in the line of duty. I never wanted to experience that reality firsthand and have to confront my own mortality as a firefighter. My hope all faded on May 24, 1997. That was the day that Tim Goff died.

Kenmore is a village located about ten miles south of North Tonawanda. Most of the homes are of the two story variety and they sit close together on cramped side streets. Like the North Tonawanda Fire Department, Kenmore had a combination department consisting of career and volunteer firefighters. Their career department staffed the fire station during the day when many of the volunteers were at work. At night, the volunteers compromised the entire staff of the department.

A stubborn blaze started in a paint store in Kenmore's fire district during the late afternoon of May 5, 1997. The Kenmore Fire Department responded to the scene, as did several other fire departments because the fire was fairly large and it involved a commercial site. Firefighting operations were going fairly smoothly when suddenly something went terribly wrong. An explosion occurred. The front of the building collapsed trapping several firefighters under mounds of heavy cinder blocks. One of those firefighters was Tim Goff.

I went down to the fire hall during the late afternoon on May 5th. The captain of our company, Ron Reynolds, was there before I arrived. I placed my electronic entrance card into the slot and I quickly removed it. A buzzing sound told me that I had about five seconds to open the door before it locked again. As I pulled the door open I was surprised to see Ron standing there.

"Did you hear about the news?" He questioned. "No, what news?" I asked. "There was an explosion at a paint company in Kenmore. The front of the building collapsed. They said that five firefighters from Kenmore were injured, some seriously. They were taken to a couple of different hospitals. There's no word on their condition yet." he replied.

A flood of questions filled my head. I wondered why the explosion happened. Was the fire still going on? How badly were these firefighters hurt? I talked to Ron for a while longer about the incident. I then headed to the bathroom. I stared at the wall that supported the urinals and I said a silent prayer asking for God to look after the injured firefighters. I asked for small injuries if any: a sprained ankle, a broken arm, anything that would not be life threatening.

My fears diminished that evening as the local news stations gave updates about the conditions of the firefighters. Four out of five firefighters had suffered non life threatening injuries. Tim Goff had been more seriously injured. He was in the trauma intensive care unit. The trauma surgeons however were confident that Tim would pull through his ordeal.

About a week after the explosion, a news station interviewed Tim's doctor. He said that he had made a remarkable recovery given his injuries. Their footage even showed Tim sitting up in his hospital bed, smiling at the camera. Everyone was amazed. A terrible explosion and a building collapse and now Tim was on the way to recovery. He was doing great. After some rehabilitation he would be fine. His future seemed to hold no boundaries.

Tim's death on May 24th shocked the members of our company as well as the community of volunteer firefighters in Western New York. We trusted the news reports and the doctors, but the overwhelming trauma took its toll on Tim's young body. Just as we were ready to rejoice in his victorious survival we now had to confront the reality of a death of a brother that we had never met.

Tim had been employed by Twin City Ambulance. He worked as a wheelchair van driver, transporting disabled senior citizens and others to medical appointments and other destinations. He had a fiancé. He loved firefighting. He was just starting to live.

The date and time for Tim's calling hours were posted and about twenty firefighters from Sweeney Hose planned on attending the wake. We met at the hall and proceeded to the funeral home, packing ourselves into members' minivans as we assumed that parking would be difficult to find. We wore our parade uniforms. The pants were dark blue and had a gold stripe running down the out seam of each leg. Our shirts were sky blue with navy blue lapels. Our company patch garnered our right shoulder while the American Flag was sewn onto our left shoulder. Our cap was navy blue and displayed a silver company badge. This occasion was a time for mourning. Fire companies with ample means had Class A uniforms which were basically like our uniforms but they included an outer formal jacket. They had white gloves. Their badges were covered with a black horizontal piece of cloth to make a mourning badge. The Sweeneys passed around a roll of electrical tape to create mourning badges. In later years the Sweeneys would purchase Class A uniforms. On this day, the uniform didn't matter to us. We were firefighters, here to pay our last respects to a brother we never knew.

Nearing our destination, we witnessed many fire engines surrounding the funeral home. We found parking two blocks away from the funeral home. We took our place in a long line of firefighters that meandered out the door of the funeral home. The news reporters who had earlier proclaimed news of Tim's recovery now stood in the parking lot. Their cameras pointed towards our mourning line. They did not approach us. They respected our purpose. Half an hour after arriving we crossed the threshold of the building. We removed our caps and put our irrelevant signatures next to hundreds of other irrelevant signatures that would eventually and hopefully form a significant memento for Tim's family.

We entered the viewing room and I caught a glimpse of Tim, lying in a casket in his Class A uniform. A uniformed firefighter stared straight ahead on each end of Tim's casket standing at attention. They were from the Kenmore Fire Department. I thought of the tremendous grief they must have experienced, seeing firefighter after saddened firefighter walking up to Tim's casket to pay their final respects to a brother they hardly knew.

When my turn came, I slowly walked to the casket with my head lowered and my eyes on Tim. I said a silent prayer for his family. Here in front of me laid the body of a volunteer firefighter just two years older than me. He woke up on May 5th never dreaming that he would be injured fighting a fire that day that would eventually claim his life. He looked peaceful. I silently thanked him for his service to his community. I turned to the right to face his family. A solitary tear came down my right cheek. I told the family that I was sorry for their loss and then I exited the viewing room.

Gathering my emotions outside of the viewing room, I waited for the other Sweeneys to make their egress. When everyone was accounted for we proceeded out of the funeral home. The sun had almost set. The line of brother and sister firefighters waiting to pay their final respects still streamed outside of the building. We silently walked to the cars. We would go home to sleep. Tomorrow Tim would be laid to eternal rest.

The next morning was crisp and cool and I arrived at the Sweeneys' hall early. A steaming cup of coffee carefully touched my lips in the hope that it would make me ready for the upcoming long day. The Sweeney Hose parking lot was the official meeting site for all of the fire companies from Niagara County who were to attend the funeral. The companies would travel as a group to the Lester Wendekindt Funeral Home. A small service for the family was to be held in the funeral home before the public mass at St. Edwards Church in Buffalo. About twenty five fire companies had gathered at our hall. Each company had about four or five members decked out in their Class A uniforms. Each company drove in a front line piece of firefighting apparatus. The Sweeneys, because we were part of a combination department, would pile into our private vehicles.

I opted to leave my Ford Mustang at the hall and rode with Sam Garson in his large Ford pickup truck. Two other members rode with us. Harry Markson was a long time member of the hall. Many considered him to be an alcoholic with a short fuse. When not intoxicated, he was a likable and fun loving person. Harvey Martin was a soft spoken firefighter who was three years younger than me. Harvey, like his father who had recently passed away, was a dedicated member of the hall who would always lend a helping hand whenever he could. Sam Garson was over thirty five when he joined our hall. Our by-laws stated that you had to be between eighteen and thirty five years of age to join the hall. We realized that putting an upper limit to age as a pre-requisite for joining our hall was discriminatory. We changed our by-laws welcoming Sam as a new, but middle aged member. Sam was a dedicated volunteer and he served as a line officer for many years. He told many interesting stories and was very active in the hall. Little did I know that day that Sam would spearhead a major fundraising effort together with the Kenmore Fire Department. This fundraiser would help to assist those firefighters who were injured in the fire that claimed Tim's life.

Sam's pickup was dwarfed by the fire engines that surrounded us. We traveled to the funeral home through the cities of North Tonawanda and Tonawanda, traveling up Delaware Avenue and stopping half a block short of the funeral home. We parked on this busy four lane thoroughfare that had been shut down for the funeral procession. I stepped down from Sam's truck and I was amazed by what I saw. There were fire trucks lined up three lanes wide for as far as I could see. During the procession the trucks would travel in two lines side by side forming a procession that would be over a mile long. I thought to myself that this was quite a tribute to a man that few of these firefighters even knew.

After a short wait, we were ordered to stand in one of two lines. We faced the funeral home and waited. A faint sound in the distance hummed. It was a bagpipe. An order was shouted out, "Company, present arms!" As we had participated in many parades, we all knew what this order meant. A right hand salute was performed while we stood at attention. The distant drone of the bagpipe continued and then quite suddenly it stopped. Deafening silence prevailed on this street that was usually a hub of traffic activity at this time of the morning. A slight wind blew. A casket draped with the American Flag was being hoisted onto the hose bed of a Kenmore engine. A faint odd sound partially eclipsed the silence. It was an air tool being operated to remove lug nuts from a car wheel. A grease monkey from a local repair shop was oblivious to the respect that this occasion deserved. A minute or two passed. A faint but crisp distant voice ordered, "Company, order arms!" We snapped our slightly throbbing arms to our side. We were ordered to fall out and we got into Sam's pickup that was surrounded by quarter million dollar red giants.

When we fell into place in the left line of the procession, Sam noticed that the fire trucks had turned on their warning lights. He quickly turned on the massive blue light bar that stretched the width of his pickup truck. I thought that this was especially fitting for the procession. Tim had probably responded numerous times with his fire engine from the Kenmore Fire Department. Red lights would have been lit up and sirens would have been blaring. He would have arrived at the fire station by means of his own car. He likely had a silent blue light that respectfully signaled citizens to yield to him because he was on the way to a call of help. Today, thousands of commuters would yield to Tim as the procession headed south down Delaware Avenue into the Village of Kenmore.

The pace of the procession seemed to be slowing as we approached Nash Street, a short side street where the Kenmore Fire Department was located. Career firefighters from Kenmore stood at attention near the foot of Delaware Avenue. Two aerial towers with their ladders partially extended across Delaware Avenue flanked each side of the street. We passed under a large American flag that was flown from the end of the aerial ladders.

We continued southward, watching as cars lined up on side streets and waited for us to pass. An occasional onlooker saluted. Others just stared in amazement. In downtown Buffalo our cavalcade snaked through the turns of some older side streets. The procession stopped abruptly and we got out of Sam's truck. We could see Tim's casket being lowered from the fire engine in the distance. We walked towards the church which had large speakers set up outside of its front doors. We would not be going inside the church. Family and firefighting brothers who had known Tim would get a break from the now sweltering late morning sun.

Hundreds of firefighters stood quietly outside of the church on the street. This was a Catholic church and the service seemed to go on and on. Tim's closest friends read eulogies. Some of the eulogies were cut short due to the overwhelming grief of their readers. An officer of the company read a touching tribute to Tim, recalling the day that Tim had put out his first working fire. The officer was with Tim on the fire attack and they made quick work of the fire and contained it to one room of the house. Now Tim would fight fire no more.

Shortly after the eulogies, "Tears in Heaven" by Eric Clapton was played over the loudspeakers. I heard a slight rustle behind me and then I felt a heavy weight on my back. I couldn't believe that someone would get into a brawl at a firefighter's funeral. I was being pushed to my knees. Instinctively, I flailed myself backwards. As I looked over my left shoulder I saw the blank stare of a well built female firefighter who was now falling backwards to hit her head on the pavement. We gathered around her and Sam loosened her shirt. Another firefighter poured cold water on her neck. She slowly became responsive. The heat of the day had likely caused her to faint. She had stumbled forward into me and I unwittingly pushed her backwards to add concussion to the list of her medical maladies for the day. She was helped to a shaded area. I went over and apologized endlessly to her, making sure that she had plenty of water to drink. I talked to her for awhile, looking for any signs of a serious head injury.

The mass ended and once again we silently saluted as Tim's casket was placed on Kenmore's pumper. I could see the face of one of the pallbearers who was one of Tim's close friends. He looked as if he couldn't cry any more tears. Utter sadness showed on his face. The next stop on our journey would be Elmlawn Cemetery, which would become Tim's final earthly resting place.

As we headed north, Sam lit up a cigarette and said, "I see you had another fat chick falling for you." I let out a short chuckle. On any other day Sam's comment would have sent all of us into uproarious laughter, but today our moods were somber. Loudmouthed firefighters were quiet and soft spoken. As we passed through Kenmore there were more people on the streets. They were waving American flags. Elderly people stood with their hands over their hearts. Our procession turned left onto Sheridan Drive. At least two hundred children stood in front of an elementary school. Some waved flags. Two teachers held up a sign that said, "Thank you Tim, we'll never forget you". Reading that, my eyes welled up with tears. I wondered if this had been Tim's elementary school. Did he sit in one of its classrooms and dream about becoming a firefighter? Did a fire prevention week visit from the fire department set his mind in motion? I wished that I could travel back in time to May 5th. I would have known the outcome of the fire. I could have pulled the firefighters back from that waste of a building. Somehow I wished that I could have prevented this tragic loss of a young life.

Ten minutes later we entered the cemetery. We parked a distance from the graveside and walked briskly towards the graveside so that we could salute Tim one last time before his body was returned to Mother Earth. We informally lined up and snapped our hands to attention as Tim's casket was carried past us. His coffin was placed in front of the grave.

The solitary bagpiper was present and remained silent for a moment. The priest offered some brief words about returning to the earth. My mind wandered from the priest's words. I glared at the bagpiper. I knew what was next. He started playing. His song was "Amazing Grace". I could feel the firefighters around me and their collective sorrow. I knew very few firefighters who wouldn't break down at the sound of Amazing Grace being played on the bagpipes. Tears flowed down my face. The song seemed to go on forever and then it abruptly stopped.

We heard helicopter blades shearing the air in the distance. The region's medical helicopter, Mercy Flight, then passed overhead in honor of Tim. Smoke trailers plumed from the helicopter and then it flew out of sight. The priest said a few more words and then gave the benediction. And that was it. The life of a volunteer firefighter had ended and we were supposed to just get in our cars and leave. I felt emotionally empty. I now fully realized that Tim was not some brother firefighter that I did not know or hardly knew. I knew him like he was my own flesh and blood – because he was.

Tim was just like me and the hundreds of firefighters who attended his funeral. He had hopes and dreams. He answered the call of help, not because it was his job or he had to, but because it was what he wanted to be doing. He, like me, had left his family hundreds of times never knowing if he would return home again from the next call. Yes, I knew Tim Goff, even if we had never met face to face before. I knew Tim because he was exactly what I was – a volunteer firefighter. I will always remember what Tim Goff did for his fire department and his community. God bless you brother for you have served this world well. May you forever rest in heavenly peace, Kenmore firefighter 44.

15

City Hall

As a collective body, North Tonawanda firefighters were always extremely passionate about their duties. They wanted to get to fires quickly and practice their skills. They wanted to face the fire and extinguish it while preventing the loss of life and limiting property damage. Both the career and the volunteer firefighters' pride became evident whenever the politicians of the city planned to make drastic changes to the structure of the fire department.

Any casual bystander in North Tonawanda would know that something was brewing if they walked into city hall on a Tuesday night when a fire department issue was on the agenda of the common council's minutes. It was difficult to appreciate the outdated 1970's avocado green décor in the public meeting room of the council when the seats were filled with angry firefighters. The gaudy walls were wallpapered by the standing room only firefighters. An ordinary common council meeting would arouse maybe ten denizens to leave their houses to make their presence known in public. There were a few taxpayers who would attend every common council meeting. Some citizens would comment on nearly every issue brought up by the council. When I attended the occasional meeting dealing with fire service issues, a particular woman named Sharon would criticize the council for things that I didn't even know were going on in the city. After attending a couple of the meetings, it was easy for me to surmise that Sharon either suffered from some type of a mental illness or she had way too much time on her hands. It may have been a combination of both. She provided great comic relief for most of us and she always publicly voiced her proud support of the North Tonawanda Fire Department.

The first hint of the city politicians wanting to downsize the fire department came in the early nineties when I started to see small posters in local businesses around town. The posters called for Truck 2 to remain open. Truck 2, a 1973 Sutphen ladder truck, sat next to Engine 7 at fire headquarters. On a box alarm, Truck 2 would respond to any location in the city that was west of Walck Road. Truck 1, located near the eastern border of the city at the corner of Nash Road and Deerfield Drive, would take any box alarm that originated east of Walck Road. The posters had been placed by members of the career department who I believed had surmised that taking any piece of apparatus out of service would lead to the loss of four positions on the paid department. The career firefighters were never terminated from their jobs, but when a firefighter retired, the retiree's position was not filled.

The common council and the mayor faced a room full of angry firefighters when the subject of Truck 2 closing came to the floor. Rage fueled normally soft-spoken firefighters to speak. Many common council members argued that there wasn't a need for two ladder trucks in a city the size of North Tonawanda. Some career firefighters did their homework and cited National Fire Protection Association recommendations that suggested that a city of North Tonawanda's size needed to have two ladder trucks. The Tonawanda News reported on and on about the debate.

And then one day it happened – Truck 2 was permanently out of service. No big fanfare, it was just taken out of service. There was a quick but deafening silence on the evening radio check after the Truck 1 driver announced that he had received the check "loud and clear". Rescue 1 then called in loud and clear when Truck 2 normally would have called in next. I don't recall a big rebuttal being put up by the career firefighters' union. Their ranks didn't suffer any tangible job loss and I always believed that was why there was no big outcry after Truck 2 was taken out of service. Posters and shouted words at meetings gave way to a quiet passing of a piece of North Tonawanda firefighting history.

Chief Davis was livid. A normally quiet man of few words that were generally kind, he blew up several times at the common council meetings. He carried a large stack of papers with him to the council meetings. These papers contained the evidence to refute the common council's belief that they should close fire stations. The council wouldn't listen. When I talked with Chief Davis in private, four letter words sprang from his mouth at the mere mention of the common council.

Truck 2 had faded into history and now Truck 1 was assigned to cover the entire city in the event of a working fire or a box alarm. Reserve Engine 3 sat next to Truck 1 at the Nash Road fire station. The Truck 1 driver would often respond to EMS calls with Reserve Engine 3 as it was easier to maneuver a relatively small 1955 pumper down narrow side streets when compared to a full length ladder truck. If an alarm of fire was toned out when theTruck 1 driver was on an EMS call with Reserve Engine 3, a simple solution existed. Truck 2 would be sent to the call. After Truck 2 closed, the Truck 1 driver would be in a real predicament if he had responded to an EMS call with Reserve Engine 3 and an alarm of fire ensued.

During the next several years, the city fathers fed their ravenous need to attempt to make cuts within the fire department. Closing scenarios were placed in front of the fire chief by the common council. Chief Davis always replied back that he was opposed to the closing of any fire station or the elimination of any fire apparatus. The council retorted with brightly colored maps that showed how moving fire apparatus around the city would only slightly increase response times to incidents. They were quick to point out that these increases in response times were insignificant. For several years debate as to whether fire halls should close swept throughout North Tonawanda. All the stations remained open after Truck 2 was removed from service. The career firefighters continued to operate Car 10, Rescue 1, Truck 1 and five engines. Those days were numbered. The beginning of the end came when a wealthy North Tonawanda resident by the name of Bernard Danson was elected to the office of mayor.

Bernard Danson had made his fortune in the construction business. His mansion along the Erie Canal confirmed that. Two story white pillars stood proudly in front of his house, supporting the roof of his palace. Mr. Danson made it clear from day one in his office of mayor that he was going to cut spending in the government of North Tonawanda. He said that he wanted to save significant money for the taxpayers of North Tonawanda. Saving money ultimately meant making cuts in various departments throughout the city. The fire department, as it had been with other mayors' administrations, was an attractive target to hone in on to make some cuts.

Chief Davis ended up retiring during the tenure of Mayor Danson. I think that he was just fed up with the entire political game of having to constantly fight to keep fire stations open. Soon after Chief Davis retired, Assistant Chief Gregory Frank was appointed to the position of fire chief. Soon after Chief Frank's ascension to chief, the mayor started enlisting policies that would ultimately change the structure of the North Tonawanda Fire Department.

The mayor was determined that no new firefighters would be appointed to the career department until a commission was formed to study the structure of the fire department in North Tonawanda. Initially this wasn't a problem for the department because there were enough firefighters on the department to staff all of the apparatus. The city, however, had offered monetary incentives for any firefighter with twenty or more years on the job to go into retirement. With these incentives and the overall future of the fire department in question, a number of the career firefighters jumped at the chance to retire. Vacancies reared their head in the department and the mayor insisted that no overtime be used to cover the shifts for which there was no driver for an apparatus. This meant one thing – revolving fire station closings. On a day to day basis, certain fire stations throughout North Tonawanda would be closed.

Few people experienced the nightmare of the revolving station closings more than the fire dispatcher. He depended on an antiquated but effective card system to determine what apparatus to dispatch to an alarm of fire. With day to day closing of stations that were meant to be open, depending on the card system seemed like it might be a waste of time. I thought that the dispatcher may have forgotten the card system at times and just used his gut instinct as to which engines to send to an alarm of fire. If things were frustrating for the fire dispatcher they must have been sheer terror for Henry, a long time volunteer firefighter with the Rescue Fire Company.

One day Henry was home and noticed a smell of smoke in his house. He went down to his basement and noticed that a small fire had started. Being a veteran firefighter that possessed common sense he got out of the house with his wife. Having no means of calling 9-1-1 and not thinking to use his neighbor's phone, Henry did what any reasonable firefighter would do. He got into his truck and drove three blocks to Engine 5's quarters. He frantically knocked on the door but there was no answer. He noticed that the truck room was dark. He went to the front overhead doors and read a piece of paper that was taped up in one of the front windows. It read, "This fire station is currently unmanned. In the event of an emergency call 9-1-1." He heard sirens in the distance and realized that somebody must have called 9-1-1. His house was saved but it did manage to receive some extensive smoke damage. Henry's story made it to the front page of the Tonawanda News.

The mayor knew that he could not permanently close a fire station on a whim. The mayor therefore contracted a fire department study consultant at the cost of $60,000 to the taxpayers. Several areas of the fire service in North Tonawanda were looked at: Career versus volunteer firefighter responsibilities, station locations and physical condition of the stations, emergency medical services, and response times. The consulting firm hailed from a southern state and had performed consulting work for other fire departments in other states. Many of their recommendations for North Tonawanda seemed to come from offshoots of their other consulting jobs. I felt the firm did a poor job of doing a thorough evaluation of the entire department. A random group of volunteers was told that they could meet with the consultant if they stopped by fire headquarters at a certain date and time. This information was presented to the volunteer firefighters the day before the consultant was to be at fire headquarters. We were told that the consultant would also be meeting with some members of the career department to discuss their individual perceptions of the department and how it should be managed. In my view, the consultant did a quick job with lots of smoke and mirrors and then skipped town. It seemed as though the firm did an excellent job of reaffirming the ultimate aspirations of the mayor: to eliminate fire stations and active fire apparatus from the fire service.

The study called for the elimination of some fire vehicles while other apparatus was to be moved to different locations. The study made recommendations that seemed to range from how many times a week that fire department toilets should be cleaned to how many full time career firefighters should be employed. The recommendations were made and a timeline was set up for the initiation of the different recommendations. The career personnel were to prepare their response to the recommendations of the study as were the volunteer firefighters. I was asked to present the views of the volunteer firefighters concerning the provision of emergency medical services in North Tonawanda. Our views were to be presented to a "fire study commission review panel". This panel was another dog and pony show that was set up by the mayor to give the appearance that he actually cared about the firefighters' opinions.

A group of volunteers and I reviewed our collaborative decision on what we thought was the correct system for the delivery of emergency medical services within the city. I let them know that I might be somewhat critical of the current policy of sending three pieces of equipment each with lights and sirens to every EMS call. I explained my rational to the group and they supported my decision to question the lights and sirens response mode as they could see that it made sense for the EMS responders to arrival safely to a call for help. I presented my section to the fire study commission. I thought that I enlightened many members of the commission about the various options that were available for the delivery of EMS within the city, either with or without the utilization of the fire department.

The Tonawanda News consistently presented the story of the upcoming fire commission recommendations. Firefighters followed the news closely. Many of the firefighters were very upset with the mayor's stance in beating down the fire service. Questions arose as to why other non-essential services such as the parks and recreation department didn't receive the burden of the cuts in the way that the fire service did. Anger boiled into the words and minds of the firefighters. Rotating fire station closings had been occurring for some time. The mayor and the council then made their decision to permanently close a fire station. Their actions pushed me over the edge. I turned to the keyboard of my computer to vent my frustration. The city had recently spent several hundred thousand dollars to provide a trash container to each household in North Tonawanda. The letter that flowed through my fingertips was soon printed in the editorial section of the Tonawanda News.

NT residents will pay for Danson's decision

During colonial times in America, citizens were required to keep buckets outside of their houses. These buckets were used by firefighters to put out fires. Technological advances produced hand pumpers that gave way to steam engines which were replaced by today's modern firefighting pumpers. Unfortunately for the serfs (citizens) of the manor (city) formerly know as North Tonawanda – of King Danson, they may soon be required to provide these buckets outside their residences.

It seems as though King Danson has once again used his short-sighted wisdom to remove another firefighting pumper from service. The king had said in the past that he would not remove a pumper from service, yet now he is planning on doing just that. Now King Danson has many knowledgeable people at his disposal. One would assume that a good leader would seek input from his fire department marshal (chief) concerning this matter. The marshal has considerable experience in the firefighting field and he knows what the citizens of the manor need for fire protection. Despite this King Danson has turned a deaf ear to the rightfully concerned and just minions of the manor.

It is a sad time for the citizens of the manor, their lives and property being put at risk because the king only cares about one thing – MONEY! I would think that the king doesn't know much about using money wisely about the manor. It was only a few years ago that the taxes levied upon the manor's serfs went to pay for a brand new firefighting pumper. Now that $250,000 piece of equipment shall gather dust and provide no service whatsoever to the manor.

Now, fellow serfs of the manor have no fear, for King Danson has unwittingly provided each and every one of us with a firefighting protection device for our houses. Over a year ago your taxes provided you with a 95 gallon green firefighting water container (trash can). Cast your naked refuse to the curb! You need your green water container to protect your house! Time to grab your buckets! All hail King Danson!

My letter appeared in the Tonawanda News on an evening when a common council meeting was being held. The topic of fire house closings was going to be on the agenda of the common council. It was standing room only once the meeting was called to order and concerned firefighters spilled three deep into the hallway outside the room. The council meeting went about with its usual business and then the floor was opened up for any public comment on any matter. The mayor and the common council must have thought that a stampede was coming towards them as firefighter after firefighter waited for a turn at the microphone. Each participant had to clearly announce his name and address. After that it was time to set frustrations loose on the people who had supported the decision to reduce the fire protection of the city.

I was third in line that night. I stood up and talked about the importance of quick response times in responding to patients who were in cardiac arrest. I questioned the mayor directly, "Mr. mayor, can you tell me how long someone in cardiac arrest can go without suffering permanent brain damage from a lack of oxygen?" He told me that he didn't know the answer to my question. I then directed the same question to the members of the common council. No one on the council could answer my question. After a brief silence I spoke again to the mayor and the common council, "So, as a collective body you don't realize how long it takes to suffer permanent brain damage from a lack of oxygen? You don't know that and still you're going to close fire stations whose engine could bring an EMT to the house of a victim of cardiac arrest and through his actions prevent brain damage and even death? What you're doing is unthinkable. You should all be ashamed of yourselves."

I stepped away from the microphone as my brother and sister firefighters cheered loudly. The mayor started to mutter something but I kept my back towards him. I had a feeling that he had a comment concerning my letter in the Tonawanda News. I wanted to ignore him at that point. I felt as though I had warmed the audience up somewhat and I wanted the momentum of politician bashing to keep steaming along.

Although he was not a North Tonawanda firefighter, I immediately recognized the next figure that walked up to the microphone. His voice boomed over the microphone, "My name is Luke Marracado and I'm a professional firefighter with the Buffalo Fire Department." His name, even though it meant nothing to the seemingly clueless politicians at the front of the room, meant something to me. Luke was a truckie with Truck 11, one of the busiest ladder companies in the city of Buffalo. He was a prominently decorated firefighter. He had saved a number of people from the horror of perishing within a burning building. Tonight however, he told the stories of the people that he was unable to save because his company had arrived a minute too late. He stressed the importance of having fire protection. He made it clear that no amount of tax money saved could replace the loss of a single person who had died because of supposed fiscal responsibility. Luke, who would later be appointed to the office of fire commissioner of the city of Buffalo, garnered tremendous applause.

Firefighter after firefighter stepped up to the micro-phone to voice their own opinion concerning the upcoming fire station closings. Some were better spoken than others but the overall message was clear: The firefighters, both volunteer and career, of the North Tonawanda Fire Department opposed the closing of any fire stations. The chief stood silently outside in the hall. Ten years ago he would have been spitting fire at the mayor but now the mayor was, in essence, his boss. A recent charter change in North Tonawanda had given the mayor and his office a great deal of power. It would have been unwise for Chief Frank to voice his personal opinions in this public forum but I felt that he must have struggled with the constant need to bite his tongue. After half an hour passed, every firefighter seemed to make a great point, but I felt that something was missing from everything that we were saying. All of the concerns about the fire department were coming from us. A career firefighter could be losing his job. A fire company could lose its engine, making the prospect of recruiting new members to their hall somewhat dismal.

I felt that we desperately needed some input from some members of the community. I leaned over to the firefighter sitting next to me and said, "Wouldn't it be great to hear from the family on Pioneer Drive who had the house fire last spring?" My neighbor replied, "Yeah that would show these jerks what we really do."

It was a cold spring morning when my scanner awakened me for a working house fire on Pioneer Drive. The hour was around four o'clock. I had run some statistics in the previous years and the least number of our calls came in between the hours of 4 a.m. and 5 a.m. The number of calls that occurred between those hours was few but nothing good ever happened at that time of the morning.

I pulled up to the scene less than five minutes after the fire had been toned out. I donned my gear as I hustled towards the front of the house. I had heard over the scanner that there were occupants trapped in the house. A wall of flame was being propelled out the front room and heavy smoke billowed from every vented window. I was standing next to Assistant Chief Jarantz who was doing a size up of the structure. He turned towards me and started to blurt out an order when he recognized me. He said, "Stay here, we're going to need you in a second." I didn't fully comprehend what he meant, but I figured someone might need medical attention shortly but I didn't know who that could be. The house that was being engulfed by flames before my eyes couldn't conceivably be sustaining any salvageable life at this point. My assumption was quickly proven to be wrong as shouts rose above the pump of Engine 7. A female was being wheeled past me on a stretcher to my left. She had some burns and she was wheezing. I joined the other firefighters and the paramedic who were rolling the patient to the ambulance. We lifted the stretcher over charged hose lines and the curb. Orlando Christopher was the paramedic and I knew him well. I trusted him to take care of anyone. I asked him if he wanted me to ride along with him to the hospital. He told me that he thought that the patient was stable for now and said he would take her to DeGraff Hospital initially. I walked back to the fire ground and I learned that the patient's husband had been transported shortly before I arrived on the scene. Weeks later I learned that both the husband and wife had recovered. I took a drive down Pioneer Drive later that summer to see if the house had been remodeled. I slowed as I approached the house. It had been remodeled. The husband and wife were sitting on their front porch talking. I stared at them until they gazed at my truck. They didn't know me from Adam, but they shot a polite smile my way and I returned the smile as I drove away.

The next person that came to the front of the council chambers and approached the microphone was a girl in her twenties. She stated her name and address and then started speaking. She said, "My mother still doesn't feel that she can talk about what happened to her last spring, but I'm here tonight to support you. I'm here to let everyone know that my mother and father are alive today only because of the actions of the North Tonawanda Fire Department." This is what I had hoped would happen. A member of the community was finally coming forward to express how their life had been positively impacted by the efforts of the fire department. The daughter went on to explain how the fire department had rescued her mother and father from the toxic smoke and gases that had invited themselves into her parents' home. She begged the politicians not to close any fire stations. She ended her speech by saying, "My mom and dad are living proof that the North Tonawanda Fire Department works like it is."

I felt tears welling up inside of me and after some more firefighters spoke their minds, another citizen made her way to the microphone. It was the woman who had been rescued from the fire. She looked well compared to that early morning when I had seen her covered in soot and struggling to breathe. She told of her long road to recovery and stated that her husband was still having some breathing problems.

She said it was very difficult for her to get up and speak in front of the audience. She said, "Even though it is difficult for me to relive my terror, I figured that I could come out and let you know how grateful I am to the North Tonawanda Fire Department."

The audience got to their feet as she finished speaking. Applause abounded and hands went up to wipe away tears that had cascaded down faces during this woman's story. She was the greatest victory we could ever hope to have. We had worked together as a team against all odds and saved two lives that morning. This was what firefighting was all about – to train hard for years to one day deliver another being from the arms of a conflagration. The newspaper and several local television news stations interviewed various people as they walked out of the common council meeting. The news kept our fight alive and in the minds of the community for a time. We hoped and prayed that the city would see the flaws in closing fire stations. We hoped that they would recognize the lives they would be putting in danger.

It was only a couple of weeks later when our hopes were extinguished. City hall ultimately decided to close Engine 2 and Engine 5. Engine 2 would no longer answer several hundred calls a year from its Oliver Street station. The citizens of the section of the city called Martinsville would have to wait at least two minutes longer for help when Engine 5 disappeared from its Strad Avenue quarters. With these vacancies, the fire chief decided to move Engine 6 from Ward Road to Rescue 1's old quarters at the corner or Payne Avenue and Walck Road. I thought that this left a significant portion of the northern part of the city with less protection. Rescue 1 moved into Engine 2's old quarters at the corner of Oliver and Sommer Streets. The social hall of the Active Hose Company remained in the basement of the station.

The face of the department had changed a great deal since I joined the hall in 1990. We now stood one ladder truck and two engines shorter. But, we still stood. Concerns about being able to effectively deal with the new situation rolled throughout the department. We had suffered again because of the decisions of a group of politicians. We came to the realization that we had to once again pull up our proverbial boot straps to do more with less.

16

The Wedge

I knocked on the fire station side door and looked around with nervous anticipation. Frank Rexinger stood silently next to me. Fred Chilsholm answered my knock and greeted us with a friendly but puzzled look. Fred was a Sweeney Hose member as well as a member of the career department. I offered Fred an explanation for our unannounced early evening visit. His puzzled look turned into a smile as our motivation became apparent. Fred stepped aside, letting Frank and me into the truck room. Sitting silently before us was the red beauty whose dimensions we came to measure.

"So you're here to measure the Wedge?" Fred asked.

"Yep," Frank and I replied.

"May I ask why?"

"Well Frank here told me that the Wedge will be going out of service soon and the chief had the intention of putting it up for public auction," I said.

"And?"

"Well I talked with the chief yesterday about the possibility of the Sweeneys getting the Wedge for a parade truck.

He cautioned me to make sure that it will fit into our storage garage before we start salivating about getting it. That's why we're here to measure it."

"Oh, go ahead," said Fred who had run out of probing questions.

Frank and I took a slow walk around the Wedge, a 1955 American LaFrance Spartan pumper that had formerly served North Tonawanda as Engine 7. It was put into reserve status as Reserve Engine 3 once the city's current Engine 7, a 1973 Ward LaFrance Ambassador pumper was delivered to the city. The truck room was dimly lit and the Wedge, named because the back of the rig was wider than the front, seemed like a runt next to Truck 1, a Pierce ladder truck that was twenty five years younger.

With a slight trembling in my hand, I pulled out a tape measure from my pocket. Frank and I walked to the tailboard of the Wedge, its widest point. "Seven feet, eleven inches," Frank whispered as we both breathed a sigh of relief. "We made it by a foot and an inch," I exclaimed. Earlier in the day we had measured the overhead door width and height of the Sweeneys' storage garage. We had also measured the length of the garage, which was being used to store miscellaneous junk from the hall as well as Canal Fest equipment.

We moved on to measure the length of the classic rig. I was on the business end of the tape measure this time. I aligned the end of the tailboard with the mark on the tape measure. It read twenty nine feet and eleven inches. I called out the measurement to Frank at the front of the truck. "About two feet of breathing room for the length," he called back.

I volunteered to balance myself on the front bumper of the engine to get the height measurement. I thought the biggest obstacle to getting the Wedge into our garage was going to be its warning light or "gumball light" that was mounted to the top of the windshield. I eyeballed the measurement several times and then called out my guess,

"About eight feet eleven inches." Frank replied, "Shit. The door's only nine feet high. That's really close."

We now had our measurements. Our first obstacle to getting the engine had been, for the most part, overcome. The rig would, somehow, fit in our storage garage. Frank and I stuck around for another hour, badgering Fred about all the details concerning driving the Wedge. I sat in the driver's seat and like a little child imagined myself driving this twenty nine foot eleven inch hunk of beautiful red steel down a city street during a parade.

Making sure the Wedge would fit in our garage was the easy part. Next I had to plead my case before the fire chief, Roger Davis. I met with the chief the next day and told him that the rig would fit snugly into our garage. The chief said, "That's great! Now all you have to do is prove to me that the other members of the company want to have the Wedge."

A feeling of warmth came over me as if I was in a college classroom about to take a test that I didn't study for. I knew the chief had to make a decision as to whether he was going to put the engine up for public auction in the next week. Unfortunately, the Sweeneys had just had their monthly meeting three days earlier and the next scheduled meeting was over three weeks away.

I whined and pleaded with the chief. I told him of our meeting situation. He sat back in his high-backed leather chair and said, "I don't know what to tell you Jason. I can't just give the truck to the Sweeneys because you and a couple of your friends think you should have it. I'll need a majority yes vote from a membership meeting that has a quorum of members before I'll consider approaching the common council with the proposal to use this piece of their property as your parade truck."

My hopes plummeted as the chief continued to talk. Most of the other volunteer companies in town had at least one of their own parade trucks. These trucks served as a source of pride for their companies. They were a tangible link to the past when firefighting was simpler, but followed the same basic principles of action. I felt as though I was about to pass out.

"Jason," the chief said slowly bringing me back from my state of self pity, "does your company have any provisions for special meetings?" A slight grin slowly adorned the chief's face as he noticed the light bulb being screwed in and turned on over my head. I got up from my seat and shook the chief's hand. I said, "Thanks chief, I'll be in touch soon."

The chief had been a volunteer at the Gratwick Hose Company No. 6 before I was even a twinkle in my parents' eyes. He knew that the volunteer companies often included provisions for special meetings in their by-laws. Now I had to find the special provision in the Sweeneys' by-laws. I got in my car and raced home. I dug through a mound of paper and finally found the object of my frantic search, the Sweeney Hose Company by-laws. After three minutes, I found the special meeting provision. I would need a quorum of fifteen members to make a special meeting concerning the wedge mean anything at all.

I spent the rest of the afternoon on the phone, calling or leaving messages for thirty members who I knew would support my quest to obtain the Wedge from the city. The day was Thursday. The next Monday seventeen members showed up at a special meeting of the Sweeney Hose Company. After some brief discussions, they unanimously voted in favor of asking the chief to get the engine for the hall. A provision was passed that only certain trained members would be allowed to drive the apparatus. I called Chief Davis at his house, letting him know that the seventeen members of Sweeney Hose had unanimously supported the move to preserve a piece of Sweeney Hose history. The chief said that he was meeting with the common council the next night and he promised to try and save the Wedge from the public auction block.

Chief Davis ended up writing a beautiful yet simple letter to the mayor and the common council. He explained the hall's desire to keep their former front line pumper as a parade truck. He also helped our cause by informing the common council that the engine would be of little value on the auction block as it had failed its last pump test. The majority of the council voted in our hall's favor and the Wedge was to become a working part of the history of Sweeney Hose.

A beautiful piece of irony was involved with the delivery of the Wedge to our storage garage. The chief decided that he would drive the engine from its quarters and park it in our garage. The chief had been a career firefighter one day in 1972 when the Sweeney Hose Company moved from its quarters on Schenck Street to its present day location on Zimmerman Street. On that day, Firefighter Roger Davis had driven the Wedge from its old quarters to its new quarters. We had an old picture of the chief walking around the back of the engine, his trademark white socks showing above his black shoes. I couldn't help but think that the chief wanted to be the last person on the career department to drive the Wedge before the Sweeneys took ownership of the rig. I imagine that he took the Wedge for its final in service ride that day and remembered all the fires he had responded to in it. I bet he probably took a little longer ride than required so that he could reminisce about his past service as a firefighter to the city. He may have even taken the rig to a stretch of open road on the west end of the city to see how fast she could still go. As to the exact route that he took to deliver the Wedge to our garage, I may never know. I hoped that his last run with the Wedge was fun.

I drove into the Sweeney Hose parking lot on the day that the Wedge had arrived there. It was a weekday and there was probably no one there when it came home. The lot was mostly empty except for the career firefighter's cars. I parked my car in front of the storage garage and I placed my key into the man door lock. I slowly opened the door to see that my dream had come true. The Wedge was now a part of Sweeney Hose. After I opened the overhead door of the garage, I briefly inspected the rig. I noticed what appeared to be blue paint on top of the gumball.

I closed the doors and I headed over to the chief's office to thank him. His secretary Cathy, who always carried a warm smile on her face, greeted me. I saw that the chief was in his office. He invited me in. He said, "I had no problem getting it over here, but the fit was kind of tight getting it into the garage." I replied, "A scrape or two of blue paint on a gumball light is a small price to pay for a fire engine."

17

Close Calls

Firefighting is a dangerous job. For the volunteer firefighter, the job doesn't provide a wage and it is not considered full time employment. The job is a far cry from the average office job. The average worker has a pretty good idea of what will happen to him in his eight hour work day. The firefighter however faces each call as a new challenge. A fire or EMS situation may have been encountered before, but each one is unique in its own way. The office worker has time to think about the challenges of the day that might arise. The firefighter needs to use his past training and experiences to act quickly when faced with a problem. In the back of the subconscious mind a constant dialogue is playing through a firefighter's head when he is at work – "How will I get out of here if the exit is blocked?", "Who is with me?", "Where is the fire?", and "Are there any victims?"

The questions stream on and on and the change in pace can be strenuous, especially for volunteer firefighters. One minute they are having dinner at home with their family. A call goes out. Fifteen minutes later they are in a room with ceiling temperatures near one thousand degrees Fahrenheit putting up a fight against a monster that man has fought to control since he discovered it. Their hearts will race. There might be a close call. Some firefighters will think and think about a close call and they might give up firefighting altogether. Others will shrug a close call off. Everyone will learn something after a close call. Sadly some calls will be too close and they will make the ultimate sacrifice that a firefighter could make.

Firefighting provided me with plenty of close calls to think about. Sometimes I was in the right place when something bad happened. Other times, I was in a bad place at a bad time when something that was not too bad happened. Often I moved away from a bad situation quickly. In a critical situation that happened one night, my early arrival might have cost me my life. A brother Sweeney's early arrival ultimately made him a hero.

There were relatively few chances for volunteers to ride the apparatus to calls in North Tonawanda. This was unless the volunteer had a great deal of spare time on his hands. That was something I sometimes possessed. The chances of riding the rig improved if the driver knew that he could be helped by your presence at a scene.

One sultry August day, Engine 7 had returned from an EMS call and I happened to be sitting at the hall watching television. A thunderstorm advisory scrolled across the bottom of the television screen. I peered out a front window of the hall and noticed that the sky had turned a menacing shade of gray. I decided to go next door to see who was driving Engine 7. When I walked into headquarters, all of the overhead doors were open. The firefighters and the assistant chief were staring into the western sky watching the lightning spectacle that was quickly approaching. I asked who was driving seven and a skinny beanpole of a man named Lyle Jollers said that he was. I asked him if I could ride with him and he quickly said that I could. I knew Lyle would say yes as he had been a volunteer firefighter with the Gratwick Hose Company for some time. Even after becoming a member of the career department Lyle had continued to participate in the activities of the Gratwick Hose Company. I ran out to my car and brought my gear back into headquarters. I took my shoes off and put my bunker gear on, knowing that it would only be a short time before we were toned out on a call.

The winds kicked up outside, yet no rain had fallen on the ramp in front of headquarters. Without warning, a bright flash came across our field of vision. This illumination was followed closely by a deafening clap of thunder. The assistant chief walked slowly towards his command vehicle as if a fortune teller had told him it might be a good thing to do. As he reached for the door handle of Car 10, the first tone of a two tap was put out. The dispatcher announced that a fire alarm had been activated. This was a common occurrence with blasts of thunder. Each activated alarm due to thunder usually turned out to be a false alarm. I started heading for Engine 7 and I stepped away from the rig as I heard the address of the call. I knew the box number well and knew that only Engines 2, 4, and 6 and the ladder truck would be rolling on the box.

As I walked away from the engine, a single tap came across the speaker from within headquarters. Lyle answered the radio box when the dispatcher called Engine 7. I walked towards the passenger's door of the rig and hopped up into the captain's seat. In a fully paid department, the captain of the engine company would sit in this seat, but in North Tonawanda the driver usually went to calls alone. I placed the lap belt across my lap. Although few firefighters responding in engines wore their seat belts, the long panes of front windshield glass on this Ward LaFrance gave me the idea that staying inside of the cab in the event of an accident would not be a bad idea. Lyle hopped up into the driver's seat. I didn't hear the nature of the call and I asked him where our trip would take us. "Downed wires on Revere Street," he replied.

Revere Street was a four to five minute drive in regular time. Driving lights and sirens would make our response time around three minutes. Lyle turned his switches to start the rig and the diesel engine roared to life, spitting a choking cloud of black smoke from its exhaust. Lyle turned on the overhead gumball lights and tapped his foot on the mechanical siren as we cleared the doorway. We turned right and came to a green light at the corner of Erie Avenue. Even though he had the green light, Lyle laid on the air horn. It was no wonder that the career drivers were always pumped up when they got to a fire with all their sirens and horns blaring. We made a quick left turn onto Walck Road and went over an inactive railroad crossing that was on the top of a small incline. Lyle was lifted out of his seat as we went over the tracks, but my seatbelt prevented me from hitting my helmet on the roof of the cab. Lyle picked up speed as he came down the incline and I could see that the upcoming traffic light at Nash Road had just turned red. Cars were already lining up in the center and right hand turning lanes so we would have to swing into the lane of oncoming traffic. Lyle seemed to be pushing the rig especially hard. I looked over at the speedometer and it read fifty miles per hour.

Lyle was inching his way into the opposite lane when he hit the brakes. The rig didn't respond like I thought it would. It started turning slightly sideways. Lyle shouted, "Hang on!" Those were the two words I never wanted to hear in a fire truck barreling out of control. I had hydroplaned a time or two in my own car before. That was scary but it was no match for the feeling of riding shotgun in a multi ton bullet that was hydroplaning. Lyle quickly released the brake and then tapped it repeatedly as we went into the intersection. I hoped that he was just going to pass through to the other side and then find another route to Revere Street. That idea was not in Lyle's head. He brought the runaway beast under control near the middle of the intersection just as the light turned green. I wasn't sure but I thought I had just seen some moments from my earlier life pass before my eyes. Even though seven's siren was still going, everything seemed to be silent and going in slow motion. I rolled down my window, giving my flat handed sign for "stop" to the motorists who all looked astounded. Lyle cranked the wheel hard to the right and we turned onto Nash Road on our way to Revere Street. A half a block after our thrill ride was done, I looked over towards Lyle. He looked at me with wide open eyes and a slight smirk on his face. He didn't say a word and he didn't have to. His expression clearly communicated what was in his head – "Holy shit, I can't believe that just happened!" The rest of our trip to Revere Street was uneventful and we sat in the rig for the next two hours in a downpour as we watched as a downed power line dance in the street before us.

A different dancing power line presented another close call for me. It was a hot afternoon in June. A two tap had come out for a working fire on Ganson Street, a side street that wasn't much wider than an alley. After a short drive from my house, I pulled my gear from my car trunk and walked quickly towards the fire scene. A thick brown smoke covered the street. Engine 7's rear gumball lights were barely visible in the smoke. The loud hum of an engaged pump and the breaking of glass welcomed me to the scene. The house that was on fire stood next to the Herschell Carrousel Museum. It housed the history of one of the oldest and most prized industries in North Tonawanda. That history was bound to be carried away in smoke if we didn't act quickly.

I grabbed an SCBA off of Engine 7 and walked up to the fire scene. Volunteer firefighters were wedged in between the house that was on fire and the museum. They were using a two and a half to soak the walls of the wooden carrousel museum in a desperate attempt to prevent any radiant heat from catching the museum on fire. My job would be to make entry into the house to suppress the fire. I finished packing up and I stood behind Rich Gleason, a rookie career firefighter who was at the front door. Rich held the attack line as he was attempting to open a locked screen door. Then it happened. A live overhead electrical line had burned off the building from the fire's heat and was snaking across the ground on the sidewalk not more than five feet from us. The other firefighters had moved away from the hazard but we were concentrating on gaining entry into the building. Loud pops were heard and a crackling noise from the wire caused my anal sphincter to tighten. Rich was still fumbling with the screen door. I didn't know Rich too well yet and I'm not sure if he had any street smarts at all. All I knew was that I wanted to be inside the building and away from the slithering electrical line that seemed to be moving closer to us. I pushed Rich to the side. I punched my right hand through the mesh screen and I popped the screen door open by forcefully pulling backwards on the inside latch. With the screen door open a simple turn of the handle of the main door revealed that it was unlocked. I crouched low and surrendered my spot back to Rich who took the line into the building as I backed him up on the hose line. We had escaped the electrical line only to be confronted by a thick blinding smoke. We knocked down the fire, most of which was in the ceiling. The house was a complete mess, with numerous piles of old newspapers strewn all over the place. We stayed in the structure for about twenty minutes cooling off the contents of the rooms of this one story residence. Rich and I walked out the front door to find that the black snake that had scared us into the house was now lying lifelessly on the ground. The power company had arrived to do their job. The Herschell Carrousel Museum was also standing with only some minor paint damage to the side of the building. The North Tonawanda Fire Department had saved an historical building from the ravages of fire. At the next month's meeting of the Sweeney Hose Company, we were awarded with a gift from the Herschell Carrousel Museum. It was the only tangible compensation I would ever receive in my service as a volunteer firefighter. The gift was a family pass to the museum with one free ride on the carrousel included. I have saved the pass to this day.

Another fire where I experienced a close call came during a late winter night one February. North Tonawanda had been experiencing a very cold winter. Apparently it was cold enough for a family on East Goundry Street to set their thermostat a little higher. After a couple of hours they noticed that it was very warm in their house. They turned their thermostat down but it kept getting warmer in the house. Eventually a call was placed to 9-1-1 to report a structure fire.

As I drove to the scene I shivered in my car. A light snow had recently fallen onto the ground but a clear moonlit sky now prevailed. As I approached the scene, I drove my Volkswagen Rabbit more quickly. Another volunteer firefighter pulled out from a side street in front of me and I had to hit the brakes. I started to skid sideways but I then brought the car back under control by letting my foot off of the brake. I tapped the brakes to prevent their further lock up. Brake tapping was a skill that anyone near Buffalo had to know and use for winter driving, especially before the advent of anti-lock brakes. I made the turn onto East Goundry Street and I parked my car. Several firefighters had already arrived on the scene. I couldn't even see the apparatus down the street due to the thick black smoke. It was going to be a long and cold night. What I didn't expect was to have the crap scared out of me in a few short minutes.

I coughed in the smoke as I found Engine 7. Ken Rojek was at the pump panel, looking calmly intense. I opened the SCBA compartment door and found two SCBAs. I removed my helmet and lowered the tank and harness over my head and onto my back. The Sweeneys liked to store our packs upside down, although other companies loaded them right side up. I was satisfied that my seal was tight on my face piece and I put my helmet back on as I went towards the front door. A charged inch and a half hose line was waiting at the front door and a career firefighter was in front of me. His muffled voice called through his face piece as he questioned me as to my identity. I told him who I was, realizing that the firefighter who I was with at a front door again was Rich Gleason.

Rich was able to open the door quite easily this time and he didn't require my assistance. A light smoke filled the long downstairs hallway as we moved into the house. There was no intense heat. I knew that the fire had to be somewhere above us. We walked past a nice table in the dining room. Rich walked into the kitchen. There was a laundry room off of the kitchen and still no sign of fire. Rick couldn't advance the hose any further as it had become caught by one of the chairs in the dining room. I went back and freed the hose line. I pushed the table towards the outside wall of the house, effectively widening our path in case we needed to vacate the building quickly. Another firefighter arrived with a pike pole and he started to tear down the ceiling in the laundry room. Rich must have seen fire because he started to shoot water into the ceiling hole that had been created. I had one hand on the hose and it indented freely with the pressure of my grip. That was a sign of low water pressure. I was standing in the doorway between the between the dining room and the kitchen. A loud crashing sound from behind me pushed me into the kitchen. I looked behind me. The entire dining room ceiling had just collapsed. I had just been in that room minutes earlier.

Apparently something that happened at the time of the ceiling collapse also scared the assistant chief in charge of the fire. The sounds of at least three mechanical sirens from the engines screamed into our ears in the house. Rich shut the nozzle down. We knew what the sirens meant. Something was wrong. Everyone had to evacuate the building. This was not the time to second guess the signal. The chief had seen something dangerous and potentially life threatening. Our quick escape would be hampered by the collapsed ceiling in the dining room. Rich, the other firefighter, and I exited the house through the back kitchen door, leaving the hose line on the floor in the kitchen. As I emerged from the house I looked up and saw a surreal sight. Small areas of flame were popping up around nearly every shingle on the roof. I walked around the side of the house where I discovered the reason why the siren prompted our evacuation. A roof ladder sat up on the roof unmanned. There was a large hole in the roof beneath most of the ladder and flames spewed forth from the hole, scorching the ladder.

Everyone had climbed down from the ladder before the roof collapsed. I surmised that the roof collapse had caused the dining room ceiling to collapse next to me.

After the roof collapse, the vast majority of our firefighting efforts were of a defensive exterior nature. We would throw water at the house from the outside. We waged the battle for hours and hours. Truck 2's aerial bucket was put into service to direct water on the fire from above. When the bucket operations were over, a career firefighter fully closed the water nozzle in the bucket. Doing that when it was warm outside was not a problem. When the weather was in the single digits, as it was that night, water froze quickly in pipes. The water that night froze so quickly that the ladder on Truck 2 could not be fully retracted. Truck 2 returned to headquarters somewhat longer then when it had responded to the house fire earlier that night. It was partially backed into headquarters with the hope that its water supply pipe would thaw. It eventually did. I returned home about seven hours after the initial call for the fire had been received. I placed my frozen turnout coat on the cellar floor and the ice imbedded in its fibers caused it to stand upright as if it were at attention. My monitor went off. It was a one tap call for Engine 4 to return to the fire scene for a rekindle. We had been taught that there was no such thing as a rekindle. There were only fires that weren't fully put out the first time. I felt completely exhausted as I turned off the monitor and went to bed.

Myron Anders and I also got to share a close call at a house fire. Myron and I had stopped over Kurt Nesterson's house on a Saturday night. Kurt was living in his grandmother's house as she had recently passed away. In true bachelor pad fashion, Kurt had taken the table out of the dining room and replaced it with a used pool table. We were taking turns playing a game of nine ball. There was one tap from Kurt's monitor and then another. Was it a box alarm or a working fire? We listened intently as the dispatcher called to Engine 5. The dispatcher gave the address of a house on Meadowbrook Drive in Wurlitzer Park, where many of the newer and more upscale houses in North Tonawanda were located. The dispatcher had received several calls about a house fire at the address. Engine 7 always responded with Engine 5 on any box alarm. We dropped our pool sticks on the floor as we raced out Kurt's front door to our cars.

Kurt and Myron drove north down Payne Avenue but I drove south. My plan was to get into Wurlitzer Park from Erie Avenue. I would encounter fewer traffic lights than Myron and Kurt. I could also push fifty miles per hour going down Erie Avenue which had a posted speed limit of forty miles per hour.

As it turned out, all three of us arrived at the fire scene at the same time. We parked on a side street perpendicular to Meadowbrook Drive and walked towards the incident. From what we could see one of the front rooms was fully involved with fire. Myron and I went to Engine 7 and quickly donned SCBAs. We went to the front door and Mark Peters, a volunteer from Engine 5, was crouched at the front door waiting for our arrival as he could not enter the building alone. Mark had the nozzle and we followed him into the house. It was hot and it was hard to see our hands in front of our faces. We didn't see any fire. Mark went to the right and went about five feet and then stopped. Something was wrong with his mask. He was gasping for air. He shouted through his mask that he was leaving the building. We turned backwards to visually make sure that Mark made it out of the house. I was now on the nozzle, searching for the beast that was making all of the heat inside of the house. We pressed forward and ended up at the back of the house against a patio door. We backtracked and I saw a gleam of orange underneath a door. The fire had revealed itself. Just as we were about to open the door an excited voice yelled out over Myron's radio, "Everybody out!"

I wasn't sure what the command was for until I heard the blaring sirens outside. We were close to attacking the fire. I didn't want to leave but Myron was going to make sure that I had no other choice. He grabbed my SCBA chest strap and started pulling me towards the front door. I grabbed the hose and took it with me. As we passed through the living room I noticed that the floor felt spongy. The piece of carpet I had crawled over felt like the softest carpet in the world. I wondered what was wrong with it. We got closer to the front door and encountered a traffic jam of firefighters. Guys on the front stoop were yanking guys out of the house and before I knew it I was lying on the front lawn. I regained my feet and took long deep breaths through my mask. Myron stood next to me. We watched from outside as the front room became fully involved in a flashover. No one was going back into the house at this point, but I was still wondering why we had been pulled out of the house.

Kurt was standing in the front of the house. He had pulled off his mask and was yelling at Wayne Jameson from the Gratwick Hose Company. Myron and I listened to them, intently hoping to gain some insight as to why we were called out of the building. Kurt and Wayne's argument was quickly shedding light as to what had happened. They apparently had come in behind us after we had entered the house. They went straight up the stairs. When Wayne was near the top of the stairs he got caught up on something and tumbled head over heels to the bottom. Captain Mike Davies from the career department was standing in the front doorway when Wayne tumbled onto his feet. Kurt hadn't come down the stairs with Wayne. That was when Captain Davies decided to send out the evacuation signal. Kurt was upset with Wayne. Wayne's unscheduled departure from the second floor left his ego bruised but his body was intact.

The firefight had temporarily gone into a defensive mode. We regrouped to plan our attack. Myron and Kurt were sent to the roof to ventilate. Recent cutbacks to the department had Truck 1 out of service for the evening. Truck 1 carried a powerful gasoline powered saw called the K-12. It would have made easy ventilation work of the roof if it was on the scene. Kurt and Myron got their workout for the night using good old fashioned dull axes on the rooftop.

I took my face piece off and inhaled the fresh air of the cool night. Everyone was accounted for after the exodus from the house. Soon after that some guys went back into the house and knocked down the majority of the fire. Captain Davies then called for more guys to go inside and do overhaul. Overhaul was a term that was used for a variety of activities. It meant wetting down the smoking charred structure of a building that someone used to call a home. It meant pulling down ceilings and walls with a pike pole. Things were moved or sometimes tossed out of the way during overhaul.

As I walked into the living room where Myron and I had crawled just a short time before, I was astonished by what I saw. The carpet had been pulled back to reveal the chasm of the cellar eight feet below. Only a good strong carpet was between me and the basement floor when I had exited the building. There was a hole in the floor. From the reports of the crew that had made entry into the basement, it was fully involved when they descended into it. If Myron and I had fallen into the basement we surely would have had our names placed upon the National Firefighters Memorial Monument. I stared at the floor in disbelief. Later I would silently thank God for watching over me and for good carpet makers.

Perhaps the closest call for anyone in the Sweeney Hose Company occurred in the early morning hours of December 10, 2003. It was just after midnight and four of us sat around the bar at the fire hall talking and watching television. It was getting late and I had a lecture to give for the emergency medicine program in the morning. I was the EMS fellow in the department at the time and I was going to explain the EMS system in the city of Buffalo to the emergency medicine residents in our program. Before going home, I had planned on stopping at Walmart in the Town of Amherst to do some late night Christmas shopping. I glanced at my watch and it was 12:25 a.m. I said goodnight to the guys sitting around the bar, telling them I would see them at the next one, a phrase used when saying goodbye to a fellow Sweeney. It referred to seeing them at the next fire call. One of the guys I said goodbye to was Kurt Nesterson. Little did I know that the next call would be so soon or that after that call Kurt would forever be deemed a hero.

I drove a short ten minutes out to the Walmart on Niagara Falls Boulevard. The parking lot hosted only a handful of cars. I drove up to the door and realized that the store was not open. I would have to wait for another time to do my Christmas shopping. I drove home and backed up my EMS response vehicle into my driveway.

Upon entering the house, my ears became focused on an unusual amount of radio activity on my fire monitor. Someone was calling out for an accountability check of all personnel at the front of Truck 1 at Robinson Street. Something big was going on but I didn't know exactly where it was happening. I usually carried my portable monitor with me. I didn't have it with me that night. I had started to wash some dishes and I was hoping to get a better location of the fire. Another transmission had mentioned Oliver Street. I let my wife know I was leaving and when I stepped out the back door I immediately smelled smoke. Now I knew that something big was happening.

I turned left onto Erie Avenue and I encountered a thick haze of smoke that was highlighted by the street lights. At the corner of Erie Avenue and Zimmerman Street Car 14, the fire investigator's vehicle, pulled out of fire headquarters with its warning lights on. I followed Car 14 up to a point but then I took some side streets to get to Oliver Street. As I was a late arriver to this fire, I parked nearly three blocks away from the scene.

As I pulled up my bunker pants I looked to my right and saw flames soaring fifty feet into the air above the second story of a building that housed the Clover Club Bar on the first floor. Fire ground operations were well underway and I knew I would have to fit in somewhere. I stopped by the front of Truck 1 where a volunteer from another company had been given the boring but essential task of collecting and keeping the accountability tags. I tossed him my tag and I headed towards Engine 7. Something big had happened at the fire scene but there was no evidence of anything being unusual when I arrived except for the fact that the building was spewing flames from the roof.

Jack Phillips, a young and dedicated member of our hall, was pulling several lengths of two and a half inch hose towards the fire. I helped him as it was difficult to drag two and a half inch hose, especially in icy conditions. To my left I heard the sound of a chainsaw. Two twenty foot trees were being cut down. They were hampering the water streams that needed to be directed onto the fire. I backed up Jack on the hose and he directed the water at any spot on the building where there was an opening. To our right, several firefighters were hitting the powerful fire from the back of the building. They were attempting to prevent the spread of the fire to a funeral home that was not fifteen feet away from the inferno. Jack and I took turns directing the nozzle, shutting it down until only a trickle of water flowed through it when we changed our positions. To our left, the unmanned aerial ladder of Truck 1 was sending a powerful master stream of water onto the fire. After about forty minutes of sitting on the hose, I needed to take a break. Another firefighter took my place on the hose and I headed towards the front of the building. The chief of the department was on the fire scene. We never saw the chief at a fire unless it was a big one. His presence let everyone know that this was a general alarm fire.

Near the front of the building I looked up and saw Kurt. He was wearing his SCBA but had removed his face piece. I knew that he was one of the first ones at the fire because he had a pack on and we were now in a defensive mode of firefighting. I greeted him cheerfully and said, "Long time no see." He smirked and then quietly stated, "I pulled a guy out." He said this but it didn't sink in with me. I questioned him, "You pulled a guy out from where?" He replied, "From the fire on the second floor."

Now this was the same Kurt that I was shooting the breeze with just an hour earlier at the fire hall. Now he had saved someone from one of time's most feared enemies, uncontrolled fire. I was starving for more information so I pulled him aside and he told me the story of what had happened.

A police officer had arrived on the scene before any member of the fire department and he ascended the stairs of the building that led to second story apartments. Apparently the conditions on the second floor were not favorable and the officer entered the apartment of a man who was trapped. The officer then called 9-1-1 from the apartment and informed the police dispatcher that he was trapped in the apartment and needed help. Kurt and Patrick Madison, a volunteer from the Active Hose Company, found the officer and the resident. Pat was taking the police officer down the stairs and Kurt was helping the elderly man down the stairs when a backdraft occurred. The group tumbled to the bottom of the stairs, followed closely by a thick cloud of smoke. The elderly man was transported to the hospital. Word made it back to the fire scene that he was in serious but stable condition. The assistant chief who was on duty that night remarked that he had never seen conditions in a fire deteriorate so quickly.

The weeks that followed the rescue were full of activity for Kurt. The Tonawanda News called him a hero. He was featured as one of Buffalo's Bravest on a local television news station. He received constant good natured harassment about being a hero at the fire hall. Kurt remained humble and graciously accepted the congratulations that were passed his way.

After that night I wondered why I wasn't at the scene with Kurt from the beginning. I drove off to a store at an ungodly hour and that store wasn't even open. Would I have been hurt or even killed if I was the one who went upstairs with Kurt instead of Pat? I don't dwell on that thought too much. It seemed to me that for some reason I didn't have my portable monitor that night. I wasn't meant to be one of the first firefighters on scene that night, even though any firefighter would likely admit that they love being first on the scene. Author Michael Perry put it best when he said, "Until courage meets circumstance, there are no heroes."

Kurt has dealt well with his new title. He sometimes gets some ribbing about being a hero. I gave him a piece of advice concerning the nature of heroes in the fire service. On June 17, 2001, the Fire Department of New York lost three of its firefighters in an explosion at a working fire. Battalion Chief John Moran, who later lost his life on 9/11, was questioned by a member of the press as to whether or not the firefighters who died were to be considered heroes. His answer was simple yet profound. He said, "The firefighter performs one act of bravery in his career and that's when he takes the oath of office. After that, everything else is in the line of duty." Kurt's close call was closer than most. He did his duty well that early December morning.

18

Celebration

The Sweeneys had always been known for their "never say die" attitude. We were branded with the name "fighting Sweeneys" very early on in our existence. This was not due to the early Sweeneys' great ability to fight fires. It was given due to the numerous fights that had broken out among our own members. A close review of the minutes from the late 1890s meetings of the Sweeneys usually included a long list of fines against members who had found it necessary to communicate their feelings with their fists.

The volunteer job of firefighting could often be very stressful and we always liked to play as hard as we worked. Each year the ultimate "play night" for the Sweeneys had been the Annual Installation of Officers Dinner and Dance. The Annual was always held on the third Saturday of February, the anniversary of our acceptance as a fire company by the city of North Tonawanda in 1894. The Annual was anything but dull.

As with any good dinner event, the Sweeneys started the night with cocktails. Silver bowls of Manhattans and Whiskey Sours were unceremoniously set out on a table.

Beer flowed steadily at the bar until dinner and then we ate. Sometimes dinner was served family style and at other times a full plate of dinner was delivered to us.

A memorial service to remember the members who had passed away in the previous year followed dinner. This was usually a very solemn time, especially if we had lost a fairly young or active member during the previous year. One of seven candles was lit for each deceased member. If there were less than seven deceased members then our chaplain, Mark Willington, would always come up with some touching sentiments or dedicate a candle to the well-being of the Sweeney Hose members. Mark was always good at improvisation. I usually agreed to play *Taps* on the trumpet each year for the service. Although Mark was an accomplished and nationally recognized player of *Taps*, he felt it was his duty to preside over the memorial service ceremony.

At the beginning of each memorial service I would excuse myself from my table. I walked into the board room and I left the hallway door open about six inches. I pulled my trumpet from its case and blew silent air through it to warm its silver body. After Mark had given his secret audible signal, which always changed from year to year, I would softly play *Taps*. I often got nervous for some reason before playing but I relaxed, perhaps too much, when I started playing *Taps*. High notes cracking were a sign of my indulgence in too many Whiskey Sours before dinner. The mistakes were few but obviously noticeable. Several members often harassed me after the ceremony about my performance for the evening.

After the memorial service the master of ceremonies introduced the audience to the guests that the Sweeneys were hosting for the evening. Career firefighters and their wives were introduced. State and local politicians were then introduced. Sincere applause was usually extolled on each guest, but the Sweeneys were not above offering a few hisses towards a local politician who had taken unpopular stances towards the firefighters throughout the year and then had the gall to show up at our Annual.

The master of ceremonies would move the evening along with the presentation of service award pins to members. Members received their discharge from active service certificate after five years of service. This signified the official end to a member's required service to the city as a volunteer firefighter; although many Sweeneys, including myself, would go on to serve for longer in the capacity of an active exempt firefighter. Only soft applause would be given for service awards because for the most part a member only had to stay alive long enough to get his or her service years. At twenty five years of service a person became a life member of the hall and was then exempt from all fines and dues. Fifty year members always received a standing ovation when they received their service awards as they really stood the test of time in their service to the fire company. A couple of years ago a member had his name called to come up to the front to receive his fifty year pin. He was seated at the back of the hall. Time had slowed his gait down but his spirit was never broken. It took him more than a minute to walk up to the front. The loud applause from everyone in attendance never dulled during his long journey. It only got louder. Fifty year members were few and far between and the Sweeneys treated them like gold.

Special awards were the next things to be given out on the night of the Annual. Certain awards were given some years and not at all during other years. A great deal of what was awarded depended on who was sitting on the board of directors at the time of selection of the recipients.

In 1992 I became the first lieutenant of the hall. As first lieutenant I was second in charge of all the Sweeney Hose firefighters on the fire ground. Ron Reynolds had joined the hall shortly after I did. He initially came across as a quiet person, as most of us did when we walked into a hall of time-honored friendships, cliques, and people that were just plain rowdy. Ron had completed his Firefighting Essentials class and he was the most active rookie in the company. As line officers, we looked for people like Ron because we knew that they could be counted on in the short term. We also knew that if people like Ron stayed active, they would likely become future officers in the company. I thought that he had put forth a great effort in 1992 and so I proposed to the board of directors and Duncan, who was captain at the time, that we give Ron a rookie of the year award. My proposal came late in the year, and we didn't have time to have a plaque made for him. I thought that Ron would enjoy a practical gift so we decided to award him with a year's subscription to *Firehouse* magazine.

The annual night came and Mark Willington was the master of ceremonies for the year. I pulled him aside before the awards program started that night. I said, "Mark, remember that I'm going to present Ron with the rookie of the year award tonight." He replied, "Yeah, I remember, but make sure that you let everyone know that his award is for rookie of the year." I thought that it was odd for him to say something like that because I wasn't sure what else I would call a rookie of the year award besides the rookie of the year award.

The time came for my presentation and I stood behind the podium that bisected the head table at the front of the hall. One side of the head table was reserved for the president, vice president, secretary, treasurer, and their wives. On the other side of the head table sat the fire chief, the master of ceremonies, and the department chaplain.

In my speech, I spoke in general about the kind of year we had with firefighting in 1992, recalling some of the larger fires that we had fought. I said that it wasn't possible to do this without the continued efforts of the Sweeney volunteers. I then focused in on Ron's accomplishments – his call attendance, his drill attendance, and the extra things he did to make firefighting better for the company and the department in the previous year. I concluded by saying, "And it's because of these things that the 1992 rookie of the year award goes to Ron Reynolds." Ron came up to the podium and I told everyone that this was a new award this year. I handed him a magazine subscription card and I asked him to fill it out. As Ron returned to his seat, I tried to follow his lead but Mark grabbed my arm. "We need you help for presenting the next award," he said. I didn't know of any other awards being given. I stood there perplexed as I listened to Mark talking. He mentioned some things about firefighting and talked about commitment to the fire hall. I gazed out into the dimly lit hall wondering who would be marching forward to receive the next piece of award hardware. Then Mark started rattling off fire call percentage statistics. I had done the statistics for the past year and I had turned them over to Duncan for his perusal. How had Mark received access to the statistics? Mark went on to mention that the firefighter had joined the hall in 1990. More information was revealed concerning the recipient and my heart began to race. Mark's next words astounded me. He said, "The 1992 firefighter of the year award is presented to Jason Borton."

I lowered my head in shock and disbelief. Duncan had pulled a good one on me. I never saw the award coming. I accepted the award and said a few words into the microphone. "I'd like to thank the membership for giving me this award. I'm sure that there are many more people in the audience that deserve this award more than me," I said. What I didn't realize at the time was that those members had won the award in years past.

I returned to my seat and showed the award to my friend and date, Anne. I would win the award for firefighter of the year once again in 1997. In 1999 I would be the first volunteer firefighter in the city of North Tonawanda to be awarded the North Tonawanda firefighter of the year award. In 2000 my brother firefighters bestowed upon me a simple but heartfelt gift. It was a desk plate that read "Jason Borton, M.D". To the left of the nameplate was a simple Maltese cross that said "Volunteer Firefighter". To the right was the caduceus, the snake wrapped around a staff that symbolizes medicine. I think the members realized how hard it was for me to attend medical school while still attending drills and going to fire calls. This gift said a simple, "Thanks for hanging in there with us".

Other awards typically presented at the Annual included a meritorious service award and the Eldridge Hunt Memorial Award. The Eldridge Hunt award was given to a member, usually with more than twenty five years of service to the hall, who had really made Sweeney Hose an integral part of his life. The Eldridge Hunt Memorial award was the highest award that a Sweeney Hose member could hope to attain.

Gag gifts would follow the real awards and the Sweeneys had some good ones. The Sweeneys' beloved 1973 Ward LaFrance pumper had seen some hard times and some better days. Rust had left its mark on many of its compartments and it was a rig begging to be put out to pasture. One day while walking in the truck room after a call I glanced upwards noting that in place of the two rear mounted gumball lights of Engine 7 there was a foray of tangled wires. As I was curious I asked the Engine 7 driver what had happened. He replied, "Oh that schmuck Harry Lomans clipped them off on the overhead door when he was backing in. He had the overhead door on the timer and it came down right onto the lights." Within two weeks, the old drab lights were replaced with impressive looking modern lights. They made the rig look like it might have been made in the 1980s. The lights impressed me so much that I decided that Harry needed to receive an award at the next Annual.

At the Annual I stepped forth and described the deplorable condition of Engine 7. I reviewed in great detail which areas of the rig were rusting. I commented on the small pond of water that formed beneath it when it sat in one spot for too long. I then enthusiastically described the awesome new pair of lights that were mounted on Engine 7. I told of how Harry had single-handedly started the refurbishment process of the rig. I showed a certificate of appreciation from the Sweeney Hose Company. I announced that Harry was the official chairman of the Engine 7 restoration committee. With a red face, Harry came forward to accept his award. He shook my hand and leaned forward. "You're a son of a bitch," he said. "Don't I know it?" I replied.

In 1994 we had some pretty bad structure fires but thankfully, no people lost their lives in these fires. The same luck didn't carry over for two members of the bird family who both perished in their cages that year. Because these two birds had died on his watch, I felt that it was my duty to present our captain, Duncan Fanners, with an award memorializing the death of the birds. I purchased a bird perch from a local pet store and then constructed two bird-like figures from paper mache. I hung them upside down on the perch to symbolize their demise and then I painted the entire award black. My speech that year was somber. I reflected on the fire from the birds' perspective. I said, "Initially there was probably a light wisp of smoke in the air, the bird probably thinking that dinner had been burned again. Then the smoke would have become heavier. The bird would now start becoming more alarmed, perhaps flying into the side of the cage several times in an attempt to escape its choking episode and the intensifying heat. Finally it might have noticed the smoke arising from its own feathers. Thankfully it would pass out, being spared the memory of being cooked to a well done char."

The best gag gift that I can remember was given to Luke Joseph, a young firefighter whose ability to run off at the mouth was only tempered by his sincere desire to make Sweeney Hose a better place for everyone. Ron Reynolds was the captain of the hall and Luke had badgered him for months about getting his red triangle removed from his helmet. The red triangle was plastered on the front of every rookie volunteer firefighter's helmet. Its presence forbade its wearer from donning an SCBA and entering a structure. Ron never liked to be forced. He would remove a triangle when he thought a firefighter was ready to have it removed. Luke's constant pestering probably bothered Ron but no one could tell. He could have gone up one side of Luke and down the other. Instead Ron took his retaliation to the Annual. He had already presented a pacifier to Yale Edwards, a friend of mine who had pestered Ron throughout the year. Luke was presented with a helmet with large triangles, in the form of slow moving vehicle placards that were seen on farm equipment. The placards were screwed into the front and the back of the helmet. Ron announced that night that he had decided to remove the triangle from Luke's helmet. A red faced and embarrassed Luke posed for scores of pictures with his super rookie helmet that night.

After the awards ceremony people would swarm towards the bar for drinks. The DJ would start to play music in an effort to coax people out onto the dance floor. Everyone would talk and catch up and have a good time. That was not the case at the second annual that I attended.

Stan Lawrence and Evan Kendricks never got along well with each other. Apparently Evan hade made a comment to Stan during the awards ceremony. As soon as the ceremony was over, they were outside brawling in the middle of Erie Avenue. They made their way back into the hall and then all hell broke loose. Evan was fighting with Stan near the men's bathroom when Evan bumped into Bob Frank. Bob's son Tim saw this and got Evan into a headlock more quickly than a professional wrestler had ever done. Tim was on the floor with Evan in his grasp telling him to cool down and knock it off when Larry Johnson came over and got into Evan's face. Dale Loter saw Larry's action as an unfair aggressive move towards Evan, who was already being subdued, so he hit Larry. That was a big mistake on Dale's part. Larry was an easy going guy until someone pissed him off. A Tasmanian devil was let loose in the front foyer as a crowd gathered around Dale to help protect him. I was in the unfortunate spot of being behind Larry when he brought his fist back to strike Dale. Larry scored a double hit, striking me in the nose and then Dale in the jaw.

The fight was quickly broken up as the invited politicians scrambled for the doors with their mortified wives in tow. The fighting Sweeneys had lived up to their namesake. Stan and Evan would be expelled from membership at the next month's meeting. Everyone eventually cooled down and headed back towards the dance floor. A smile came across my face as the words of the song "Celebration" by Kool and the Gang struck my ears, "There's a party going on right here."

For me dancing was always one of the most fun parts of the evening. For some reason, alcohol always seemed to make me a better dancer or at least a better dancer in my mind. One year I came up with a crazy notion. I walked over to the DJ and said, "Play something provocative for me, something stripper like." "You got it doc," was his reply and two songs later I was the only one on the dance floor with the exception of a solitary chair. I removed my sport coat and flung it into the crowd of onlookers. Next came my tie, shirt, and undershirt. My belt and pants left me shortly after that and I danced in my underwear, socks, and shoes. I made nineteen dollars in tips from the female spectators the first year. I've grown accustomed to putting on this show each year and after my dance I would gather my clothes from around the hall. Unfortunately for me, my drunken firefighter brothers must have surmised that I always liked to be nearly naked. One year I was standing around minding my own business when suddenly a herd of six or seven firefighters swarmed around me and stripped me of my clothes, leaving me only with my socks and underwear. They then carried me to a door and hurled me outside onto an awaiting February snow bank. On my return trip into the hall, I walked through the back parking lot. An auxiliary police officer was coming into the parking lot to park his car for the night. I smiled and waved to the officer as he looked on in bewilderment.

Over the years I had different dates that I brought to the Annual. During the end of medical school I had asked one of my classmates to come to the Annual. She was crazy and a fun person. My brother firefighters kept pulling me aside on the night when I brought Brittany, telling me that they thought she was awesome. The night was moving on and the hall was getting warm and smoky. Brittany and I decided to step outside for a breath of fresh air. I glanced at the garage behind the fire hall. I told Brittany to walk with me as I headed towards the garage. I opened up the overhead door to let her look at our antique pumper which we affectionately called the "Wedge". She looked at it with half-hearted interest. She was getting cold and wanted to go back into the hall. My glasses fogged up as we walked back into the warm hall. I went behind the bar to wipe them off with a towel. Brittany went to the front of the bar where Ron Reynolds and Chuck Peterson were standing.

Chuck had been in the hall for less time than me. In his previous life he had been a career firefighter in another state. His department had been downsized and he had lost his job. Chuck could be the ultimate goofball, especially when he was drunk. He could be loud when he was sober and he remained loud and added obnoxious and boisterous to his repertoire when he was drunk. Brittany was standing next to Chuck at the bar. I hoped that Chuck wasn't about to make an ass out of me, but I knew that he just might make an ass out of himself.

"So where were you guys, Jason?" Chuck queried. "We went out back to look at the pumper," I replied. Chuck said, "So Brittany, how did you like the Wedge?" The music must have been too loud because the next thing she said to Chuck was, "I can't have a wedge you ass, I'm not wearing underwear."

Brittany was a wild girl, but I never expected her to make a confession like this in such a public place. I felt sorry for Chuck and Ron. I felt the need to step to the other side of the bar to help them lift their jaws off of the floor. After their initial amazement wore off, they broke into laughter over Brittany's confession. We never did let her know that "the Wedge" was the nickname of our beloved antique fire engine.

At times the focus of our Annual has seemed to have changed. We sometimes go to other banquet facilities besides our hall for our dinner. Sure these places embody more elegance than our meager sixty by forty foot social hall, but I feel that they lack something vital. A something that says, "This is the home of the Sweeneys". The last time we had our Annual at an outside banquet hall was a disaster. They couldn't keep up with the need for alcohol of our members. People were waiting in line to get a drink for twenty minutes. That had never happened at an Annual held in our own hall.

It is now February again. The Annual will be held at our own hall this year. Plans for the program are progressing. Drinks will be poured in a few short weeks. Awards will be given. We will mourn our losses. Good food will be served. I am determined to dance, celebrate, and make at least twenty dollars this year.

19

Some Characters

On May 7, 1990, I stood in the front of the Sweeney Hose hall with my right hand raised. I repeated an oath. A brief silence ensued when I had finished the oath, followed by a round of half-hearted applause. The person that had sworn me in shook my hand. I glanced to my right and there were seven people standing there. They were the board of directors and they had garnered enough votes the previous December to earn the right to be where they now stood. On my left was the general membership of the hall. On initial inspection these two groups appeared united for a single cause – to efficiently suppress fires within the community. After a brief session of hand shaking I turned to my left and found a seat with the general membership at the back of the room. Little did I imagine it that night, but in time my buttocks would adorn the seats of the first lieutenant, vice-president and ultimately the president of the hall.

One meeting night after what I deemed to be an unpopular decision that was made by the board, I approached the hall secretary, Allen Michalis. I badgered him for some justification for the board's decision that evening. Our discussion started out civil, but soon became heated as I was even more upset with the decision that had been made. Allen always had a short fuse. The tone in my voice had just lit it. Wisps of smokes were pouring out of his ears when he finally blew up and said, "If you could do better, why don't you run for an office? Let me tell you, it's a whole different ballgame when you're sitting on this side of the table though." I kept silent as we walked away from each other and the surrounding members were silent too. His words resonated through my mind. I vowed that night that someday I would sit on his side of the table.

Our company was set up like many volunteer companies. The board of directors was the executive committee. They dealt with managing the finances of the hall and helped to run its day to day functions. The line officers served as the operations branch of our hall team. They were in charge of the firefighters at a fire scene. They provided leadership to the firefighters on the fire ground.

The board of directors consisted of seven members: president, vice president, secretary, treasurer, and three members who were directors. According to our by-laws, the president was there to enforce the by-laws and preside over the meetings of the company. He was in charge of assigning committees. When things went wrong the members looked to the president for an explanation. When things were going well the president seldom received praise. The vice president was there to step in when the president couldn't be present. If the president and vice president were friends, the vice president would often take on some tasks to relieve part of the president's burden.

The secretary of the company always seemed to be the real work horse of the operation. He took the notes at all of the company and board meetings. He received the new member applications. He compiled fines and dues lists. The newsletter was created by the secretary. If people needed a question answered and the president wasn't available, the secretary was the next person to ask.

The treasurer kept the financial records of the company in order. He paid the bills that the membership approved. He would often give financial advice to the company regarding whether or not he thought an expenditure was a wise decision based upon the fire hall's financial situation.

There were three official members of the board of directors and they were to, according to our by-laws, "have charge and they shall hold in trust the real, personal, and other property of the company. They shall present an annual inventory of all property and supervise all uses of Company property. They shall see that properties are kept in good repair and make suggestions as to property to be excessed." In reality I cannot recall the board of directors ever presenting an annual inventory of the company property. In essence the board of directors, who each served for a three year term, acted as further governors of the Sweeney Hose Company and they rallied for the direction that they wanted the hall to follow.

The Sweeney Hose captain had the job of directing and watching out for the Sweeney Hose members on the fire ground. He was to assume command of the company at drills and parades. He was to give new members an overview of fire equipment. He collected parade uniforms and gear. He was in charge of making or getting food for meeting nights. Evaluation of members on a semi-annual basis to see if they were in compliance with their requirements also fell on the captain. The 1st and 2nd lieutenants basically assisted the captain in the performance of his duties. They also could act as the captain in the event of his absence.

My first elected office in the company was to the position of 1st lieutenant. After the November membership in 1992 I approached the first lieutenant at the time, Larry Babinski, and questioned him about his plans to run for the 1st lieutenant position in 1993. He flat out told me that he wasn't running again because he had just been hired by the North Tonawanda Police Department. I submitted my name on the ballot for 1st lieutenant and when the nominations were closed, I was running unopposed for the position. I took the office of 1st lieutenant on January 1, 1993. Duncan Fanners was my captain and Ron Billings was the 2nd lieutenant.

Duncan was always a no nonsense type of guy. He carried his no nonsense beliefs into the firefighting arena. He expected active firefighters to be at every drill. He wanted to see his firefighters at every call they could make. In the early nineties, active members were very few, but Duncan wanted to make sure that everyone did their part. He pulled gear if members weren't keeping up with their duties. His actions likely caused some members of the company to resign. I agreed with his leadership style even though I believed that it ultimately got him elected out of the position of captain.

Ron Billings was the pretty boy of the fire company. He wore expensive clothes and he didn't seem to like to do all the down and dirty activities of firefighting. Despite this, he put forth a great effort and did his job of being a lieutenant very well.

As line officers we were expected to set an example for the company. We had to make every call that we could. Volunteer firefighters wore black turnout gear with black helmets and career firefighters wore yellow gear with yellow helmets. Line officers were assigned a blue helmet so that we could be identified quickly on the fire ground. We became affectionately known as "Smurfs" because of our blue helmets.

As line officers Duncan, Ron, and I tried to make things better for the Sweeneys. We convinced the company to purchase bunker pants, which were made out of the fire resistant material Nomex. The city issued the volunteer firefighters three quarter length boots that were pulled up upon arrival to the fire scene. These offered little protection to the legs during intense firefights. We decided that we would protect our members to the best of our ability as the city had yet to provide bunker pants to the volunteer firefighters.

The board of directors stipulated that the money for the bunker pants would come out of the bingo funds. For

Duncan this meant working bingo in order to get a set of bunker pants. I had never seen Duncan at a bingo since I had joined the hall. Rumor had it that he had once worked a Sunday night bingo. At the end of the three hours the regulars had gotten to him and he was reported to have been seen running for the door. Duncan did return to bingo each week and he got his pair of bunker pants. He kept coming down to work bingo and his wife would often play bingo while he worked the floor.

We also convinced the company of the need for fire ground radios for the line officers. This would enhance our ability to communicate with each other on the fire ground. As volunteers we were not allowed to use the career firefighters' radios, even when entering a burning building. These radios, we hoped, would help us to improve our safety. The radios also provided a vehicle for us to end up in some embarrassing situations.

I had a couple of friends that would come to bingo nearly every week. My friends and I would often go out to eat after bingo had ended. One of my female friends was overweight and the guys at the hall would never let me forget that. She and Dan Stevens were with me one bingo night when we went to eat at a restaurant about seven miles outside of North Tonawanda. I had my radio on the table and we had just finished eating when a two tap came in for a chimney fire on Miller Street. I encouraged my friends to move as I had every intention of going to the call. We drove through the back roads of the Town of Wheatfield and when we hit the North Tonawanda city line, I illuminated my blue light. I had been in broken radio contact with Duncan and Ron. When I was about four blocks from the fire scene they called me over the radio to question my whereabouts. Duncan's radio call sign was 7-1. I was 7-2 and Ron was 7-3.

Ron called to me, "7-3 to 7-2."

I replied, "Go ahead 7-3."

"How far out are you?"

"Four blocks, be there in one minute."

"10-4. By the way, do you have the fat chick with you?"

I felt a pot of anger boil over me as the radio transmission came through. Luckily it was partially filled with static as my female companion questioned me as to what Ron had said. Dan had heard it all and he started rudely laughing in the back seat. I quickly changed the channel on the radio to prevent further awkward transmissions. Thirty seconds later I was at the fire scene. I jumped out of the car, leaving a laughing Dan and a bewildered girl behind. I briskly walked towards Engine 7 searching for the short 2nd lieutenant who had made the inappropriate comments over the radio. I spotted Duncan as I walked towards the engine. "Where's Billings?" I shouted. Looking at me Duncan later said he could see the smoke coming from my ears. At that moment, Ron stepped out from the other side of the engine. I was starting to see the humor in Ron's comment but I wanted to make him sweat. "She was in the car you asshole," I said as I shoved him backwards as I broke into a grin. Ron had trouble breathing for a couple of minutes because he was laughing so hard. He couldn't believe that she was actually in the car.

Being a lieutenant meant that I had to give orders on the fire ground. This was initially difficult for me as I had always been taught to follow orders. I slowly gained the trust of the active firefighters once they saw that I knew what was going on at a fire scene. Some of the older firefighters seemed to show doubt in their eyes sometimes, but they always followed my orders without question. We were taught to always follow orders on the fire ground, even if we weren't sure why a particular order was being given. Exceptions to this rule did exist. If a firefighter didn't feel he had the skills or the confidence to complete a task that was assigned to him, that firefighter was to immediately inform the ordering officer of his inability to perform the task. A firefighter could also refuse to follow an order if he felt that following that order would put his life in immediate danger. Fortunately because of the training of our firefighters, these situations were not frequently encountered. As a line officer it was important for me to know each firefighter's strengths and weaknesses. This knowledge was gathered from observing the firefighters at training sessions.

The North Tonawanda Fire Department offered a three hour training drill for the volunteer fire companies each month. The career department personnel had their drills on a separate day. Duncan and I thought that we needed to offer additional training for our members. We often invited members of the Rescue Fire Company to join us at our "in house" drills. One Saturday morning we held a drill at our hall. We were going to test mask confidence of the firefighters and we set up a maze. Teams of firefighters would enter our darkened social hall with their SCBA masks made impervious to light by the aluminum foil that we placed over the face piece. The object of the drill was to get through the maze, which consisted of banquet tables turned sideways, locate a fire victim, and remove the victim from the maze.

On one particular Saturday morning, Wayne Boyer had come to drill. Wayne had a slight speech impediment and was unfortunately harassed by many members of the hall. He worked a third shift job and couldn't come to the hall to work bingo. Instead of working bingo, he set the tables up for bingo early Sunday mornings. He often employed the help of his children who always seemed to be running on high octane. I had once stopped over Wayne's house to drop something off to him. He offered me a beer and we sat on his front porch watching traffic. We made small talk and as I got up to leave, one of Wayne's kids appeared out of nowhere. I walked toward my car and he decided he would open the door of my Volkswagen Rabbit for me. Unfortunately the door was locked, the kid was determined, and my door handle had seen better days. When he had finished, the door remained closed and my door handle was dangling from the side of the car. A half-hearted apology of "sorry mister" came from his mouth and he ran back to his backyard to play with his siblings. I somehow managed to put the guts of the handle back into place. I eventually used a strong adhesive glue to permanently fix the handle and I always left my car doors unlocked whenever I visited Wayne.

As line officers we knew that Wayne had a problem with mask confidence. I volunteered to be his partner to lead him through the maze. Wayne and I put on our masks. Wayne was doing well until the foil was put over his mask. Then the sound that emanated from his mask resembled that of Darth Vader breathing like he had just ran the Boston Marathon while smoking a pack of Marlboro Reds. We removed his mask and tried to calm him down. After five minutes he said that he felt like he was ready to try the maze. Darth Vader breathing returned with the aluminum foil mask. Wayne and I got onto our hands and knees and we entered the hall. I was doing a right handed search and we were moving forward in the maze. My left foot had started to feel numb as Wayne had formed a death grip on my ankle. We went thirty feet into the maze and Wayne's low pressure bell started ringing. Our SCBA cylinders were usually good for thirty minutes of air and possibly twenty minutes if a firefighter was working hard. Wayne had managed to polish off his bottle in less than seven minutes. I turned him around and we made our way back to our entry point as my left hand now kept in contact with the wall. We stood up in the hallway and Wayne ripped the mask off of his face. I casually turned off my air and took my mask off, bending down to catch a couple of breaths of air. I noticed something shiny at the toe of my left boot. It was steel, as in steel toed boots. Wayne had managed to scrap the overlying rubber right off of my boot. Everyone at the drill knew that they would never go into a burning building with Wayne. As line officers, we were intent on making sure that Wayne didn't receive the go ahead to become an interior firefighter unless he showed a dramatic improvement in his mask confidence.

In 1994 I was re-elected to my position as the 1st lieutenant, but in 1995 I stepped down from the position as I was residing at Niagara University and I couldn't give the position the dedication it deserved. The next year I ran for the office of vice president and I served under Tim Frank who was the president at the time. I learned a great deal during my stint as vice president. I learned that what went on or was said at board meetings didn't always get communicated to the general membership of the hall. I learned to watch my back, but I also learned how important it was to be honest and open with the members. Tim always went on vacation in August and I got my one and only chance that year to run a meeting. I stumbled with some of the proceedings, but I was able to run the meeting, from start to finish, in forty seven minutes. Our meetings usually lasted at least an hour and twenty minutes.

The next time I took a shot at running for office was for the office of president in 2003. I had been listening to a number of younger members in the hall and they were telling me that they felt that the current board was being too strict with them. They felt that their freedoms were being taken away. I decided that I needed to run for president. I needed to see if I could make the hall a better place for the members to be. I kept my plans confidential. My wife didn't even know that I was going to be running. Nominations for elections closed at 9 p.m. ten business days after the night of the November meeting. I arrived at the hall at ten minutes to nine on the tenth business day after the meeting. I walked into the hall at five minutes to nine and dropped my office nomination into the ballot box. Paul Andres, a young active member of the hall who seemed to jump from job to job because he had problems finding one that could accommodate his laid back lifestyle, was at the hall. He started asking questions.

"Whatcha running for?" he questioned.

"To help my fire hall," I replied.

"No, I mean what office are you running for?"

"An elected one. I'd appreciate your vote."

With that I walked out of the hall. I called people that I thought might come down to vote on election night. I also mailed out some letters that outlined what I planned to accomplish if I was elected president.

Election night came in December and when all the voters were tallied, over fifty members had come out to vote. Before the December meeting a fish fry was always held. This seemed to entice members to come down to the hall to cast their ballot.

The election committee disappeared into the back room at the start of the meeting to tally the votes. We were allowed to have a representative present for the counting, but I didn't send one. Oscar Keating, who was the president, ran the meeting. He was my only rival in the race for president. He eventually called out the election committee and they announced the winners of all the offices except for the president. The vice president winner was not called off because no one had submitted a nomination to be elected to that office. I thought it was strange that there was no mention of the presidential winner. The election committee chairperson then spoke, "We have a tie for the office of president."

My racing heart throttled up to a faster pace. I hadn't won. With all of my campaigning I didn't get enough votes to become president. All of the members present at the meeting would have to vote again. This sucked. I knew what would happen next. Scraps of paper would be passed around the hall for a secret ballot. Then the election committee would gather the pieces and retreat to the secrecy of the board room to once again tally the votes to see who would be the president of the hall in 2003. The pressure seemed to be mounting. Suddenly, a voice from the front of the hall silenced the whispers circulating through the membership. I was staring at the floor, dreading a re-vote. I glanced up. Oscar was speaking. He said, "My health hasn't been that great in the past year and I think it's time the hall lets a new guy take the reins and try this thing called being president. I'm conceding the win to Jason, your new president for 2003." I was in awe. I knew it was hard for Oscar to do what he had just done as he was very active in the hall. After the meeting I went up to the head table and thanked him for his selfless action. At the January 2003 meeting an election for vice president was held and Oscar was quickly elected to that position.

My dreams of accomplishing great things quickly became tarnished as I learned that being the president of the hall was not about making big changes all at once. Being the president seemed more like being an actual firefighter. I had to put out little spot fires before they amassed into an inferno. Sometimes I felt like the chief babysitter of the hall, putting members in their own little corner when they didn't play nicely with the other kids in the sandbox that we called a fire hall.

I kept my notes from the meetings when I was president in 2003. The board would meet at 7 p.m. on the night of the general meeting. We would also sometimes meet on another night during the month as there were often additional issues that needed to be addressed and one hour was not long enough to get this accomplished. I felt that every board member needed to be given some time to express their thoughts and concerns. During our board meetings I let each person blurt out any concerns or things they thought needed to be addressed.

Kevin Richards had been a member of Sweeney Hose since I was a year old. He was a director and a no nonsense guy who was quiet. He kept his concerns to a minimum occasionally complaining about the hall not being clean. Things were usually fine with him.

On the other end of the blurting spectrum was Luke Joseph. He constantly seemed to be whining. He was the chairman of the building and grounds committee and seemed to want everything he could get for the upkeep of the outside of the hall. Once I looked past his whining however, I realized that he was a dedicated member of the hall, who was never afraid of a great deal of hard work if he could help make the hall as best as it could be.

Chuck Peterson, like the rest of us, always had an opinion about someone else's opinion. Most of us were content to keep our opinions in our heads on most issues. I came to believe that Chuck, as a child, suffered a head injury that interrupted the brain circuits that prevented thoughts from being verbalized. Chuck would give his honest opinion, free of tact, about anything that was said concerning the fire hall. He often thought that he had a better way to do something. At times, he would get extremely passionate about what I thought were little things going on at the hall. He seemed to want everyone to accept his opinion. Those were the times when I would start calling the fire hall Peterson Hose. He would see my point at times and back down a bit. He was one on the most dedicated Sweeneys I had ever known. Chuck was a fun guy to be around. His pants would often hang low and I would never hesitate to toss a penny towards his gluteal cleft when his belt failed to perform its intended job.

Doug Jarret liked to talk about the Wedge in the board meetings. He kept us appraised of what was going on with it and what expenditures that we might be looking towards in the future. He became very passionate about some issues. He was a fairly quiet board member who always seemed to remain optimistic about the hall and its future direction.

Ken Davis was the secretary of the hall and he always seemed to be looking one step ahead of where we were at the present time with the fire company. He worked hard with the by-laws committee to update our by-laws. He pushed hard to make sure that the Sweeneys got class A parade uniforms. He did not complain. He made it his goal to make sure that all members of the hall were treated with respect.

Oscar was present for a handful of meetings during the year. For the most part, he kept quiet and let me have my shot at running the company. Ron Reynolds was the captain of the company and he was always present at our board meetings. He told us of any firematic concerns that he had with any of the members. He wouldn't make an outright decision about pulling someone's gear or disciplining someone without explicitly getting the board's permission to do so. I let him know that it was my position that he should be completely in charge of the operational aspect of firematics as he was the captain, but he still sought the board's backing with any firematic issues that involved disciplining a member. Ron's predecessor Duncan never sought out the board's approval before pulling someone's gear. Over time, Duncan seemed to become less popular. I thought that Ron always remembered this and why I thought he always sought the board's approval.

The fire hall was a melting pot of people from North Tonawanda. In our ranks were businessmen, city workers, EMTs, electricians, factory workers, teachers, managers, auto mechanics, and a doctor. Amazingly, these people were able to come together time and time again to suppress the fires that occasionally upset the humdrum life of our bedroom community. When these people weren't working or fighting fires they often spent time at the fire hall. Sometimes the time spent there could be too much and that's when trouble always seemed to begin.

I had found out that there were a couple of things that someone had to possess to become a successful volunteer firefighter in North Tonawanda. First and foremost a person had to have the drive to be a firefighter. Nothing could take the place of the drive. If that wasn't there the other firefighters would sense it and there would be a lack of respect. I could spot firefighters without drive a mile away on the fire ground. They would hang around the truck on the scene. They would only do something if someone asked them to perform a task. Firefighters with drive would find something to do on the fire ground even if it was the smallest of tasks.

Another ability a firefighter needed to become a respected Sweeney member was the ability to take a ton of verbal abuse from his fellow firefighters. Guys would constantly taunt other members about their looks or something they said and they wouldn't let it go. Anyone that was going to remain an active member had to be able to take the teasing and then start dishing out some of their own. These remarks weren't made to truly put another person down. Members only gave shit to others that they truly liked. A young member who had been in the hall a couple of months was receiving his induction papers from the city one night at our monthly meeting. His name was read off by the secretary and one of the board members commented, "Mark Sheblonsky, sounds like a good German name." The membership exploded into laughter and as the laughter died down a pissed off voice from of the back room said, "It's Polish." I stared at Sheblonsky and knew right then that he would never truly make it as a Sweeney. He didn't. He resigned after a couple of years, having only made a handful of calls.

Certain guys constantly received crap from other members and sometimes it was excessive. One day Jack Phillips had enough and he threatened some members from the hall when they had asked him to do something. Jack's threats were not idle and the members reported him to the board, saying that they feared for their safety. Jack didn't deserve all of the taunting he received, but as president I had to look out for the safety of the members of the hall, whether they were instigating Jack or not. Jack was a reasonable member and he was suspended from the hall and from responding to fire calls for thirty days. I thought that the time away from the hall did him some good and he returned to the hall with a more relaxed attitude.

I had to deal with some serious issues during my tenure as president of the hall. A young man in his early twenties by the name of Dennis Brandt had joined the hall. He had spent a short period of time with an all volunteer fire company in a nearby county and then he had moved to North Tonawanda. Dennis came off as a know it all who didn't know much about dealing with people. One meeting night Dennis pissed off Luke Joseph. The two of them ended up outside fighting behind the fire hall. Luke got Dennis in a head lock and then Dennis was begging for mercy. Guys that had Dennis' attitude seemed to join the hall every three years. They would get the membership in an uproar and people looked for ways to get them expelled from the hall. I had seen three Dennis like characters before and I knew that it would only be a short period of time before Dennis secured his own demise.

For Dennis it turned out to be an error in parking at the scene of an incident. He had parked illegally at the scene of a motor vehicle collision and a North Tonawanda police officer, Larry Babinski, who was also a Sweeney member, ran Dennis' license plate through his computer. As it turned out, Mr. Brandt was driving a car with switched plates. He also had no registration or insurance for his car. A letter to the fire chief was quickly drawn up by the Sweeneys and the next month Dennis handed in his fire gear and he became an ex-Sweeney Hose member. Dennis wrote a letter to the hall a few months later saying that he had moved back to his old town. He went on and on about how great Sweeney Hose was. Towards the end of the letter he asked if I, as president, could write him a letter of recommendation for reinstatement into his former fire company. The members at our meeting were quite verbal about not wanting this to happen so Dennis' request was entered into the circular file, our term for the wastepaper basket.

A constant warning from the board that went out to the general membership was "what goes on in the hall stays in the hall". Apparently someone had been discussing Sweeney business with a member of another fire company. News of this discussion apparently made it back to one of the Sweeney board members. This seemed to be a good policy to me as the Sweeneys' truly private business really had no real reason to be discussed outside of our hall.

Towards the end of my year as president, I received a message from Oscar that he wanted to talk to me about a matter concerning the hall. I called him back but I was unable to reach him by phone. I had the next day off from work so I decided that I would stop by his wife's restaurant on Oliver Street. His wife did most of the work at the restaurant while he mingled with the customers, probably downing at least a half a dozen cups of coffee each morning.

I walked into the restaurant the next morning and I didn't see Oscar at the sit down counter. A wall separated the restaurant into two halves. As I turned the corner what I saw shocked me. Oscar and two board members from the Sweeney Hose Company were sitting at a table with papers in front of them. They ignored their papers when they saw me. It seemed like they might have been discussing company business. To me, talking about company business outside of the company with other Sweeneys was a minor sin. The fact that two other volunteers from two different fire companies were sitting at the table with them elevated their actions to a major sin if they were indeed discussing company business. I wished that I could have called every member of the company down to the restaurant to see the meeting that was going on. I never questioned them as to what they were discussing and for all I know they might have been discussing world politics. I just had a bad feeling about what was being discussed. When I sat down at the table their discussion stopped and I made small talk with them. I quickly guzzled a lukewarm cup of coffee and Oscar told me briefly about what he had called me for.

As I sat and listened to Oscar my mind wondered. It was there at that table that I decided that I would not run for the seat of president for the following year. I never found out what the group was discussing but it could have been about Sweeney business. I said good bye to the group and I headed outside into the cool fall air. I headed to my truck feeling like an isolated solitary speck, not the president of an organization. I was mostly disappointed in myself. I hadn't given the hall all of the attention it deserved when I was president. I thought to myself that I would go back to run for president someday in the future. I did however make up my mind that it would be a long time before I strolled down that contorted road again.

20

Marching On

Today is the third Sunday in June. Yesterday we had the annual Tonawanda and North Tonawanda Inspection Day Parade and it was a great celebration of firefighting. It was a day when we showed the pride in our company and in ourselves. The citizens of the community got to see just who would be showing up if their house caught on fire. It was a day for remembrance and catching up with old friends. It was a time to reflect on the roots of our fire companies. Parade day was a day that has changed from year to year. As I grow older the focus of the day has seemed to change.

Inspection Day was originally set up as a day for the officers of the fire department to inspect their men and the fire equipment. Each member would present his gear to be inspected by the company captain and ultimately the chief of the department. All of the fire companies would then march in a parade in the city of North Tonawanda. Citizens would watch the parade and give a visual "inspection" of each company and its apparatus.

Today the tradition of the firefighters' inspection day continues. Each firefighter does not have his equipment inspected by the company captain or the chief but each fire apparatus is washed and waxed and brought to the most presentable appearance that is possible. Tonawanda has joined with North Tonawanda in the Inspection Day activities. The start of the parade alternated between the cities each year. The parade always ended in the opposite city.

On parade day firefighters brought their uniforms out of the closet. When I joined the hall the Sweeney Hose uniform consisted of a shirt that was sky blue with lapels and pocket covers that were navy blue. The right shoulder bore an American flag while the left shoulder hosted a Sweeney Hose patch. Navy blue pants with a mustard yellow stripe going down the outside of the legs made up the lower half of the uniform. A black tie and a navy blue cap adorned with the Sweeney badge completed the outfit. The Sweeneys decided to improve the look of the parade outfits by purchasing Class A uniforms. The original parade uniform remained the same in color but a black belt, white gloves, and a blazer complete with a new Sweeney Hose badge accessorized the old uniform. Members only needed to supply a pair of black socks and black marching shoes to complete the uniform.

On parade day, the Sweeney Hose members would need to arrive at the hall by noon. If a member was unable to march that day, a written excuse would have to be delivered to the captain before noon on the day of the parade. An unexcused absence from the parade would make any member with less than twenty five years of service subject to a fine. Members would arrive at the hall and sign the company ledger, which signified that they were indeed present for the day's activities. Beer flowed freely from the taps and old friends rekindled their friendships. Rookies were assigned to the color guard for the day. The American flag and the company flag needed to be carried. In the past, color guard members carried white wooden rifles with each rifle assigned to "guard" each flag. The hall had recently retired the old white rifles and replaced them with silver headed pick axes engraved with the Sweeney Hose name and the Maltese Cross. White helmets with special color guard badges topped the head of each color guard member. Yellow aiguillettes were held in place underneath their left arm lapels. A navy blue scarf buttoned around their neck and tucked into their shirt replaced their black ties.

Transportation to the parade line-up was provided by two school buses. Our parade band, a bagpiping group called the Mackenzie Highlanders, occupied one of the buses while the members rode the other bus. Some members drove to the start site in their own classic vehicles. Magnetic signs on the side of the cars let the public know how many years of service the riding firefighters had under their belt. A select few firefighters rode on the Wedge, the company's 1955 American LaFrance pumper that we had purchased from the city for a dollar.

Before boarding the buses and the private cars, the company was lead in prayer by our chaplain, Mark Willington. Yesterday Mark continued the tradition. This past year Mark was elected as the chief chaplain of the volunteer fire service for the State of New York. Mark had always thrown his heart and soul into Sweeney Hose. He always helped when he could and he had delved into many projects at the fire hall over the years. He had a great respect for the history of the Sweeney Hose Company and for the fire service in general. He had been criticized in the past for doing things for the hall that did not always turn out perfectly, but he was often the only member of the hall who would stick his neck out to try new things to benefit the hall. He was someone you could talk to and confide in. He knew that life was hard. He had worked at odd jobs to support his family until he found his niche in the computer field. Mark was someone that was fun to be around. He did not take a holier than thou attitude and he could swear with the best of them during a heated game of Euchre.

After Mark's prayer, where he had asked God to be with us and our fellow firefighters throughout the day, we boarded the bus. Members of the color guard also served as our "pitcher bitches". These rookies were responsible for carrying two full pitchers of beer each time they came on the bus. They were to provide a member with a full cup of beer when they were summoned. They would be relentlessly chastised for spilling any beer onto the bus floor, or even worse, another member. Yesterday's event started like any other parade day with the exception that we had only twenty minutes to arrive at the start of the parade before the 2 p.m. sendoff.

The bus headed out of the parking lot as we waved to the members of the career department who were standing at fire headquarters. We reached Robinson Street and made a right turn. A red light stopped the bus at the Twin City Memorial Highway. It was known as the TCMH in North Tonawanda and it was a four lane divided highway that cut through the city of North Tonawanda, dividing it roughly into eastern and western halves. A two lane, one-way street called Division Street bordered the TCMH in North Tonawanda. There were ramps that lead onto the TCMH from Division and there were ramps from TCMH that allowed a driver to get onto Division Street. The key to yielding was very simple. The driver on Division Street was always required to yield the right of way. People didn't seem to grasp this concept however, as the merging lanes had often been the site of many car collisions over the years.

The bus accelerated at the change of the traffic light as members talked loudly with each other. My body suddenly jerked forward as the bus came to an abrupt and complete stop. To my left a rookie who weighed about two hundred and fifty pounds moved six feet forward in less than a second. Captain Ron Reynolds was now wearing the vast majority of the pitcher bitch's spillage. Shouts and cursing swelled from the back of the bus towards the driver as the bus moved forward again. I looked out a window and saw what we had just missed; a small beat up blue car that had decided to turn in front of the bus. Ron was smiling and cursing at the same time. He shouted, "Who the hell hired this guy? I've never gotten my parade uniform wet on the bus before the parade!"

The bus driver received another round of harassment as he braked quickly on a bridge when we entered the city of Tonawanda. Auxiliary police officers had blocked off the parade street and then diverted our bus to a side street. We arrived at Isle View Park along the Niagara River with five minutes to spare before the start of the parade. We passed other North Tonawanda fire companies as we walked to our place in the line up. Firefighters I hadn't seen in years were at the parade. I had bowled with some of them or had sat on different committees with them at one time or another. I hadn't seen some of the guys for nearly ten years, yet we still knew each other's names as we exchanged a heartfelt handshake.

Blaring sirens heralded the start of the parade. Ron Reynolds informed the company that we would perform a hand salute at four different places along the parade route, the last place being the judging area. The Sweeney Hose Company had won the best appearing fire company trophy for the past four years. Questions had been raised as to who actually had judged the fire companies on their appearance. We had our company name engraved into the trophy for each year that we had won the award. This parade marshal had taken the trophy from our hall this year and he displayed it at the beginning of the parade for each company to see.

A scorching late June sun beat down on us as we marched out onto Niagara Street. We aligned our feet to the beat of the drums of the Mackenzie Highlanders who marched ahead of us. It felt good to have a cool breeze blowing across the Niagara River. The cars followed the marchers and Engine 7 with its complement of career firefighters followed the cars. The Wedge was absent from the parade as it was having repair work done at a local truck shop.

The sparse crowd along Niagara Street became denser as our group approached Tonawanda City Hall. Patches of spectators applauded as we passed them. I looked forward and Mark Willington was working hard to keep the rookie firefighters of the color guard in step with our band. They were without flag holders and their usual array of color guard garb as the bag that contained all of the equipment had been misplaced.

We continued our march as I looked off to my right to notice an old oak tree. It was during the parade two years ago that I looked up to see Mark Willington marching with the American flag. He had not been carrying it just thirty seconds earlier. Out of the corner of my eye I saw Don Rabinski, who I used to work with at the Riverside Chemical Company, dashing towards the tree with a hurried stride. He disappeared behind the tree and we laughed as we knew what was happening. His bladder was near bursting capacity and he decided to water the poor tree in broad daylight. Luckily the judges weren't strewn along the parade route. Don caught up with the company before we even made it to the bridge into North Tonawanda and he reclaimed the American flag. We won the trophy for the best appearing fire company that year.

As my thoughts returned to the present time, I realized that my strides would have to get longer as we turned onto the bridge that led into North Tonawanda. We were headed to Webster Street, which had once been the hub of North Tonawanda city life during the late 1800s and early 1900s. Webster Street always stood as a reminder to me of the big fires that could get occasionally break out. Ahead of us on our left was the spot where the old Salvation Army Thrift Store stood until a suspicious Saturday morning fire in 1992 all but burned it to the ground. Next to the space stood a tanning bed parlor which used to be Murphy's Department Store. It had burned for hours and hours one spring night in 1987. I was returning from an outing with a friend and we noticed the smoke from quite a distance away. We dropped my friend off and my mother and I proceeded to the fire. We gazed in amazement as we saw large columns of smoke billowing from the structure. I wondered if the building would be a total loss. The building was saved but Murphys became a Webster Street memory.

We neared the judging stand and the cheers from the crowd became louder. A shiver went up my spine. These people actually seemed to appreciate what we as volunteer firefighters had done for the community. The wailing siren of Engine 7 echoed between the two story buildings of Webster Street. We approached the corner quickly as the captain yelled out, "Company, present arms!" A sharp right hand salute was displayed by all the marching members of our company. We turned right with the chiefs of the Tonawanda and North Tonawanda Fire Departments on our left. Various politicians filled up the space next to the fire chiefs.

I looked straight ahead. I couldn't help but think that we looked damn good. I had felt this way during this part of the Inspection Day Parade each year and this was no exception. I felt proud to be a firefighter. We crossed over Main Street and our band continued to play for us as they split to form a line on each side of the street. We kept saluting and then we split into a line on each side of the street. The band then reconvened and marched past us followed by the parade cars and finally Engine 7. Once it had passed the last firefighter, Engine 7 gave a blast of its air horn as it accelerated through the old part of the city on its return trip to fire headquarters.

Ron Reynolds gave the company orders to fall out and the members all seemed to open their jackets at the same time. Caps were removed and we wiped beads of sweat from our foreheads. We walked a short distance to the parking lot that hosted our buses. Behind the parking lot was a wooded area whose foliage had flourished mainly because it had served as a urinal for many firemen with overdistended bladders throughout the years. Some rookies were standing around and I told them how I was a line officer in 1993 when the temperature was in the mid forties on parade day. I told them how I had carried our treasured and extremely cold parade trumpet for over forty five minutes. After the parade I ran to the wooded area and peed for at least five minutes straight. The gave me bewildered looks as I finished my story, but I had always felt that that it was important to hand down some tidbits of hall history, whether important or trivial, to the newer members. I had hoped that they would appreciate this and pass on their own stories to future hall members in their good time.

The Sweeneys slowly made their way onto the bus with some stragglers finishing their cigarettes while others chatted with members from other halls. We finally got underway and I hoped that our bus driver was going to do a better job of driving on the way back to the hall. The bus came to a slow gentle stop at the side entrance to the hall and Ron Reynolds told us that the bus we were on would be returning to the bus company. Several rookies were told to get a garden hose. He ordered them to drench the inside of the bus to remove any dried or sticky beer from the floor and the seats. It just wouldn't be right to have a third grader getting drunk from the fumes of our beer mess as he rode the bus to school two days later.

Cool air enveloped me as I walked into the hall. I went behind the bar and poured myself a Pepsi. It felt too warm out to continue drinking beer and I felt somewhat sick anyway. I went into the main part of the hall expecting to see a feast laid upon the buffet table. There were only empty pans and cheap white paper table cloths. We had almost been late to the parade and the food today was also late. The hall seemed crowded and loud and I went outside to stand in the shade.

In the shadows of the hall I shook hands with Matt Lavelli, a long time Sweeney member who always came out when he could lend a hand at any hall function. Matt had worked for the city for many years but he had recently suffered some setbacks in his health. He said that he was now starting to feel better. Matt's long time friend, Sam Rallers, was standing next to him. Sam had been a long time Sweeney member and had recently retired from the career department. Matt and Sam asked me what hospital I was working at, just like they did every year. They also asked me if I was still stuck in the emergency department. I hoped that someday they would realize that the emergency department was where I wanted to work. Sam proceeded to tell us several stories about his run ins with various chiefs on the paid department. I had never heard them before and they were hilarious. Now I was the younger member of the hall, hearing stories from a seasoned firefighter.

I noticed some younger members entering the hall and thought that the food might now be out to eat. The smell of roast beef wafted out from the opened doors. I briefly talked with the fire chief and some of the assistant chiefs as I made my way towards the lengthening line of hungry guests. I got my food and sat down at a table. As I looked up from my plate, I saw Myron Anders sitting down across the table from me. Myron was a good friend and he had become a Sweeney Hose member in 1997, shortly after witnessing his neighbor's garage being completely destroyed by fire. In the past I would often visit Myron at his parents' house and I was almost always invited to have some dinner. Myron knew that he wanted to become a career firefighter and he obtained an associates degree in fire science as well as a bachelor's degree in fire service administration. He worked odd jobs and became an EMT. In 2005 his break finally came and he was hired as a career firefighter with the North Tonawanda Fire Department. Myron and I talked about his upcoming wedding. He had met the girl of his dreams. I had told Myron after meeting her that she was the one for him and we now laughed as my prediction was about to come true. He said that his family was doing well. It was always good to catch up with Myron.

Ben Timkins, another Sweeney Hose member and recently appointed career firefighter, had come to join us at our table. Tim was well respected on the career department and he was always an aggressive volunteer firefighter. He had just completed his associate's degree in nursing when he was hired by the city to be a career firefighter. He is now an Engine 7 driver. He will likely go far in the department.

Our traditional parade day meals of roast beef and pasta noodles were now finished and our plates revealed their stained white tops. Noticeably absent from the menu this year were scallions. In the past we had always enjoyed eating this offensive cousin of the onion each year. Someone had simply forgotten about them. Limburger cheese and onions and rye bread were on the banquet table though. All the rookies were "encouraged" to voluntarily eat one of these sandwiches. Those who refused were usually assisted in eating their sandwich. Luckily this eating tradition for rookies had not become a tradition until a few years ago, long after my rookie days had passed.

I stood up and headed towards the bar for a drink. Myron and Ben had excused themselves as they had plans for the evening. The drone of the bagpipes from our band started in the far corner of the hall. This was another tradition. The MacKenzie Highlanders went through a lively medley of songs for us for about ten minutes. They always ended their medley by playing Amazing Grace. This song always brought tears to my eyes as I remembered all of the firefighters and friends who had passed away.

As the last notes of Amazing Grace echoed in the hall a loud round of applause was given for the band. Soon the cry went out for members to board the bus. The Sweeney members made yearly stops at the volunteer fire halls of the North Tonawanda fire companies. The Tonawanda fire halls used to be open to both the North Tonawanda and Tonawanda fire companies. Tonawanda had recently stopped this practice as several fights had broken out between different companies. They now hosted a single picnic at their firemen's park. Families were welcome to attend. No fights had occurred at the park since their move. In North Tonawanda individual volunteer companies still chose to host their own parties. They continued to have brawls.

I had never witnesses a bloody or particularly nasty fight between our company and a Tonawanda company. I do remember being ready to leave on a bus and seeing a rustle in the bushes in front of the Delaware Hose Company of the

Tonawanda Fire Department. The next thing I remembered was Ken Rojek, who was our company captain at the time, yelling at the top of his lungs and dragging one of our drunken brother firefighters onto our bus. The bus driver quickly closed the door and hit the gas as Ken was still going up one side of Henry Kavinski and down the other for his participation in an altercation. I always felt sorry for the line officers on parade day. They had to limit their alcohol intake so they could be a responsible babysitter for the rest of us drunken fools in the company.

Several fights had occurred between just the North Tonawanda companies throughout the years. Most of the scuffles seemed to occur between the Active Hose Company and another company or companies. The Actives had many strong personalities in their hall. On a normal day this was not a problem. However, when strong personalities were combined with large quantities of alcohol and then coupled with strong feelings of company pride, as often happened on parade day, trouble often ensued.

The recipe for a fight was perfect one parade day when the Sweeneys had gathered with other companies at the social hall of the Live Hose Company No. 4. The Lives had a small social hall in the basement of their quarters which was directly beneath their truck room. I was drinking at the bar with Mike Mallard and we convinced one of the elderly Live Hose bartenders to hand over one of the antique fire nozzles that adorned the back of the bar. We inspected it closely and saw the number "7" engraved into the coupling of the nozzle. We were drunk and we decided to have some fun with the bartender. We insisted that he immediately surrender the nozzle to us as it was obviously the property of the Sweeney Hose Company as it bore the number 7. The bartender looked very concerned and he stepped closer to the bar. He started to look visibly upset and I thought that he had visions of us taking the nozzle. I was worried that we were going to give this poor guy a stroke so we handed the nozzle back over the bar. We thanked him for letting us have a little fun.

To our left some bantering was going on and then I heard a distinctive shout from one of our rookie members. He was in trouble. A crowd of Sweeneys hurried towards the sound of his distressed voice. He was being held by a member of the Actives. Our altruistic efforts to help him were temporarily halted as we looked towards the stairwell. An indiscernible shout came from the stairwell. No one was there. Then from out of nowhere there came a flying Sweeney. It was our brother in need's biological brother. He had heard his brother's cry for help and had quickly jumped down the stairs into a crowd of firefighters. He was swinging his fists like a madman as he made his way towards his brother. The Active Hose perpetrator was quickly removed from the building by his captain. The Sweeneys decided that it was time to move on and we boarded our bus, ready to arrive at our next destination.

We often sang on the bus as we went along. "No Beer in Heaven" was the classic favorite of the Sweeneys. When we were in Tonawanda a simple two word song called "Tonawanda Sucks" could be heard emanating from the open windows on our bus. It would not be uncommon for a passing motorist to observe a pair of ass cheeks pressed up against the glass of the bus. We would sometimes shout things at people walking down the streets not because they did anything wrong but they just happened to be there when we happened to be passing by.

The new millennium brought what seemed to be a decrease in the number of firefighters at each hall. Friends that I had met in the early 1990s had either left the fire service or didn't come around for parade day any longer. As a few older members and the younger members made their way towards the bus for the hall excursions, several people encouraged me to get on the bus. I gratefully declined their offers. The meaning of parade day had changed for me. It was no longer a day to get totally drunk and act irreverently. For me it was now a day to remember what the fire service stood for and to remember what a great privilege it had been for me to serve my community. I felt very tired that day. I said goodbyes to my close friends. I then got into my truck and headed for home, a twenty five minute drive from the city where I had once served as an active firefighter.

21

We Fly to Save

I write this final chapter not from my home several miles east of the city of North Tonawanda, but in North Tonawanda at the Sweeney Hose Company. I felt the need to come back to the place where my time as a volunteer firefighter began. I needed to be surrounded by the walls of the building where so many memories of my early days of firefighting seemed to linger. For years, the four walls had gathered so many volunteers and they will hopefully continue to welcome willing servants for years to come.

I left my home this evening after my wife and children had fallen asleep. As I walked to my truck I looked up in the sky and saw a late autumn Orion seemingly lying on his side. Taurus the bull appeared to be claiming his victory over this downed warrior. I got into my truck and headed down country roads towards North Tonawanda. A classic Jerry Lee song played on a CD. The chorus of the song rang out, "When your hot you're hot, when you're not you're not." Tonight I can't help but feel that I'm not as hot as I used to be. I used to get up at all hours of the night to help to protect the lives and property of the citizens of my old town, but tonight I am merely a visitor. My name has been removed from the active exempt roles of the company. I am now an exempt member whom had presumably done all that he could do to help make a difference in the lives of strangers that were called neighbors.

Time makes me feel as though I am the late fall Orion, lying on my back and succumbing to the veracity of the bull. For me, moving ahead in life unfortunately meant moving further and further away from the life of firefighting. I met my wife at a Buffalo bar one night in March of 2000. She was an EMT for a local ambulance company. We had informally talked for the first time a couple of weeks before our bar meeting. I was a second year emergency medicine resident at the Buffalo General Hospital and I was attempting to place a breathing tube in a very sick patient that she had brought in by ambulance. When I visualized the patient's vocal cords she handed me the endotracheal tube and I said, "Thanks." I had noticed her before in the emergency department and I thought that she was quite attractive. I noticed her right away on the night that we met at the bar. I saw that she was with a paramedic from her ambulance company, but I decided to talk to her anyway, seeing that I had the strength of at least four or five beers in me. I talked to her about the patient that she had brought me two weeks earlier. We both agreed that taking care of the patient was a big fiasco as the attending physician I was working with that day seemed to be very close to the border of being clinically competent to practice emergency medicine.

We talked throughout the night as I bought drink after drink for her. I could see that her boyfriend was getting somewhat perturbed by my presence, but I didn't care. One of the nurses from the hospital was bartending that night. After a couple of more drinks the music was sounding really good to me so I stood up on the bar and started dancing. Shortly after that my pants came down and I finished dancing in my boxer shorts. The bar was hopping. Soon after I came down from the bar, Sue asked me for a pen and a piece of paper. As I didn't have either, she asked the bartender Janet for the same two items but she came up empty handed. Then to everyone's amazement she bolted out the front door.

Five minutes later Sue returned to the bar. We went out onto the dance floor and as her hand touched mine, a small piece of paper was discretely delivered to me. I casually put the paper in my pocket. The night was bursting into the wee hours of the morning and she left the bar with her boyfriend. I reached into my pocket and saw her home phone number and her pager number. I paged her later that day and we had dinner that night. We dated and soon moved in together. We were married nineteen months later.

We initially lived in the city of Tonawanda, but we were within a mile of the North Tonawanda city limit so I could still respond to calls with the North Tonawanda Fire Department. After we married, my Grandma Borton had decided to move out of her house and move into the senior apartments in North Tonawanda. She graciously offered to let us buy or rent her house. Sue and I decided to rent as we had dreamed of building a new house.

Our first child was born in the spring of 2003. Today she is a beautiful, intelligent and complex seven year old. Our second child was a boy and he was born in August of 2004 and he is a considerate and playful five year old who loves trains. My grandmother's house was comfortable yet somewhat cramped. With the expected birth of our third child, who would become Mr. Talkative, in 2006, Sue and I had looked at several pieces of vacant land in the country. We had both grown up in areas where the next door neighbor's house was no more than fifteen feet away from our own house. One day while driving in the country, Sue saw a vast area of open land. The land had no "for sale" sign but she noticed stakes in the ground and she assumed that the land had been subdivided. She stopped at the nearest house she could find. She got the name and phone number of the farmer who owned the land. It was indeed for sale and we quickly jumped at the chance to buy one of the lots. We found a builder, designed our house, and moved into our new home late in the summer in 2005. It was during the time when our house was being built that I realized that my days as an active volunteer firefighter in the North Tonawanda Fire Department were numbered.

My transition to becoming an active exempt firefighter had been a slow one. I wasn't able to make all of the calls that I could when I was single. My children deserved my attention and I knew that they needed a dad to look after them. The fact that we were moving out of North Tonawanda automatically sealed my resignation as an active firefighter in North Tonawanda. I would be living too far outside of the city to respond to calls.

It was a bittersweet day when I turned in my fire-fighting gear. No longer would I be an active firefighter who would be able to go into burning buildings to fight one of nature's oldest enemies. I couldn't answer first aid calls and other calls for help. My daughter was with me the day that I drove to fire headquarters to turn in my gear. What normally would have been a twenty five minute ride turned out to be a forty minute ride as I seemed to want to hold onto my firefighting gear for just a little more time. We took the back roads and just before we got into North Tonawanda we stopped at a park along the Erie Canal. I got out of my truck and opened the plastic bin that had held my fire gear for many years. The bin was devoid of my helmet as I had written a letter to Chief Frank and asked him if I could keep it as a memento of my service with the department. He accepted my plea. I slowly pulled out my turnout coat and searched the pocket for any of my personal possessions. I pulled out a pocket guide to firefighting. I looked over to my then two year old daughter as she watched me from her car seat. I said to her, "I want you to remember this. I want you to remember that your daddy was a fireman." She replied slowly in the speech of a two year old, "Daddy, fireman." I told her, "Good job Bean," and we headed off to fire headquarters.

Chief Frank was out of the building when I arrived at headquarters but I spoke with Manfred Johnson, an assistant chief and Sweeney Hose member. He told me that I could leave my turnout gear on the floor. That's what I did. Unceremoniously, I laid my gear onto the truck room floor and I walked out the door leaving my gear for another firefighter to don in the future.

As I drove into North Tonawanda this evening, I was met at the bottom of the Robinson Street Bridge by a twelve foot inflatable Santa Claus. Something made me turn left and I proceeded left down Sweeney Street, which closely followed the meanderings of the Erie Canal. I headed towards downtown North Tonawanda where over one hundred years ago, the area thrived due to the lumber shipping business. Tonight the water was open. Not a single lumber barge was docked on its shores. Gone too were the towpaths that mules walked along to pull the early boats of some long gone North Tonawandans. I turned right down Vandervoordt Street and passed Engine 4's quarters and the social hall of the Live Hose Company. Engine 4 rested alone in its three bay station. The presence of a couple of cars in the parking lot suggested that a member or two from the Lives were possibly imbibing in an early holiday drink. I next drove down Oliver Street, passing by the closed drinking establishments that had somehow failed to make it. I passed the old fire headquarters which was now a multi-unit apartment building and bore no resemblance to a fire station. I went past the old home of Engine 2 where Rescue 1 was now stationed. The lights were on in the station but Rescue 1 was out. A short ride took me past my old house on Chipman Place. There was a darkened house with a car in the driveway. My parents had moved two weeks earlier, moving closer to our house so that it was easier to see their grandchildren. I drove past the fire station at the corner of Payne Avenue and Walck Road. Engine 6 was barely able to fit into the old structure which perfectly housed Rescue 1. I then headed for the Sweeney Hose hall. I pulled into the parking lot and it was half full of cars. Antennas on several of the cars let me know that the ARATS, a group of ham radio operators, were having their monthly meeting at the hall. As I looked in the door, I saw that they were having their Christmas party. A member of the company, Ken Michaels, met me at the door and let me into the hall. He told me that the hall was rented. I asked him if he could let me into the board room because I had some work to do. With a flick of his key tag in front of a door sensor, the door unlocked. I plugged in my laptop and here I now sit, reflecting on my years as a Sweeney Hose Company volunteer firefighter.

The hall has changed a great deal since I became a member in 1990. The old bar that was at the end of the hall is gone. The new bar is located in the area where the old coatroom with the beer dispensing machine stood for years. The old ratty floor is gone, covered by a new tile floor that makes the hall fairly competitive as a host for small weddings and parties. The hall that usually sat empty when I was a new member is now regularly occupied at night by young members who have come down to socialize and watch sports events on TV. For a couple of years, games such as foosball and darts made an appearance in the hall, but their popularity has seemingly faded. A large screen TV sits at the front of the hall. Gone are the light and navy blue painted cinderblocks that decorated the inside of the hall. Wood paneling covers the lower half of the walls while Navajo white painted drywall fills the upper part of the walls.

From what I have heard, things have also changed quite a bit on the fire ground. Our company still clings to the tradition of having a captain and a 1st and 2nd lieutenant. The lieutenants for all purposes are reportedly figureheads and they get to wear an officer's hat during summer parades. The captain serves as a citywide lieutenant. Each volunteer company has a lieutenant to help with officer jobs on the fire ground. Three volunteers have been elected by a fire chief appointed commission to serve as citywide volunteer captains. Their job is to ultimately oversee the volunteer firefighters at the scene of a fire. They get their direction from the assistant chief of the paid department who is in charge of any incident. Interior firefighters are known by their tan turnout gear. In the past every career firefighter wore yellow turnout coats and every volunteer wore black gear. Now only exterior volunteer firefighters wear black.

The people of the hall have changed too. Duncan Fanners got a job as a police officer in Virginia after twenty years of taking police entrance exams. Allen Michalis moved to North Carolina. I saw him recently and he plays golf at least three times a week. Oscar Keating moved to Florida. Over the years the Sweeney Hose Company lost several brothers, hopefully to a better place. Tim Frank ended a long battle with cancer in 1997. At Tim's wake, I greeted his family and his brother Greg leaned over and said, "Tim was really proud of you and he was glad you chose to go into medicine." That had always been a source of comfort for me, especially when things have seemed stressful at work. Sadly, we lost Greg Frank to cancer in 2008. His father Bob died later that year. Ken Paulis had become paralyzed after a tragic fall. He died from complications from his injuries nearly a year after his accident. Ken's mother and father had always been active in Sweeney Hose. It was heart breaking to watch them as Mark Willington led Ken's memorial service at the funeral home. Don Galling was diagnosed with advanced lung cancer that had metastasized to his brain. I talked for a long time with Don at the Sweeney Hose family picnic about four months before he passed away. He was in good spirits and he truly seemed to be at peace. A couple of months later at a fundraiser that was being held for him, he looked uncomfortable. About forty Sweeney Hose members turned out for Don's memorial service. Several guys from the hall helped to install a new furnace in his house after he died.

I've changed a great deal since I first stepped foot into this fire hall the day before my eighteenth birthday in 1990. I was recently at a fire hall meeting and a member with less than two years in the hall got up and questioned the actions of some of the members of the board. The president silenced him in front of the membership when he said that the roof was in dire need of repair. The member was fuming after the meeting, especially when the president butchered his last name. I saw the old me in him that night. I used to be very active in the hall and I used to cry foul when a policy seemed suspicious or not to be in what I thought was in the best interest of the hall. I strived to always do my best for the hall. I wanted to make sure that my fellow firefighters were treated well at the same time. Today, I believe my ideals are the same, but I don't feel quite as passionate about them. I used to make every meeting and every drill. I don't attend drills anymore and I'm lucky if I make three meetings a year. I don't have the "lowdown" on everyone's business and I don't want it. I think that having children has helped me to drastically change my overall perspective of the fire hall. In the past I would lie awake; troubled about something that was going on in the hall. Now I realize that when it comes to hall business, many members seem overly passionate about what goes on. There's nothing like a controversy in the hall to turn a bunch of perfectly competent firefighters into a bunch of German washwomen. I couldn't say this if I hadn't been a German washwoman in the past. Now my focus has changed. If every firefighter makes it home from every call they go on, then it has been a good day.

I do miss the experience of firefighting itself. Every time I hear a fire engine siren or see a fire truck racing to a fire where I live now, I feel that a part of me is racing away with that fire truck. That's not to say that I don't retain some of my skills. Recently the drip pan on my propane grill caught fire when I was grilling a piece of steak. My son was out in the driveway with me. He watched as his dad calmly grabbed a glove, removed the drip pan, and set it on the concrete. I then managed to fully extinguish that blaze with a couple of sprays with the garden hose. He looked at me in amazement as the steam from the fire rose skyward. If he had a larger vocabulary I'm sure he would have said, "Wow", or "awesome" or "cool". For me his intrigued, wide-eyed silence confirmed that he has the firefighting itch somewhere inside of him.

When I was in the first two years of medical school at the University of Buffalo, I would often emerge from three or four hours of mind numbing lectures to hear the rigs of the Buffalo Fire Department wailing in the distance. At times I wondered if I was put on the Earth to be a firefighter in a fully paid department. I had ranked high on the North Tonawanda Fire Department civil service test with a score of 90. The list was good for four years. It ran from November 6, 1995 until November 6, 1999. That was basically the same time that I was enrolled in medical school. Not a single soul was hired onto the career department from that list. I think that ultimately I would have become restless if I had become a career firefighter in North Tonawanda. The thought of staying at a fire station waiting for something to happen would have eventually driven me bonkers. I have many friends in the career department now. They all seem to love their job. I'm happy for them and I know they'll never forget their roots as volunteer firefighters.

The ARATS' Christmas party is now over and they have left the hall. There are several Sweeney members in the hall tonight, talking and watching TV. It seems that every five minutes a good natured dig is thrown at another member who is sitting around the bar. There are certainly some cliques in the fire hall, but I never felt that I had been purposely shunned from any group or activity. Even though I don't frequent the hall as much as I used to, I am convinced that I could call any Sweeney Hose member to ask them for their help with anything. They wouldn't give a second thought to helping out a brother or sister firefighter.

So here I sit, coming to the end of my reflection on my past fifteen years as an active volunteer firefighter. I'm sitting in the room where I was first welcomed as a brother firefighter by some twenty members from all different walks of life on the first Monday night in the month of May in 1990. Good friends have walked out of these four walls never to be seen again in this life. Many friends have remained and continue to serve their community. New friends will walk through those two doors on the first

Monday night of some month of some year in the future. They may walk timidly towards the front of the hall and raise their right hand, not knowing exactly what lies ahead of them in their service as a firefighter. They will state their name aloud. They will promise to abide by the rules of the fire company and uphold the Constitution of the United States. They will be welcomed as a member of the fire hall. They will probably find a seat near the back of the hall and sit alone. In time, they will sit with others. They will learn to fight fire and how to respect it. They will learn to appreciate the unique smell of their smoke laden turnout gear after a tough working fire. They will feel the joy of being able to help save a neighbor's house or even their neighbor's life. They will come to realize that there are times when even a superhero couldn't make a difference in the way things turn out. They will be taught and they will teach. They will ache. They will follow in the footsteps of their patriotic colonial fathers. They will fight off sleep and get out of bed at an ungodly hour of the morning. They will leave their families at inopportune times to go and help a complete stranger. They could become a well respected fifty year member of the hall. They might never return home from the next call.

A short time ago I was looking through some of the historical papers of the Sweeney Hose Company. Many of the original notes and requests from the company were written on small pieces of stationery that was specially printed for the Sweeney Hose Company. What is written on these notes is very interesting. Most of the notes are from the early years of the fire company in the late 1890s. There are requests to the city council to add and remove members from the city rolls. There is even a request to the city council to move a fire alarm bell so that members of the Sweeney Hose Company could more easily hear an alarm of fire. I however believe that the most interesting piece of history on these sheets of paper is the words that are imprinted on the top of each page. The sheets read, "Our motto – When duty calls, we fly to save."

A tone across the fire monitor interrupts my thoughts. The dispatcher calls out, "Fire dispatcher to engine seven." A voice answers back, "Engine seven." The dispatcher speaks, "Report of a motor vehicle accident with injuries, Niagara Falls Boulevard and Erie Avenue."

My eyes look towards the bar. The seats are empty. Unfinished glasses of soda pop sit on the bar. In the parking lot, blue lights flash and fall into line behind Engine 7 as it accelerates down Erie Avenue. It has been one hundred and twelve years since the Sweeney Hose Company was formed. Duty has just called and the Sweeneys are once again flying to save. May the Sweeneys continue to hear the call to duty to fly to save for another one hundred years.